Information
Economics

Information Economics

Linking Business Performance to Information Technology

Marilyn M. Parker

Robert J. Benson

with H. E. Trainor

Prentice Hall
Englewood Cliffs, New Jersey 07632

Library of Congress Cataloging-in-Publication Data

Parker, Marilyn M.
  Information economics.

  Bibliography: p.
  Includes index.
  1. Strategic planning.   2. Information technology.
  3. Industrial management.   I. Benson, Robert J.
  II. Title.
  HD30.28.PC15   1988   658.4′012′0285   88–5989
  ISBN 0–13–464595–2

Editorial/production supervision: Chris Baumle, Editing, Design & Production, Inc.
Cover design: Edsal Enterprises
Manufacturing buyer: Margaret Rizzi

 © 1988 by Prentice-Hall, Inc.
A Division of Simon & Schuster
Englewood Cliffs, New Jersey 07632

Printed in the United States of America

10   9   8   7   6   5   4   3   2   1

ISBN 0-13-464595-2

Prentice-Hall International (UK) Limited, *London*
Prentice-Hall of Australia Pty. Limited, *Sydney*
Prentice-Hall Canada Inc., *Toronto*
Prentice-Hall Hispanoamericana, S.A., *Mexico*
Prentice-Hall of India Private Limited, *New Delhi*
Prentice-Hall of Japan, Inc., *Tokyo*
Simon & Schuster Asia Pte. Ltd., *Singapore*
Editora Prentice-Hall do Brasil, Ltda., *Rio de Janeiro*

Contents

PART 2 ELEMENTS OF INFORMATION ECONOMICS

Preface

Since 1981 Marilyn Parker has been Manager, Enterprise Analysis, and more recently Program Manager, Enterprise Information Management, at the IBM Los Angeles Scientific Center. One of her group's first efforts was to contribute to a special issue of the *IBM Systems Journal* devoted to Enterprise Analysis. In it were articles written by her Enterprise Analysis Group and others, targeted on topics in strategic planning. From that beginning, the Los Angeles Scientific Center has been active in developing tools and methodologies, in support of their intellectual products, in strategic planning for information technology.

Bob Benson started the Center for the Study of Data Processing at Washington University in 1976. The Center now has forty-five corporate affiliates in the Midwest. The Center and its affiliates pursue MIS topics of interest, one of which is strategic planning. In 1984 the Center and IBM established the Joint Study in Enterprise-wide Information Management (EwIM). Each year since then, the Joint Study has sponsored an international conference, including cosponsoring similar activities at the National University of Singapore.

Early in the Joint Study we observed that the vocabulary in MIS and strategic planning is imprecise and overlapping. One immediate goal has been to define terms. For example, we will use three discrete terms to elaborate on what typically is called "MIS." We will refer to the technology of MIS, such as communications, database software, computers, and workstations, as Information Technology (IT). We will refer to the systems of MIS, the applications portfolio, as Management Information Systems (MIS). This embraces transaction processing through decision support systems. And we will refer to the organizational unit of MIS, the data processing department in previous years, as Information Systems (IS) as an adjective to management and organization units. Hence we'll refer to the IS director or the IS organization, the people responsible for information technology (IT) and the systems (MIS). Our attention to clear definitions will underscore the development of ideas in strategic planning and information economics.

We have also observed that strategic planning in general, and planning for information technology in particular, cannot be described as a pre-defined, step-by-step process. Rather, it is a goal-driven methodology for changing the allocation of capital and operating resources within an enterprise.

Successful strategic planning results in resources allocated to a project which, when pursued, will improve the financial and competitive position of the company. Planning is based on the systematic analysis and extrapolation of information. However, a planning methodology involves evaluation where choices and decisions are made. This is where *persuasion* is necessary. Effective planners are those who identify the projects and *convince* management to commit resources to the projects.

Persuasion is also a part of the planning the IS organization must do for application systems. That is, the IS planner's responsibility is to identify valuable MIS projects for implementation and then through some methodology persuade management to provide resources for the projects. Similarly, an IS director's responsibility is to define appropriate computer and communications architectures and then persuade management to commit the resources to implement them, providing the foundation for future MIS applications.

We began the Joint Study in Enterprise-wide Information Management with the expectation that the major topics and projects would focus on enterprise-wide data models, competitive advantage and strategic systems, and advanced technologies. These are important, but we found ourselves needing a way to evaluate their importance. We needed a way to persuade management, a way to make the case effectively based on the value these matters have for the enterprise.

Our attention turned to economics, starting with traditional cost-benefit analysis and return on investment concepts. Marilyn had worked in this area previously, so we had a good starting point. We found, however, that very little work had been done by others extending either economic theory or cost-benefit concepts to the problems in strategic planning and enterprise-wide information management. We decided to accumulate the materials and ideas that have been developed, extend them, and apply them to our work in strategic planning.

At about the same time Marilyn and Bob began working together, Ed Trainor became the head of Computer Services at the National Railroad Passenger Corporation (AMTRAK). Ed's background is chiefly business planning, and as he began to cope with the problems of planning for information systems, he developed planning processes based on business planning ideas, not solely technical planning ideas. Ed's ideas were refined in subsequent application and development at Flying Tigers and SoCal Gas. A number of these ideas were key in the formulation of the decision processes that are described here. While Marilyn and Bob have been writing about information economics, Ed has been applying it.

Ed was the Director of the Information Systems Department at Flying Tigers—the world's largest air cargo carrier—at the time information economics was being applied there. With the support of CEO Stephan Wolf and Senior Vice President Larry Nagin, Ed successfully applied the information economics concepts and contributed case material and insights from this effort. Flying Tigers, under his stewardship, also placed a great deal of emphasis on development of an enterprise-wide systems and data architecture (i.e., a blueprint). These concepts were validated as Flying Tigers successfully brought together the business and technology requirements in a demanding and competitive environment.

One characteristic of the information economics topic, and consequently of the book, is that it doesn't fit neatly into the culture and mindset of the IS organization or of business management. We are proposing a substantially different view of the role that management information systems (MIS) plays in the enterprise. In addition, we present Information Economics as a tool for defining the value of MIS to the enterprise.

The different view is summarized as follows: the value of MIS to the business is based on *improved performance* at the *line of business* level of the enterprise. Decisions regarding information technology investments are *linked to* and *driven by* business planning. The information economics function can be used to assess the value of MIS at the line of business level.

Overall, our goal is to focus on ways and means to improve the contribution of the IS organization to the success of the enterprises they serve. We believe *Information Economics* is a good step toward this goal.

Although we have not written a book about strategic planning or IS management, the ideas of information economics are intertwined with planning and management processes. We therefore find it necessary to discuss these topics at appropriate points.

We wish to acknowledge the contributions of a number of people to this project. Dr. Matthias Schumann contributed to the development of value linking and value acceleration. During 1987 Dr. Schumann, from Betriebswirtschaftliches Institut, University of Erlangen-Nuremberg, was a Visiting Scientist at the IBM Los Angeles Scientific Center. Dr. Patricia Gongla contributed to the value restructuring model and standard cost concepts. L. Conti, of the German Department at Washington University, translated reference material from German. Mike Mushet from Southern California Edison and Randy Mackles from AMTRAK have supported our efforts through the years, as have Ken Orr (Ken Orr & Associates, Topeka) and Bob Atkinson (Atkinson, Tremblay, & Associates, Toronto), two of the leading consultants in the field. Dr. Peter Sassone, College of Management, Georgia Institute of Technology, and Dr. Perry Schwartz contributed to our initial work in the application of economic theory to business decision-making. Ralph Alterowitz provided new insights in the application of new venture assessment to strategic planning. And Mary Lepage, through her work with the Flying Tigers and SoCal Gas blueprint projects, contributed many hours and ideas.

We both are most appreciative of the continuing support provided us in the Enterprise-wide Information Management Joint Study and in this effort, given by the IBM Corporation, especially Dr. J. A. Jordon and R. V. Bergstresser, and Washington University.

Don Burnstine deserves credit for bringing us together in 1984, and Randy Mackles for introducing Ed Trainor to us. Tom Bugnitz and Virgil Parker have earned our appreciation for patient criticism and stoic contribution of balance to the effort and our lives. John and David Benson kept Bob motivated; Sherman, Marilyn's aide-de-camp, kept us on track.

Marilyn M. Parker
Robert J. Benson
H. E. Trainor

PART 1
LINKING BUSINESS PERFORMANCE AND INFORMATION TECHNOLOGY

1

Introduction to Information Economics

1-1 INTRODUCTION

Our purpose in this chapter is to give a short overview of Information Economics and set the stage for the following chapters. We will consider the ideas of benefits and value that MIS applications have for the enterprise and sketch out a planning process that IS managers can use together with business managers to maximize the value MIS brings to the organization. The last section orients the reader to the subsequent chapters of the book.

1-2 WHAT IS INFORMATION TECHNOLOGY WORTH?

Apparently information technology is worth something because companies continue investing money to install computers and create application systems. They must see some relationship between the costs of information technology and ultimate company economic performance. At least the benefits received from computers, systems, and programmers appear to exceed the costs of those computers, systems, and programmers.

But do they? Twenty years ago, a manager could define costs and benefits with relative ease. A payroll or general ledger system were typical applications. Such systems were primarily intended to reduce costs; the investment needed was a computer and software. The benefits and costs were definable, and the question of *worth* determined with a simple question: Is it worth $1,000 (the cost) to produce $1,200 of personnel or other cost reduction (the benefit)?

Since then, technology changes and expanded management expectations have made both benefits and costs more difficult to define. For example, the business press has been full of ''strategic advantage'' stories. Companies (e.g., American Airlines and American Hospital Supply) have used computer systems to change the competitive performance in their businesses. In response, other companies find that they too must install more computers, create additional applications, and hire more programmers to create new products, open new distribution channels, and apply advanced marketing tools to maintain or gain competitive advantage. So now the question of benefits and costs might be: Is it worth $1,000 (the cost—plus or minus cost uncertainties since it is a new area of company activity) to produce a better product than that of the competition (the benefit—plus or minus business uncertainty whether the better product will improve company sales)?

At the same time, information technology advances have created more complexity. Twenty years ago mainframe computers and COBOL were the cutting edge, and batch-oriented transaction systems were the primary applications. Now, companies can apply a wide range of information technologies for back-office and business unit applications. New technology in communications, such as local area networks and satellite links, make new and more advanced applications possible. Personal computers and online systems, enhanced with fourth generation languages (4GL) and relational databases, extend computer power to user organizations more quickly with the prospect of greater impact on users and business performance.

Because information technology has become more complex, costs too are harder to specify—what is the cost of an advanced systems development tool or a relational database management system, and how should the cost be justified? We can identify the acquisition price of such technologies and the costs of training and culture change for professionals using the technology. However conversion and other implications of successfully managing technology change add to the overall investment in time and money necessary. Further, information technology investments tend to apply to many projects and so have benefits derived from many projects, with consequent loss of any directly assignable benefit to the investment. For example, a relational database system is costly, and requires considerable training, technical support, and computer resources such as random access storage and CPU for processing. The benefits will accrue from future applications systems not yet explicitly known. What is it worth to the corporation to make the investment?

Technology developments and advanced application systems put pressure on the methods enterprises use to make decisions about the allocation of resources to information technology. What is it worth to a company to create competitive distinctiveness in their products? What is it worth to strengthen a company's relationships with its customers?

The word we continually use here is *worth*. We use it in the sense of asking whether, and how much a company is willing to invest to produce a desired business result. In the past this has been determined by comparing cost to benefit, both narrowly defined ideas. Cost has been thought of in discrete fiscal terms such as the cost of programming expressed in hours or payroll dollars. Benefit has been defined in equally discrete fiscal terms. Actual cost reduction through headcount, or direct revenue improvement through interest earned on cash more rapidly collected is an example. Both cost and benefit so defined are too limited to be useful in guiding corporate decisions about, for example, whether the company should invest in a communications network with its customers to strengthen its competitive posture with them.

The increased complications of defining costs and benefits, and at the same time the increased sense of urgency to make decisions about information technology due to its competitive implications, poses hard management questions. "Are we spending enough or too much on information technology?" is a common concern particularly when an enterprise faces a substantial project backlog. "Which projects are the wisest use of our resources?" baffles even the wisest manager.

The approach we take to respond to the problems is based on several simple ideas introduced in this chapter and developed throughout the rest of the book. First, we expand the concept of *benefit* by developing a larger concept of *value*. The concept of benefit remains important as a measure of discrete economic effect such as cost reduction or direct revenue production, and these benefits are certainly worth something to a business. We propose *value* as a broader concept based on the effect information technology investment has on the *business performance* of the enterprise. Cost reduction and revenue production—traditional benefits—are two of several components of *value*. Cost reduction or direct revenue production are important effects on business performance, but so is competitive advantage and increased market share. *Value*—the basis for determining whether it is worth it for a company to invest in information technology—is assessed by adding business performance factors to discrete benefits.

Second, we expand the concept of *cost* to include the many ways which information technology investments can negatively affect the organization. For example, a new information technology introduces the perturbations of training and preparedness in the organization. A systems development group contending with a new relational database environment not only requires training, but also must contend with new elements of project management, changes in the systems development methodology, and problems of integration of a new information systems environment into the computer operations group. Although not discretely identified as a part of the acquisition cost of the software, these are real matters which do affect the performance of the organization for some time.

In summary, we define value based on improved business performance, and cost based on total organizational cost, which taken together define the *true economic impact* of information technology. The ability to assess improved business performance and total organizational cost makes it possible for an enterprise to make the best decisions about the investment in information technology. So, to answer the question "What is it worth?" we explore the value the investment brings to the business modified by the cost of the innovation. However, the result is a decision-making process that forces a shift in management emphasis away from the information technology to the effect technology has on the business itself. This, of necessity, requires a link between information technology planning and business planning.

1–3 STRATEGIC PLANNING AND INFORMATION TECHNOLOGY

We have spent three years studying strategic planning for information technology (Benson and Parker, 1985). Initially we thought the value of strategic planning would be found in the result, a company-wide architecture for information technology including computers, communications, and data. To create these results, we quickly added implementation ideas to the planning ideas, an action plan to get something done in a company. Strategic systems for competitive advantage—the development of new products or new means of interacting with customers—was added as well. The result has been a unified view of strategic planning that links the business use of information technology to business performance.

We have realized, however, that the real purpose of strategic planning is to affect corporate decision-making. Corporate management makes decisions about the deployment of corporate resources, including money and staff. What we want to accomplish through strategic planning is a better, wiser set of decisions derived from a better understanding of the corporate business: its problems, opportunities, and strategies. In effect, strategic planning should change the basis on which resources are allocated within the corporation to each of its lines of business and the information technology function. To do so, we need a way to assess alternative resource allocations. For example, should we buy a computer or hire more marketing staff?

This, it appears, is the heart of the matter. That is, any business organization has a limited capacity for investing in new activities. Perhaps this limit is implemented through a capital budgeting process that allocates the available resources across the best candidates for investment. Limits to resources are also implemented through the processes of operational budgeting. We face choices like hiring programmers compared to hiring marketing staff. We must make the case for information technology investment based on value to the business. However, how can a manager persuade corporate management that *his* particular project is the most important use of scarce resources? How is *value to the business* demonstrated?

We have now defined the problem. Whereas we may have an integrated view of the strategic planning processes themselves, we currently lack an effective way to measure and demonstrate the value of information technology in ways that are comparable to those used by business management to make other investment decisions. How can we compare the value of investing in communications systems compared to ten more marketing staff? That is, how can we demonstrate the true economic impact of a communications system in terms of its impact on business performance?

Our problem is complicated by the range of information technology projects we have. It is difficult to compare a systems project such as a direct company-to-company communications network or a relational database to a marketing support system. With current methods, we have no common technique to assess the desirability of (otherwise) very different kinds of information technology investments. We have no method to describe and interpret the decision criteria applied in decision-making processes that are common to corporate, line of business, and information technology decisions.

So linking information technology planning to business planning though important isn't sufficient; we need to link information technology *investment decisions* to commonly understood business decision-making processes and business investment decisions.

1–4 NEW DECISION-MAKING CRITERIA

A new set of decision-making tools and concepts, applied to information technology, is needed to cope with the problem. Company managers routinely make decisions about resources such as which information technology projects should be funded. How can information technology projects compete successfully with other corporate priorities? How do managers successfully choose between alternative investments? Clearly, the ones chosen *should* be the ones that have the most impact on the business performance of the enterprise. A set of tools and concepts that can assess the impact on performance of the information technology investment is needed.

The problem, of course, is complicated. Some investments improve the existing infrastructure: the mainframe computer, a collection of personal or departmental computers, a communications network, the database and systems development software. These investments do not themselves affect business performance, but they create the capability for many individual application projects, much like a manufacturing building and its utility and heating systems provide the infrastructure for the production of a company's product lines. Other investments improve the existing technology with new enhancements. Still other investment potentials include projects on the basis of some form of priorities. Should we install an order-entry system or a marketing intelligence system? Both infrastructure and application project decisions are ultimately priority decisions: which of the many possibilities are the best and deserve support?

We have developed **Information Economics** to give management the concepts and tools to answer these questions. Three categories are highlighted: the definition of value built on an expanded vision of benefit; the definition of cost which includes explicit consideration of the potential risk; and a decision-making process to make investment decisions in a manner consistent with business investment decisions.

The result is a framework of concepts and tools. At one level, Information Economics is a collection of computational tools for quantifying benefits and costs for information technology projects. This is the traditional role of cost-benefit analysis (CBA). Information Economics looks beyond CBA to deal with value based on business performance—to handle such as those that have strategic impact on the company. Information Economics also looks at the information technology infrastructure—the supply side investment in the infrastructure.

At a second level, Information Economics is a process of decision-making. Every proposed investment—programmer, application, hardware—should be justified, but every potential investment has unique and different characteristics to its value, costs, and risks. Resource allocation is decision-making among alternative investments, such as installing a relational database management system, buying the Financial Reporting System, or hiring a personal computer support professional. *Prioritizing* among alternatives is extremely difficult. Yet managers must make decisions on priorities all the time.

Our purpose is to take economic tools like CBA and expand them to embrace competitive advantage and infrastructure, and at the same time provide guidance for a coherent and consistent decision-making process.

1–5 NEW DECISION-MAKING PROCESS

We started this chapter by asking "What is Information Technology Worth?" We answered the question by introducing *value* as the basis for determining worth, and by expanding *cost* to include the ideas of organizational impact of change. In effect, we have created a two-part decision, one based on business value through performance, and one based on technology cost.

Information Economics applies a decision process that separates the *business justification* for information technology from the elements of *technological viability* for the proposed application. Both are necessary, but the measurements and considerations are separate and should be determined separately. From the business perspective, justification is on the basis of the project value compared to cost.

This allows us to ask the two key questions. First, what is an information technology investment worth to the business? We've described this at length in previous sections. Second, do we have the resources to complete the project—that is, to overcome all of the technology and organizational impact hurdles that the investment raises? Figure 1.1 graphically shows the decision elements from the business and technology perspectives.

From the technology perspective, viability of the investment is based on project resources available compared to the resources needed to successfully develop and implement the project. For IS organizations that use some form of chargeback to users, this translates into a cost-recovery analogous to a revenue stream for a business unit. To be viable, the cost recovery must be sufficient to cover all potential costs including items such as training, changes to development methodologies, and temporary reductions in productivity due to introduction of new technology. Even if an IS organization does

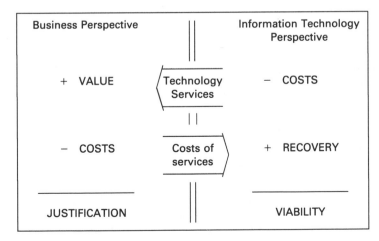

FIGURE 1.1 Information Economics.

not use a charge-back process, the problem remains: Do we have the necessary resources, such as time and personnel, to overcome the project hurdles?

From the business perspective we focus on value, meaning the effect information technology has on the performance of the business. In this sense the information technology itself has no value in the business domain; rather its value lies in the application of the technology to cause change in business performance. So any value of information technology is derived from the capability it affords the IS organization to deliver its services to the business units, whereas the value contributed to the business domain is based on the information and services actually delivered.

The justification for information technology, then, is the balance of value and cost assigned to the business, measured by the business organization in business terms, whereas viability is based on the value of the information technology to the IS organization, compared to the cost of using the technology for the service organization. Figure 1.1 shows this set of relationships.

As Figure 1.1 demonstrates, the separation into two perspectives allows determination of value and priorities for the business distinct from the technology infrastructure, staff, and facilities required. The two perspectives are useful in a decision process, precisely because they are different. In particular, the source of value is the character of the business itself, and may not be so clearly definable in strictly fiscal terms. For example, we've read about the information economy. We don't know whether it exists, but we do know that the increasingly complex and powerful capabilities of information technology provide substantial value to the enterprise. Commentators as diverse as Richard Nolan, John Diebold, and John Naisbitt forecast a new competitive order, one founded on information and information-based services. Information becomes the foundation of competition. If this is so, the basis for planning and justifying information technology projects must reflect the new value of information *to the business*. True economic impact can be determined and projects and investments can be considered and approved with more confidence by considering justification separately from technical viability.

1–6 CHANGE

We have defined the value of information technology based on its true economic impact. Underneath this idea is an undercurrent of change. First, we propose that the real benefit of information technology comes from change in the business. Products, markets, management styles, and organizational structures are changed by information technology. Second, we propose that the ways in which a company plans and manages its information technology also changes, because its business objectives are influenced by information technology.

1–7 WHAT INFORMATION ECONOMICS IS NOT

We have ground rules for this particular vision of a decision process. In particular, this is not a book on strategic planning, competitive systems development, or traditional economics. Sources for such ideas are cited in the references. We also do not define strategic planning for information technology. The Information Economics process will not produce the *vision* or *ideas* for the appropriate infrastructure or strategies. For example, whether a company should use decentralized versus centralized information technology, per se, isn't the issue we're dealing with. Rather, as further investment in the particular infrastructure strategies are required, the Information Economics processes will work to justify them.

However, we do explicitly link information technology with business performance. This is the key to Information Economics. Without linking to business performance, information technology is irrelevant. With a credible and demonstrated link to business performance, information technology is an enormously powerful tool with which managers can improve the performance—the strength and vitality—for the organizations for which they are responsible.

1–8 THE DETAILS OF INFORMATION ECONOMICS

We present the details of Information Economics in three parts. First, we explore the notion of *value* in increasing detail. The following chapters in Part One look at various facets:

1. Introduction to Information Economics
2. Challenges and Problems
3. Information Value in the Business Domain
4. Information Value and the Technology Domain
5. Information Economics and Organizational Planning
6. Costs, Benefits, and Value
7. A Process for Linking Business and Information Technology

We will consider the implications of *value* and *business performance as the measure of value* for the enterprise and its management, and for the IS Organization and its staff. We end Part 1 with an overview of a planning process that allows the use of Information Economics in decision-making about MIS investments.

Part Two presents a number of explicit tools and approaches in Information Economics. Some of these are extensions to cost-benefit analysis in that they add to the methods of measuring cost reduction and revenue enhancement due to MIS applications. Others present new ways to assess value and costs beyond the scope of traditional cost-benefit analysis. The following chapters provide appropriate case examples for each Information Economics tool.

8. Cost-Benefit Analysis
9. Information Economics Tools
10. Value Linking and Value Acceleration
11. Value Restructuring
12. Innovation

13. Business Domain Values and Risks
14. Technology Domain Values and Risks

Part Three looks at the problem of installing and using Information Economics in real enterprises. The problem of operationalizing the ideas of Information Economics is considered at length. In particular, we recognize that every enterprise is different, with different cultures, management styles, and business conditions. Accordingly, we've adopted a strong contingent approach—which explicitly provides for adjustment to the realities of individual organizations and enterprises. Similarly, in Chapters Five, Fifteen, and Eighteen we discuss how these ideas can be applied to organizations that are not-for-profit (i.e. governmental agencies and not-for-profit institutions). The following chapters reflect this contingent orientation.

15. The Basis for Corporate Values
16. The Corporate Decision Process
17. Applying Information Economics in a Corporate Setting
18. Summing Up Information Economics

QUESTIONS

1. What is information worth to you as an individual?

2. What kind of company or industry would be likely to place the greatest value on information?

3. What kind of information is most valuable?

4. What is the value of strategic planning?

5. What is an example of change that information technology has caused in a business with which you are familiar?

6. Does information have value for a non-profit or governmental organization? Specifically, would you be willing to pay more taxes to obtain such information?

2

Challenges and Problems

In Chapter One we state that decisions about information technology should focus on the relationship of the investment to business performance, that this relationship defines the value and hence the desirability of the investment.

Sounds easy. In real life there are, however, some challenges.

2–1 A CASE: RIKI TIKI TRAVEL

Companies that deal in travel have an interesting time of it. Riki Tiki provides travel services to corporations. When executives wish to travel their office calls Riki Tiki. They, in turn, make the reservation, print the ticket, deliver the ticket to the traveler, and bill the executive's company.

Information technology is important in each element. A phone system with message-taking and call-director capabilities adds productivity to the firm. An online terminal to the airline reservation system enables the airline transaction itself. An in-house computer electronically receives the confirmed reservation and prints the ticket and boarding pass on a printer located in the customer's company and connected through Riki Tiki's communications network. A back-office system keeps track of the ticket and produces periodic invoices and accounts receivable follow-up.

Riki Tiki faces a number of problems. The airlines are increasingly competitive.

The threat of their making substantial inroads to the corporate market, by providing Riki Tiki's services directly to the traveler, is growing. Other travel companies compete strongly, using their own versions of the systems Riki Tiki has installed. Corporations are increasingly interested in managing their own travel business, particularly to control their travel costs and implement their travel policies.

In addition, there is intense price competition in the business. Though service levels are also important, companies are reluctant to pay more than necessary for travel. Consequently, cost control and productivity are constant management concerns for the travel company.

The combination of price competition (and hence cost control) and strong competitive pressures, against which a company must continue to innovate in services and products, is a *real* challenge. Yet vendors, both airline and hardware and software companies, are aggressively developing new computer products to sell to Riki Tiki. For example, one large company sells a product that may allow Riki Tiki to get into the group and charter market with distinctive services to customers. The product has appealing features, including a video-disk destination coverage that should attract the interest of customers. Another company sells a complete back-office system to reduce the per-ticket back-office processing costs. Still another integrates word processing with an intelligent airline system workstation, enabling rapid correspondence (response and confirmation) to customers.

In Information Economics terms, each of these systems represents real potential value to Riki Tiki. Each promises to improve business performance, either in terms of cost control or in terms of improved service to customers. There are risks and uncertainties, of course. It isn't completely clear that the software will actually produce the promised benefit. It isn't clear that the corporate customers actually want, or will respond to, some of the improved services. And it isn't clear what the effect on Riki Tiki's business performance really will be.

And yet Riki Tiki management must make some decision, even if it's a non-decision which has the effect of saying no to every possibility. It comes down to "what is it worth" to Riki Tiki. Is it worth one million dollars to buy a first-class back-office system that controls billing and invoicing in a superior way, and also enables a better communications network for remote printing of tickets? These capabilities are probably worth something—*but is it number one on the list*?

The case shows the difficulty of the decision. That same million dollars can also acquire a competitor to Riki Tiki, it can set up a branch in another part of the city in order to compete better for suburban company business, or it can hire several more marketing staff. And it's real money, probably obtained by borrowing. The problem comes down to the degree of management's commitment to the goals, and the strength of the case made for each alternative, founded on clear *value* and *costs* (*including risks*) of the project.

Management decision-making for Riki Tiki will depend on the link between business performance and each alternative. In Information Economics terms, we see four steps to the solution: (1) identify the value, and full cost, for each project; (2) apply broad economic criteria in a decision process; (3) assess alternatives; and (4) allocate scarce resources to the most valuable projects.

2–2 CLASSES OF VALUE

As we can tell from Riki Tiki, the potential for a company to gain value from information technology is large, and also diverse. Management has been interested in value and costs ever since information technology began, of course. From the beginning, the idea of *benefit*—the benefits in cost-benefit analysis—originated with cost reduction. In order to assess the additional ways information technology provides value to the enterprise, that is, the ways information technology contributes to improved business performance, we have expanded the idea of benefit to six *classes of value*: (1) return on investment; (2) strategic match; (3) competitive advantage; (4) management information; (5) competitive response; and (6) strategic IS architectures (Figure 2.1).

Briefly, each may be defined as follows: *Return on investment* is derived from traditional cost-benefit analysis (CBA) and reflects advanced ideas on defining the financial effects (both cost and benefit) from information technology. *Strategic match* is the value derived from directly supporting an existing business unit strategy. For example, if Riki Tiki adopts a business strategy of direct consumer advertising, then an MIS application that enables direct consumer communications is within this class of value. *Competitive advantage* is the value derived from creating a new business strategy, a new product, or a new approach to overcoming a competitive force or hurdle. For example, Keep-On Trucking may install an MIS application to directly connect it to its leasing customers. This system permits Keep-On Trucking to track truck maintenance and provide customers with early warning information. This feature adds considerable value to the customer—something no competitor could do—and is an example of competitive advantage as a value. *Management information* is the value derived from information support of an enterprise or line of business critical success factor. For example, Riki Tiki Travel management may conclude its most critical factor is customer satisfaction with ticket delivery. An application that tracks the performance of ticket delivery and that allows management follow-up and control over this factor, provides this value. *Competitive response* reflects information technology projects intended to catch up with the competition. For example, if Old Ivy University discovers that its research line of business is losing research contracts to other universities capable of intense supercomputing in high energy physics, then an investment that makes such supercomputing possible at Old Ivy is a competitive response. *Strategic IS architecture* is an investment that enables other projects to occur. For example, if Riki Tiki invests in a communications network that is a precondition to on-premise delivery of tickets and boarding passes as well as on-premise delivery of itineraries and other information about travel for other corporate customers, it has invested in strategic IS architecture.

Return on Investment
Strategic Match
Competitive Advantage
Management Information
Competitive Response
Strategic IS Architecture

FIGURE 2.1   Classes of value.

Chapter Six provides considerable detail for each class of value. The point here is to introduce the classes to demonstrate the broad range of values of information technology investments that can have substantial effect on the business performance of an enterprise.

Information Economics measures each class with an appropriate value measurement and recognition. For example, a truck leasing company obtains new competitive advantage from a system that improves route and service station information to its customers' drivers. This system has no cost reduction value nor direct revenue creation value, yet has a profound effect, hence value, on the company's competitive position and business performance. Keep-On Trucking's customers gain value by the improvement in their drivers' performance, and Keep-On Trucking gains new customers. Riki Tiki Travel has the problem of its competitors already having superior in-house computing that offers their corporate clients the means to define travel policies for enhanced cost control. In simple terms, Riki Tiki has to catch up, to provide a competitive response in order to maintain its customer base.

Our goal is to provide measures to assess these values. In the case of Keep-On Trucking, how much of a competitive advantage is there? In the case of Riki Tiki Travel, how much competitive response is necessary? A million dollars worth? The challenge is to get business managers to think through the values and relate them to the potential effect on the business.

2-3 ALLOCATING SCARCE RESOURCES

A company has limited resources to invest in information technology. Indeed, a company has limited resources to invest in any aspect of its business. So management has choices to make. Should that new plant be built? Should we purchase that local area network (LAN)? Should we initiate that online order-entry system? The company also has limited organization resources to invest. The Information Systems (IS) department has a finite set of skilled professionals, and the business domain has a similarly finite set of knowledgeable managers. A decision about allocation of this scarce resource has the same basis as funds: Where should we best deploy these resources for the health of the enterprise?

2-4 ASSESSING ALTERNATIVES

A company needs to assess alternatives and make its resource allocation decisions in the most effective way. The decision process should focus on value and cost. Value is used to rank opportunities (by each of the categories of value) to best define the basis for prioritizing the use of scarce resources.

What isn't so obvious, but sensible, is that the best judges of value are the full set of managers affected by the each project. Their participation makes it possible to develop consensus among senior management, financial and planning staffs. The choices are not only between desirable technology alternatives but also between technology and investment in other parts of the business. Hence the decision process should be **understandable** and **meaningful** to *both* business and technology managers. We characterize the resource competition and allocation decision process in Figure 2.2.

Management can choose to invest in LOBs, the corporate backbone infrastructure, or the information technology utility. **The choices are not necessarily discrete. The investment may be an information system that supports both the LOB and corporate backbone.** As managers, we expect that an investment in a financial system for corporate accounting has the same result (we hope) as an investment in more accountants for corporate accounting: improved performance of that backbone activity.

For example, Old Ivy University's LOBs are (1) undergraduate education; (2) graduate education; (3) research; and (4) patient care (in the university hospital). University management can choose to allocate operating budget appropriations among these LOBs, the administrative backbone units, the information systems organization, or to computing equipment such as personal computers in the administrative and academic departments. Similarly, the administration may choose to allocate a capital gift or bequest among these categories. So the administration may decide among capital investments in undergraduate teaching laboratories, graduate student housing, scientific equipment for research, upgrade of the cardiac care unit, additions to the accounting office staff, and a computer network for instructional computing. Assuming funds are finite, these are good examples of the choices facing an administration.

We propose the decision should be determined by comparing the effect each alternative may have on the *business performance of the LOB* affected; that is, the decision should be determined by comparing the *value* of each alternative to the institution.

What about alternatives that add value to the corporate backbone or overhead rather than directly to the LOBs? We can easily define the LOB value of adding to undergraduate teaching laboratories in terms of enhanced attractiveness to prospective students or reduced costs of operating the laboratories. Both add to the performance of the undergraduate line of business. But what about an alternative that enhances the performance of the central accounting office staff?

For example, a proposed electronic mail system for the accounting department may increase the productivity of each accountant. No direct cost reduction is anticipated (that is, no staff reductions will occur), but enhanced accounting services may be provided

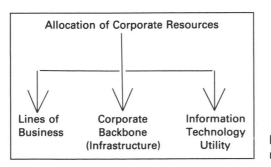

FIGURE 2.2 Allocation of corporate resources.

to the rest of the institution. How should this alternative be assessed and compared to the other investment possibilities?

For the corporate backbone or infrastructure the assessment of the value for an investment is based on the effect the innovation will have on the business performance of the *LOBs served by the backbone accounting staff*. This can, of course, include a reduction of the cost of accounting services allocated to the LOB (if corporate overhead is distributed). So the test of the electronic mail system for the accounting office should be based on the effect on the LOBs it services. If no direct connection to LOB bottom-line performance can be found, perhaps (in Information Economics terms) the investment is not justified.

2–5 ECONOMIC CRITERIA FOR DECISION-MAKING

The current tools in cost-benefit analysis cannot easily be applied to all classes of value and, consequently, will drive resource allocation processes badly. We find this most conspicuous in annual planning processes that allocate operating budgets. There, the tendency is to rely on traditional costs and benefits and ROI. However, traditional techniques do not easily consider the value, for example, in competitive response and strategic IS architecture.

To summarize, there are problems that create the need for Information Economics. First, the classes of value a company obtains through information technology are diverse. Second, a company has limited resources to invest in information technology. Third, a company needs to make allocation decisions in the most effective way. And fourth, tools in traditional cost-benefit analysis are not adequate to address all classes of value.

2–6 PROJECT ASSESSMENT

We address the problems in two ways. We apply new Information Economics tools to define value, and we create an Information Economics decision process. The implementation of both can be visualized with a simple clerical form shown in Figure 2.3.

Participant in Process	Value	Investment	
Business Manager(s)	Business Domain Feasibility	Technology Domain Viability	Agreed Ranking
Financial Officer(s)			
Corporate Planner(s)			
IS Manager(s)			
Consensus: Agreed Values and Evaluations			

FIGURE 2.3 Information economics project assessment form.

This figure is a simplified version of a decision and evaluation process conducted by the several management groups affected by a project. The process is intended to develop a measure of value and an understanding of costs and potential sources of failure, or risk. In addition, the process results in consensus on values among the management groups, or the project does not receive further consideration. The evaluation covers both business feasibility—value and effect on business performance—and technical viability, including risk identification. Business feasibility includes the classes of value such as strategic match and competitive response. The idea is to grade feasibility by business value as perceived by each of the affected management groups. This develops consensus and enhances the learning and awareness of each group about the concerns and evaluations of the others. The book develops the basis on which value is defined and measured (or assessed) and then describes value tools and details of the decision process. Cases that demonstrate both value and the application of decision value tools are presented.

The project assessment form conveys the essential ideas (Figure 2.3). First, each opportunity for investment is evaluated, whether it's infrastructure (for example, a new database management tool) or an application project (for example, a new strategic system). Second, projects are ranked in a decision process that promotes consensus among the management units represented.

The result is an enterprise view of the possible investments with a consensus view of the value of the investments. Each project has a value measured with Information Economics. This allows the company management team to determine resource allocation among the projects.

2–7 THE JUSTIFICATION FOR INFORMATION ECONOMICS

To some managers applying traditional approaches to evaluating information technology investments, it isn't clear that further investment in information technology is justified for their company. One company executive said to us: "In my view, we are wasting our dollars on computers. We have to reduce corporate overhead now, and one prime candidate may be the IS department. They spend money, lots of it, but without clear impact on our business performance. Our problem is knowing whether our investment in computing is effective, worth it to us, or whether we should be investing our resources and energies elsewhere to better effect."

His view might be correct. Paul Strassman's studies suggest that high information technology costs in companies are *not* automatically reflected in high return on investment for those companies. Further, he proposes that poor performance—that is, poor productivity—in the information technology part of the business is a cause of noncompetitive costs of American business (Strassman, 1985). These results are counterintuitive to the wisdom of most computer professionals. If he is correct, then companies face a serious risk. The situation is made increasingly dubious when the information technology investments are determined by technology managers and not business managers. Computing in companies is managed, usually, by the technology managers. Management by technology-oriented managers prevents the clear relationship between *investment in information technology* and *improved business results*. It is precisely this relationship that we are working to create with Information Economics.

The problem is one of credibility. Will information technology improve business performance? This elusive relationship is demonstrated in texts written by and for information technology managers. For example, one textbook describes information technology strategic planning as the way an organization determines its long range goals for information systems delivery. So an organization may decide that it will convert from batch to an online environment or install database management. "The effectiveness of a new information systems environment [is] the primary reason organizations should consider information systems strategic planning" (Gillenson and Goldberg, 1984, pp. 68–69). Well, yes. On the other hand, this thinking leads to higher costs and substantial investments in the absence of clear connection to the ways the investments link to business performance. The questions should be: Is it sound from a business perspective to entertain these investments? What's the economic effect these strategic plans will have on the enterprise as a whole? Is it merely an addition to cost? (A manager who has had the experience of adding substantial resources such as word processing or electronic mail where *no* cost reductions were accomplished or, worse, equipment was poorly used by the ultimate users, can be very sensitive to the issues. Seeing personal computers sitting on shelves gathering dust rather than adding to business performance is discouraging.)

Decisions about technology investments such as networks and advanced database systems, when evaluated by technology management, appear necessary and prudent to them. The linkage between them and real effect on the business, however, is illusive. Such decisions show what's involved when information technology managers are the primary managers involved in making (from a business impact perspective) basic information technology decisions.

In contrast, another company executive in the same industry as the one cited at the beginning of this section remarked: "Computing is crucial to our future and our competitive capacities. We intend to invest heavily in our computing infrastructure and in our capacity to apply computing to our business. Our problem is knowing how best to invest our resources. What can we do to make investment decisions most wisely? What can we do to assure maximum business impact from our investments in computing?"

These comments typify the fundamentally conflicting points of view in industry today. On the one hand, "competing with computing" books and articles have hyped the importance of computing in the enterprise. In this view, each company can apply computing to its competitive advantage; it is only a question of how and where. The value of information technology is that it is a major potential force for strengthening and advancing the enterprise. On the other hand, computing costs continue to escalate without clear evidence of actual contributions made to the enterprise bottom line. Corporate computing is part of the corporate overhead, and hence subject to the same forces that result in decentralization and/or elimination in corporate restructuring.

The two executive views are quite different but deal with the same fundamental issues: the value of information technology to the enterprise (and how we can measure it); and the decision process to determine the wisest investment of its limited resources in computing.

Fred Crawford, a retired CEO of TRW, noted that of the hundred largest companies in revenues in 1900, by 1980 only two of them were still around. He observed that the pace of technology is such that in ten years we have surpassed the magnitude of technology advances for the prior seventy years. Does this suggest a more rapid pace of effect on company health? Shanklin and Ryans report a CEO's perspective: "I think there are going to be more companies that get killed by the technology and particularly, they are going to get killed by their inability to see what is happening . . . they will get killed by not understanding the world that they are in and making adjustments to it" (1985, p. 109). And they'll be killed by the companies—their competitors—who *do* understand these things.

2–8 CHALLENGES IN INFORMATION TECHNOLOGY

We believe that information technology is a **fundamental force** in reshaping the business world. There are surely enough authors making the point in books ranging from *Megatrends* to *Infotrends*. Moreover, each manager must be able to determine the value of information technology in his or her organization. To this end, we assert:

1. Information technology is important to the enterprise.

2. Management decision-making about information technology investments, if made solely with an IS technology perspective, *handicaps* the enterprise in making the wisest investment decisions.

3. What's needed is a set of concepts and ideas that develops information technology's *true economic impact* on the business, both value and cost.

4. The goal of Information Economics is a business-based decision process for making information technology investments.

5. A soundly implemented infrastructure—computing and communications—is a prerequisite for effective information technology implementations.

6. The result should be a partnership between technology managers and enterprise business managers.

2–8–1 Information Technology Is Important
to the Enterprise

We gave a presentation on the importance of information technology to a group of managers. We cited the cement business as an example of a business in which information technology may not be so important. To our surprise, a manager from a cement company took great exception to this. He said that he had been greatly affected by his competitor's use of computers to provide improved customer service. To him, the computer had made a significant competitive difference.

The press has widely reported companies that have had great success in using computing to their advantage. The more often reported cases, American Hospital Supply and American Airlines, make the strong case for computing as providing significant competitive edges in their respective businesses. Even in such relatively mundane areas as back-office support and word processing, however, computing has made real differences to small and large companies. Few companies would or could abandon their existing computing activities.

A manager should ask three questions:

- How can my company compete more effectively by using computing?
- How can my company improve its productivity and effectiveness using computing?
- How can my organization plan computing most effectively?

Answers and directions for the first question are found in the "competing with computing" literature. *Strategy and Computers* (Wiseman, 1985) offers several ideas for identifying potential competitive applications. Wiseman makes the point that these applications, which he calls strategic information systems (SIS), are different in almost all respects from traditionally defined application systems—and cannot be planned and developed according to traditional information technology planning methods. The reason for this lies in the character of the application. Traditional methods focus on describing the existing business and business organizations. Data flow diagrams and data models are used to accurately portray what is happening in the system now, to enable their automation. SIS on the other hand represent completely new functions, new business activities, new management tasks. In short, traditional methods match information technology to business; the design of SIS defines the business through the application of information technology.

Based on the examples reported in major magazines and newspapers, information technology *is* important. The press has routinely reported on the potential of information technology. Feature stories highlight applications such as telemarketing, customer service, training, sales support, and improved financial management.

Some examples:

- A retail store may add distinctiveness and value by providing telephone ordering. A computer system records the order, organizes the delivery, and prints the various labels and bills. Done in a timely way, this can cause potential customers to choose this store, not for low costs, but for the convenience and service.
- A cement company may add value to its services by giving its customers data about previous, current, and future shipments. The company may be able to deliver on time and at lower cost because of the computer dispatch and order entry system. The dependability and lower costs add value to prospective customers. It may add value to that customer's customers.

Such examples are perhaps intuitively obvious. Their purpose is to look at the way in which products and services are provided to the customer, and to determine how best to make the enterprise-customer relationship of particular value to that customer.

Richard Nolan observes that information technology is the force that causes the transition from an industrial to an information service economy. New information-based industries and enterprises have already emerged. Further, the competitive balance among companies, even in manufacturing and other heavy industries, is changing from costs to intangibles such as quality, serviceability, and time of delivery. This results in the success or failure of companies to be based on such intangibles (Nolan, 1986).

We propose that this basis for competition is the value represented by information technology, which can be described in the values included in Figure 2.1.

2–8–2 IS Management-Driven Decision-Making

Management decision-making about information technology investments, if made with an IS technology perspective, *handicaps* the enterprise in making the wisest investment decisions.

Focusing on supply-side planning is all too easy. From the beginning of computing, management has overestimated what can be done and underestimated the time and costs required. The result is a real focus on the programming and computer part of projects and plans. In prior years this may have been justified because the crucial issues in information technology were delivery issues—did it, or would it, ever work? Now the issues have shifted. We can make it work. The question is, do we want to? Whether we can make a contribution to the business success is the issue.

Traditional, technology-based approaches to decisions and plans concerning information technology get in the way of real progress in the enterprise. One such technology-based approach is to think about managing the IS department as a *business-within-a-business*. The purpose is to develop a customer orientation for the IS group and hence add business emphasis to the need for the company to invest in the information technology infrastructure. Presumably, a business-within-a-business needs capital investment for the creation and maintenance of its productive capabilities, much like the enterprise itself. This new management paradigm perhaps offers some assistance in addressing the user ("they are our customers") and investment issues. However, this approach merely disguises the problem of technology-based decisions as business-based decisions. It fails to consider the basis of value of computing to the user and hence misses the values for the business it serves. The correct approach is to focus, not on the performance of the information technology activities, but on the performance of the business itself. This will ultimately justify the necessary investment in the information technology infrastructure (Allen, 1987).

The ideas represented by business-within-a-business and the previously described strategic information technology planning tend to avoid direct business impact; rather, they tend to have a *transaction* or *process* view of information systems. What this means is that the primary users—the ones buying the services of the business-within-a-business—are themselves largely the overhead of the enterprise. Their own contributions to business effectiveness and to the bottom-line are obscured and indistinct. In some ways this view only exacerbates the problem of technology-based decisions about information technology. For example, materials that describe the IBM business systems planning (BSP) processes focus on data and functions—useful items, but not clearly related to the success of the business enterprise itself. The bottom-line improvement or success is the point of the information technology investment.

The key is to subordinate technology decision-making to business decision-making. Architectures, networks, and computer delivery systems *are* important to be sure, and Information Economics needs to give information technology managers the tools to justify and apply such tools properly. Nevertheless, these are means, vehicles for business direction and application. The decisions to move forward, to make the investments, are better made as business decisions.

Lest we be accused of treating this issue only in strategic terms, we believe the issue of technology-based decision-making as a hindrance applies at least equally to individual application systems projects. The literature is full of cases where IS-motivated applications failed or where the IS-driven projects solved problems that didn't exist or weren't important. One of the messages of systems development methodologies is exactly this. The user should be directly involved in the development of projects and their objectives. The process part of Information Economics gets directly at this point.

2–8–3 Case: Keep-On Trucking

A Midwestern truck leasing company, Keep-On Trucking, illustrates the danger. Management became convinced that replacing a ten-year-old computer was the highest priority for computing within the company because the equipment was perceived as the bottleneck for effective computing systems. Company management directed the IS staff to create a multiyear plan to replace the hardware and re-do the corporate backbone systems. The emphasis was on the change in hardware.

Three years later the company has installed three new computers and new applications, but it is still running the application software on the old (now thirteen-year-old) computer. No substantial contribution to corporate goals has been made. The expenditure budget for the computer organization has more than doubled. Company management is very worried about the IS investment in hardware, but they have no vehicle to consider or address the problems. Our observation: The company focused on technology issues and not the method for adding value to the LOBs and the company as a whole. That the hardware is old really doesn't matter—unless there's a line of business rationale for the older computer as a problem.

2–8–4 True Economic Impact

The understanding of true economic impact requires both a business-based understanding of values and a technology-based understanding of the investment needed to realize those values. Once this understanding is in place, the process gives business leadership a suitable structure for making the wisest choice for investment. The solely technology-based decision-making hinders the enterprise and its leadership from understanding and making these decisions.

Wiseman's work describes this idea in an interesting way. He notes that information systems planning, driven from the technology perspective, has a limited vision as to the possibilities. This vision limitation is essentially *process* oriented—the processes necessary to carry out the business of the enterprise. He suggests that Anthony's triangle (strategic planning, management control, and operational control; see Anthony, 1965) exerts a conceptual limitation on the vision of what is possible in applying computing innovatively (Wiseman, 1985). Interestingly, a similar point is made by researchers looking at potential artificial intelligence (AI) applications. Their point is that AI makes possible new ways of doing new things, not simply automating the old ways of doing things in new ways.

For example, an information systems professional may look into the possibilities of a new system for an accounting department by doing data flow diagrams and data models. By applying Anthony's ideas, he may look at the operational tasks of the department, define the management control opportunities, and speculate on strategic planning possibilities for the activities of the accounting department. The driving question: How can he apply information technology to improve the functioning of the accounting department and its staff? Yet from the business perspective, the question may be more fundamental: How does the accounting department relate to business performance, and what does the *business* need from the accounting department? The difference between the information technology perspective and the business perspective is subtle but crucial. Starting from the information technology perspective tends to limit the vision to the needs of the business unit in question. Starting from the business perspective tends to open the vision to overall business (meaning business performance) requirements.

Business vision, business objectives, business management goals and opportunities should drive the vision and the use of information technology. A process for measuring, describing, communicating the business potential—to business management—is crucial in making the wisest investment in information technology. Process-oriented (meaning information systems processes), technology-oriented approaches, with limited vision of the potential values—the true economic impact—are insufficient.

2–8–5 Enhanced Vision of Business Effect

Our goals for Information Economics are an enhanced vision of the potential business effect of information technology investment and a business-based decision process for making information technology investments. The second goal is key; we need to transform the decision process from a primarily technology-driven one to a primarily business-driven one. The ultimate purpose is to affect the allocation of resources through planning processes.

2–8–6 Business Value from IS Infrastructure and Architectures

Even though an enhanced business vision of the value of information technology is the foundation for wise planning and investment, a soundly implemented infrastructure—computing and communications—is a prerequisite for effective information technology implementations. This gives us a particular problem in relating information technology investments to business performance, because investments in the infrastructure—though necessary—are not easily related to specific improvements to business performance.

A mature computing organization has well-developed strategies for communications networks, database administration, fourth generation development languages, artificial intelligence, and so forth. All these can make up the company's strategic architecture—that collection of services and facilities that comprise the mainline computing for the enterprise. For example, Old Ivy University has settled on an infrastructure that includes centralized IBM mainframes, departmental DEC VAXs, IBM PCs, a copper-wire communications network, and VM (IBM's Virtual Machine control program) and CICS (IBM's largest-used online systems environment) with MVS.

Key elements of the architecture, for example, the database software, are costs borne by the information systems organization without attribution to specific systems projects. The architecture—the infrastructure—is crucially important to the IS organization in the development of its services. The investment needs description and justification. Architectural components can include:

- Computer
- Communications Networks
- Database and related systems development tools
- Data—the enterprise-wide data model

Consider a state-of-the-art manufacturing facility. Such a facility is a significant asset to the business; it in itself has value. The existence of the productive capacity makes the company capable of competing effectively for future business. Without it, a company can compete only if substitute capacity can be found, or if the delay in erecting the plant can be endured. This exactly describes the role of infrastructure and architectures in the information technology arena. The achievement of the productive capacity in itself is a value that significantly affects the capacity of the company to compete in the future.

2–8–7 Technology and Business Partnership

The result of Information Economics should be a partnership between technology managers and enterprise business managers.

Two complementary ideas stand out. The first is that the full attention of the business manager should be on the values and outcomes of information technology—how to define them, measure them, and achieve them. Second, the business manager is one part of a partnership. The other part is the technology establishment, the IS organization. Achieving the values of information technology depends on effective methods for working with the technology sector of the enterprise.

Poor communication between the business organization and the IS unit is a problem. The business manager should assign explicit responsibility for the communications with IS *and* for successful accomplishment of the information technology project within the business unit. In the absence of a business sector manager taking this responsibility, the technology manager is forced to do it. Unfortunately, the technology side is not capable of fulfilling the responsibility for effective communication to and from the business unit. The reason is that the most-needed communication is about business objectives and not technology objectives. An effective partnership that sets the future course for investment and management is crucial to the future success of the enterprise.

QUESTIONS

1. Name three ways a company gains value from information technology.

2. Give an example of strategic advantage in a company you know.

3. Give an example of cost and performance value derived from information technology in a company you know.

4. Give an example of competitive advantage in a company you know.

5. Give an example of strategic match as a part of an information system in a company you know.

6. Why does a company need to make resource allocation decisions effectively?

7. In what way does it matter, and to whom?

8. Define the lines of business for a company you know.

9. Define the lines of business for IBM or a similar company.

10. Define the lines of business for a large metropolitan hospital.

11. Describe the difference between an information system that supports a line of business as compared to one that supports the corporate backbone functions. In what ways do these systems compete?

12. In what ways can business technology improve business performance for a line of business?

13. Speculate on which of the Fortune 500 companies won't be on the list in the year 2040—because of the influence of information technologies.

14. Why did Keep-on Trucking not enjoy success in the development of information systems?

3

Information Value in the Business Domain

The heart of Information Economics is *change*. We assert that **the business must change to achieve real, enduring value from information technology.** Consequently, we need ways to describe change and its effect on an organization. In this chapter we explore some of the tools available and their use in defining what constitutes important change.

3–1 CHANGE AND VALUE

From the beginning, data processing textbooks have emphasized the need for management support. The reason is simple: A data processing system requires *change* in the user's organization. For example, a simple payroll application requires the payroll office to do things differently. Data must be entered into a terminal or onto a data form, and failure to get the data entered correctly produces bad results. Consequently, the payroll office procedures are changed substantially. Further, to accomplish system goals of cost reduction, tasks, and responsibilities, organizations have to do things differently. Moreover, other organizations may change. Systems intended to have strategic value for a company do so by changing the behavior or actions of customers and suppliers.

That's the point of such systems. For example, a company using a communications system to permit customers to enter orders directly depends, for successful accomplishment of its goals, on change in customer activities *and* change in the way the company internally handles orders.

A second idea: Change is also a major source of cost and risk to the proposed system. It isn't the only cost, of course, but the planning and management of change in customer and internal organizations is a major consideration for any project.

A third element is perhaps even more important. The current business conditions reflect continual and substantial change affecting every company. Whether it's technology, patterns of government regulation, global competition, or consumer demographics, practically every element of the business environment seems to be changing. Miles and Snow cite a business executive: "Not only is it a competitive jungle out there, new beasts are roaming around that we can't even identify" (1986, p. 63). We believe information technology is both a cause of change and a crucial factor in the capability of a company to respond to other sources of change.

Change is central to Information Economics; it is the crucial element in both value and cost. The value provided by a system is founded on change in the business. To develop Information Economics, we need to understand change.

3–2 DESCRIBING AND ANALYZING CHANGE

Several useful ideas have been developed in strategic planning to assist management in understanding what's possible in the business. One set of these ideas describes the enterprise itself. Our objective is to use them to describe the enterprise in Information Economics terms.

3–2–1 Business and Technology Domains

The enterprise is described in two parts: its business activities and the supporting technology activities. The term *domain* is used to characterize the two different activities.

The purpose of the division is to emphasize the different roles of management and planning in business and technology. The business domain is the user of information technology; the technology domain is the supplier of information technology services. This supplier could be an IS department or a technical specialist in the business organization whose responsibilities include personal computing. In the business domain, the use of a computer system to store and manage personnel data creates several technology domain management responsibilities: systems design, software development, control over the data, security of information, and authorization for staff to acquire and use the information in the system (Figure 3.1).

Technology domain management responsibilities exist whether the computer is located in a centralized management department or in the business manager's office. These responsibilities are different from the business manager's responsibilities that give rise to the use of the data. It is the difference of the responsibilities—and the fact that the business domain use of the information technology creates the responsibilities in the technology domain—that makes the concept so important.

The Domains of the Enterprise	
Business Domain	Technology Domain
Staff and business units that utilize information technology.	Staff and equipment to provide information technology and services to the business domain.

FIGURE 3.1 Enterprise domains.

Technology-related problems generally are not the limiting factor in adopting information technology in business. Through the last several years, substantial progress has been made in systems development methodologies (e.g., structured concepts) and information resources management (e.g., change management). We (meaning the IS profession in general, and the IS Manager in particular) know how to manage the technology domain itself. We know how to write programs and purchase hardware. We know how to create the technology of databases and data communications. Generally, the technology part of information technology is a solved problem. What we typically don't know is how to apply the technology best to bring benefits to the business domain. Historically, the emphasis in applying information technology to business problems has been placed on the technology development for the design and implementation of the application. This often prevented a clear understanding of the potential business domain values, much less their measurement and justification by means of Information Economics.

3–2–2 Change and the Two Domains

Change is the basis for value in information technology. This change might be reassignment of staff, reorganized responsibilities, or new functions and responsibilities. For example, if a university initiates the use of a computer system to keep track of its students, the business domain management—say the registrar's office—changes the way it functions. Staff now enter data into a terminal rather than type them on cards or maintain files. Moreover, to achieve the benefit of doing this, the registrar must initiate change in the way student records functions are conducted. Presumably the effort was undertaken to achieve some objective of benefit to the university—cost reduction, perhaps, or improved data for management purposes. The registrar is the business domain manager with the obligation to achieve these benefits for the enterprise. This seems a simple idea, yet the implications of linking change in the business domain—including a management responsibility for accomplishing the change—to the use of a value in Information Economics, are significant. One of the implications is that a key element of any Information Economics project is precisely the accomplishment, in measurable terms, of the anticipated values. Surprisingly, this is harder to do than it seems, and the difficulty is one reason for focusing on the concept of two domains. When we consider strategic and competitive objectives, we will see the importance of these ideas even more directly. Incidentally university registrars do not normally think in these terms. The registrar's office is a part of the *overhead* activity of the institution. Linking the replacement of a student records system to the ultimate economic well-being of the institution is a hard matter. Without making the linkage between the investment in information technology and the institution's business performance, we cannot think about making the wisest choice.

The idea of domain separates the enterprise into two parts for the purpose of allowing us to assess responsibility, identify values and costs appropriately, and ultimately make the wisest choices for the information technology investment (see Benson and Parker, 1985).

3–3 THE VALUE CHAIN

To define the linkage between information technology and business performance, some understanding of the business itself, and its structure, objectives, and interactions with customers, suppliers, and the rest of the economic environment is necessary. The *Value Chain* provides a structure that highlights the relationship between information technology and the enterprise units. Developed by Michael Porter, the Value Chain defines the distinct activities necessary to provide products and services to the enterprise customers (Porter, 1985). It makes clear that a business has a particular relationship to its suppliers and its customers.

Each enterprise in the system buys materials, supplies, or products from the previous, or upstream, supplier, and sells materials, supplies, products, or services to the downstream enterprise (Figure 3.2). From a business strategy perspective, a useful question is, What is the value provided by a upstream business to the product or service ultimately obtained from the downstream business? What does a particular enterprise add to the distinctiveness or value of the product? Why should a buyer buy from this enterprise? In these terms, *competitive advantage* is obtained by creating distinctiveness or value that encourages the buyer to choose this enterprise's products and encourages the supplier to provide preferential treatment for this enterprise. Moreover, information technology can add distinctiveness through additions to the product itself or changes in the ways the product is provided to the buyer.

To describe the enterprise itself, the Value Chain classifies its internal activities into nine specific groups. Each activity group has a specific role to play in bringing the product or service to the buyer. Five of the nine groups are direct, or primary, activities; these are activities that acquire, create, market, and deliver the product—the line activities of the business.

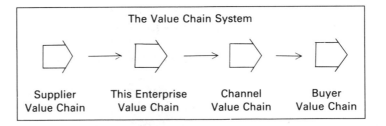

FIGURE 3.2   The Value Chain System (Adapted from Porter, 1985).

Value Chain Examples: Five Line Activities			
Line Activity Category	Example for University Research Unit	Example for Computer Manufacturer	Example for Cement Company
Inbound Logistics	Lab Animal Facility	Parts Inventory	Materials Yard
Operations	Research Lab	Manufacturing Operations	Cement Production
Outbound Logistics	Report Production	Shipping; Transportation	Truck Routing
Marketing and Sales	Federal Agency Relations	Manufacturers Representatives	Sales Force
Service	Research Update Service	Product Repair	Inspection

FIGURE 3.3 Value Chain examples of line activities.

Each activity participates directly in the sale, production, delivery, and service of the product or professional service (Figure 3.3). It's straightforward to ask how information technology can add value to each step—enhance the product itself, reduce cost or time, and add value to the customer relationship. Further, information technology can cause each of the activity groups to work more effectively together. For example, the marketing and sales activity can supply data to the outbound logistics activities and reduce time and effort in planning routes. Similarly, data can flow through production scheduling to inbound logistics and reduce inventories and hence cost, or reduce response time and hence improve timeliness of services rendered. This working together, or *linkages* (in Value Chain terms), is a crucial opportunity for information technology. Seen in this light, such innovations as just-in-time (JIT) manufacturing systems can be classified as managing the linkages. (This is discussed further in Section 10–2).

A further development is the question: What can we do to enable the activity groups of our buyer to cooperate more effectively? How can we add value through our innovations to the products and services of our buyers? How can we contribute to the competitive distinctiveness of our buyer's products and services? For example, perhaps our order entry system, coupled to our outbound logistics planning, can reduce the time required to deliver components to our buyer, thereby permitting our buyer to provide products more quickly and cheaply.

The remaining four activity categories in the Value Chain are support, or overhead, activities of the enterprise (Figure 3.4). These activities do not directly participate in product production, delivery, or marketing. Rather, they are necessary for the ongoing conduct of the business. The use of the *overhead* designation is intentional; it emphasizes that their traditional relationship to the product and customer is to add cost. The primary contribution of information technology is to reduce that cost or increase their productivity (cost reduction or cost avoidance).

The link between the information technology investment and business performance

Value Chain Examples: Four Overhead or Support Activities			
Line Activity Category	Example for University Research Unit	Example for Computer Manufacturer	Example for Cement Company
Enterprise Infrastructure	Dean; Grant Accounting	President; Finance	Accounting; General Counsel
Human Resource Management	Academic Personnel	Personnel Department	Payroll Department
Technology Development	Research Development	Engineering; R & D	Equipment Acquisition
Procurement	Departmental Business Office	Purchasing	Purchasing

FIGURE 3.4   Value Chain examples of support activities.

is especially difficult in these overhead areas. Yet, historically, the preponderance of such investments have been precisely in these areas; for example, most enterprises have significant financial and human resources systems in place. Whether they are clearly linked to business performance is a good question. Cost reduction—and future cost avoidance—is important, to be sure, as is improved management made possible by data provided from systems. Whether this results in improved business performance may be questionable, however. In particular, will investments in these corporate areas and business functions add new customers? Add competitive value?

3–4 LINE OF BUSINESS (LOB)

Real enterprises are considerably more complex than a simple Value Chain would suggest. For example, Old Ivy University is engaged in several business activities that affect a broad array of customers and involve many products. Undergraduate education is one major product; we could construct a Value Chain to represent the way the university conducts this business. We could then analyze the undergraduate business to determine how information technology could strengthen and advance university performance in it.

Information Economics links information technology to business performance. By analyzing the undergraduate business Value Chain, the question of improvement of business performance can be asked. The complexity of a real enterprise, however, is that it commonly engages in many businesses—each with quite distinct customers, products, strategies, strengths, weaknesses, and opportunities. Business performance is a function of *each* business within the enterprise. Information Economics must concern itself with the potential contribution of information technology in each of them, and each is likely unique to the particular business area.

Line of business (LOB) is the term used to describe each unique business in which the enterprise is engaged. Accordingly, a separate Value Chain is used to describe the activities, elements, and strategies followed in each LOB. Old Ivy University is in four lines of business: undergraduate education, professional education, research, and health care. Actually there are others: housing (dormitories), food service (cafeterias), and retail (bookstores). For each of these LOBs, information technology can make a contribution to business performance—and in each, this contribution is specific to the needs of that business.

In the university undergraduate LOB, the key contribution may be made in marketing and sales; information technology may provide a superior way to identify, communicate with, and ultimately attract the best qualified freshman student. The ways this contribution can be made may be quite different for professional (graduate) students. For the university health care LOB, the competitive distinctiveness from the perspective of the patient and the practicing physician may be in terms of superior bedside treatment and results information. In Value Chain terms, the undergraduate line of business key contribution may be in the marketing primary activity; in the health care LOB, in the operations activity.

The problem the university faces, overall, is the decision about best investment of information technology resources. Is undergraduate education more important than health care? Yet this is exactly the issue in allocating resources—whether capital or information technology—and is exactly the concern of the allocation decision methods presented in subsequent chapters.

3–5 LOB AND BUSINESS ORGANIZATION

Enterprises are, of course, not all alike. Many are engaged in a single LOB. For example, a passenger airline arguably is in just one LOB, with just one Value Chain needed for description and analysis. We may ask whether the business travel and personal travel are significantly different businesses. Certainly information technology innovations, such as frequent flyer programs, have been directed toward the business traveler. Yet almost all the other activities in the business are common to both sets of customers.

Other enterprises, however, are clearly in multiple LOBs. We've used Old Ivy University as an example, but large enterprises like General Electric operate forty or fifty quite distinct businesses. Indeed, the underlying ideas of LOBs—reflected in portfolio analysis in strategic planning—came from General Electric experiences in the 1960s and 1970s (Hamermesh, 1986).

For these larger enterprises, the relationship between organizational units and LOBs can become more complex (Figure 3.5). For example, the university undergraduate LOB is conducted by several autonomous business units called schools. The School of Business and School of Engineering both have undergraduate programs. The business performance of the university undergraduate LOB, then, is a summation of the performances of each of the organizational units that conduct that LOB. The same situation may be true of other enterprises. For example, General Electric, now with RCA as one of its components, may be involved in the same LOB—for example, television manufacturing—with multiple organizations. We add the line(s) of business for an enterprise as the basis for analyzing both business strategy (from the planning perspective) and business performance (from the Information Economics perspective).

Earlier we referred to the considerable literature about competitive advantage through

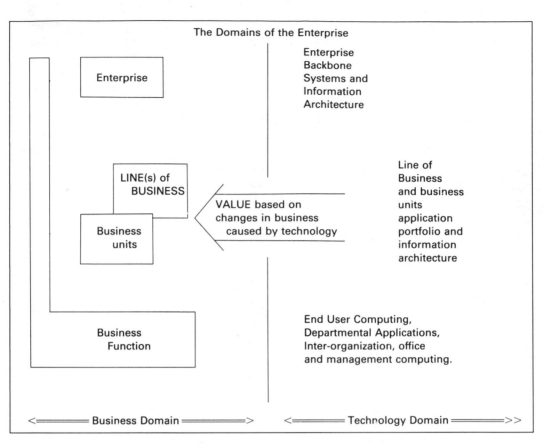

FIGURE 3.5   Multiple lines of business in the enterprise.

information technology. The value of this literature is to assist in generating new ideas about applying information technology for business value and distinctiveness. For example, we believe information technology can change the way companies relate to customers and suppliers, but actually defining which of the areas is most likely to produce value is hard.

In Figures 3.3 and 3.4 we showed an example of the Value Chain for a research unit of Old Ivy University. These two figures can be combined in Figure 3.6.

Value is obtained by changing how one of these nine elements functions and is made more productive or more effective. Porter's work in strategy focuses on ways to decide *which* activity to change in order to make a business more competitive. Information Economics is similar: Decisions about investments should be made in favor of the area with the greatest impact on the performance of the business unit.

From the technology domain perspective, the resulting application portfolio and supportive information architectures should be constructed to emphasize business performance. For Old Ivy University's research line of business, which of the nine areas will have the greatest impact on the competition for research support? To answer this

Old Ivy University			
Five Line/Primary Activities		Four Support/Overhead Activities	
Line Activity Category	Example for University Research Unit	Support Activity Category	Example for University Research Unit
Inbound Logistics	Lab Animal Facility		
Operations	Research Laboratory; Research Program	Enterprise Infrastructure	Accounting; General Counsel
		Human Resource Management	Provost; Academic Personnel
Outbound Logistics	Report Production	Technology Development	Research Administration Office
Marketing and Sales	Federal Agency Relations		
Service	Research Update Service	Procurement	Departmental Business Office

FIGURE 3.6   Old Ivy University Value Chain activities.

requires considerable understanding of the research business. It isn't something that staff from the technology domain alone can answer.

The Value Chain is a tool for defining the activities that bear on the LOB. It also can be a tool for looking at the underlying business strategy. Other tools include critical success factors (CSF) that ask us to define which area, or which activity, has to go especially well to assure LOB success (Rockart, 1979). Note that the cost reduction in the overhead areas for Old Ivy University may have little or no bearing on the success of the research activity. More than likely the research itself and direct supporting activities such as libraries, quality of available staff, and direct computational support are more important. This gives us a view about the basis for investment decisions. A new financial system or a new payroll system at Old Ivy University may not be the most desirable choice. The financial system or payroll system may be the most justifiable from the narrow ROI perspectives, but may not bear on the overall well-being of the enterprise.

3–6 THE CHANGING ENTERPRISE STRUCTURE

To this point, we have focused on changes initiated from within the enterprise. It is appealing to view change as something we choose to have in the company. As the current decade has demonstrated, however, the turbulence in business is caused by external forces. Competitive innovations, mergers and acquisitions, changing currency values, and massive foreign competition are unquestionably factors. Many of the forces and factors are certainly external to the company—environmental, technical, and competitive.

The mid-1980s created a new vocabulary in American business. **Restructuring** and **de-massing** became new business objectives. Every company, it seems, wishes to become lean and mean to combat domestic and foreign competition. Corporate leadership is on the move to attack the bloated bureaucracy of the central staff and push corporate business functions to the operating divisions of the enterprise. Corporate raiders added new dynamics; acquisitions and divestitures changed the shape of many corporations. Conglomerates abandoned unrelated businesses to focus on areas of strengths. Mergers created even larger competitors in industries such as airlines.

Information systems change because the enterprise is changing the way it does business. Enterprises now view their markets as world markets in a global economy. To compete successfully in an international arena, the ability of an enterprise to change and respond quickly is necessary. Further, the business responsibility has been driven down the organizational structure and resides in the LOB. This change requires decision and data availability to a larger group of users. For example, WALMART, a large retail chain, makes extensive amounts of information available to on-site personnel. Department managers are given mark-up information so that they will know which products to feature and promote. Decentralized decision-making can be enhanced with information systems that enable the effective functioning of the smaller-sized LOB.

Information systems facilitate restructuring into smaller, smarter lines of business to compete more effectively. Suppose a manufacturer develops an automated order-checker to assure that components ordered by customers will work together. The manufacturer makes the right components the first time and reduces the number returned. The computer configurator has a positive effect on three areas of the enterprise Value Chain—inbound logistics, operations, and outbound logistics. Analyzing market actions may also provide an edge for marketing and sales.

Information systems need to support fundamental changes in the enterprise caused by international competition, rapid technological change, and job restructuring. The ability to respond rapidly and logically to change requires a thoughtful evaluation of the affordability of the way in which we currently develop systems—with long lead times and even longer pay-backs. High personnel costs for development, long development efforts with no interim deliverables, and the inability to support change in the organization and line of business can no longer be tolerated if the enterprise is to sustain its competitive posture. The demographic changes of the labor pool (aging work force and decreased skills of new entrants) cannot be allowed to decrease employee productivity. Employee productivity must, in fact, be increased for the enterprise to sustain its competitive position.

3–7 THE CHANGING WORK FORCE

Not only must information systems support change of the organizational structure and function, it must also support change in the makeup of its labor force. By the year 2000, the U.S. work force will have undergone a major change in composition, both in the new entrants and those employed in the 1980s. The number of minority youth will increase while the total number of youth of working age (16–24) will decline. High school dropouts will increase because of the drive for renewed excellence in public school education. Of the 1980s 17-year-olds, 40 percent can't draw inferences from written materials, and 66 percent can't solve math problems with several steps (National Alliance of Business, 1986).

The impact of the changing work force on business and the economy is threefold. First, the enterprise will have to hire applicants that it would normally pass over. Second, it must plan strategically and assume responsibility for training or retraining at all levels. Third, it must develop new approaches to maintain and increase productivity and the commitment of its work force.

These forces provide distinct opportunities for information systems to facilitate more orderly change in business and the economy by developing systems: (1) with greater intelligence to compensate for the lack of work-force competence; (2) with greater intelligence to facilitate competitive edge and change; and (3) to capture competence before it is lost.

Compensating for Lack of Competence. Information systems have successfully been demonstrated in areas where lack of competence, for whatever reason, exists. The lack of competence is by no means a completely negative issue. For example, it can be created through job and enterprise restructuring. This may represent progress for some in the enterprise, at the cost of reducing the competence of the work force in new or restructured areas. This is an opportunity to apply intelligent information-based systems.

A less competent work force requires training. Job restructuring requires retraining of the current work force. Information-based systems of the enterprise contain, by definition, the data necessary for the business to function. This data in a training aid format can then be used to train or retrain the workers.

Another view of training is the effort of several companies to develop automated training aids to assist customers in using their products. In this case, they create a competitive advantage.

Decision-making and prompting systems are examples where information systems can enhance competency and productivity. Computer-integrated-manufacturing (CIM) applications such as circuit board manufacturing in IBM's Endicott plant provide for consistency in quality products. There, information technology has reduced by 50 percent direct labor content and the number of manufacturing steps. At the same time plant output has doubled, costs have dropped 20 percent a year, and quality has significantly improved (Business Week, 1986).

Facilitating Competitive Edge and Change. Decision support systems and facilitator systems are in this classification. Impetus for these systems is not lack of competence, but lack of experience, or information, or ideas for alternative action. S*P*A*R*K, a facilitator system based on brainstorming by example, provides a structure for brainstorming new ideas on using information systems to gain competitive advantage (Ives, Sakamoto, and Gongla, 1986). Here, an executive is led to consider a variety of ways in which information technology can be used to gain or maintain a competitive edge for the firm.

Capture Competence. Systems can be built to capture the critical competence of the enterprise before it is lost through retirement, competition, boredom, or cyclical change. Here, "practice capture" becomes important. Management decisions must be made about what practices need to be preserved, what ones can be eliminated or ignored, and, more important, what practices need to be created or developed. In essence, we can create our future by deeming what in our past needs to be preserved.

To summarize, a variety of technology solutions already exist to solve critical business problems triggered by societal change:

Robotics to counter a smaller, less skilled work force

Fail-safe, tutorial, and lead-by-the-hand decision support systems at low functional levels to provide consistency, quality, and functional intelligence

Decision-support systems and facilitator systems for business planning and strategy, using the time of middle and upper management more effectively

Intelligence-capturing systems for capturing the critical expert information within the enterprise before it is lost (through early retirement, competitors, or boredom)

Training and educational systems to bring substandard (for whatever reason) skills to a level of technical or business competence.

According to Paul Strassman (1985), information technology does more than simplify how a single organization operates internally. It makes possible the reorganization of an entire industry to deliver improved value to customers.

QUESTIONS

1. How does information technology cause change in a business?

2. Give examples of change you've observed in a company because of information technology.

3. Describe the business domain and technology domain for a large metropolitan hospital. Describe the domains for a company like IBM.

4. Define how change is the basis for value. Give an example of change, caused by information technology, that created a result of value for a company you know.

5. Describe the Value Chain for American Airlines.

6. Why is it important to Information Economics to link information technology to business performance?

7. How do ideas like Porter's Value Chain apply to Information Economics?

8. Describe "architecture" as it applies to information technology.

9. What forms can change take in an enterprise?

4

Information Value and the Technology Domain

4–1 VALUE AND TECHNOLOGY

IS organizations and their professional staffs find themselves caught between a complex technology and a demanding set of users. A Gresham's Law applies: Technology management problems drive out business perspective and awareness.

We see this in the many forums in which we participate, groups as wide ranging as major vendor user groups (such as SHARE and GUIDE), senior IS management groups, and our own annual conference. The problem isn't that information technology managers don't want to take on the business perspective; it is that the information technology and service management problems are themselves challenging and complex. They require full and complete attention. So we find great interest in what are essentially information technology matters: fourth-generation languages, relational database systems, enterprise-wide data networking, and information centers. These are seen as vehicles for reducing the information technology complexity of the IS activity and hence bringing services and value more quickly to the users. However, they are typical of technologies, not the applications in which they may be employed.

The measure of value is the foundation for establishing priorities for information technology. Even questions of investment in advanced technologies such as relational databases and fourth-generation languages is determined by their ultimate value to the business domain through MIS applications to be developed in the future, not their technical excellence or elegance. In short, IS management and staff need to enhance their ability to translate information technology projects into business value, and hence justify investment in the information technology.

This is a considerable shift in perspective for technology domain managers who have been taught to rely on cost-benefit analysis and technology-based service management principles. For example, information technology management may focus on keeping online systems available at the 99 percent and better level; this is a well-understood measure of performance and (they hope) user satisfaction. What isn't understood is that this sort of measure, though useful, is essentially irrelevant—second-order consideration—in determining the *value* of the service to the user. For example, an online hotel reservation system for Riki Tiki Travel has value *if* it accomplishes its intended effect on business performance. In this case that effect is improved reservation information and more timely service to Riki Tiki corporate customers. Whether it operates at 99 percent or 95 percent availability is relevant to Riki Tiki staff (certainly interruptions are frustrating) but this alone doesn't bear directly on the achievement of business performance. Moreover, further investment to improve availability (say, from 95 percent available to 99 percent available) may not be justified in terms of value, that is, its impact on business performance.

The perspective shift is profound for those that haven't considered it. Four components make up the change in perspective from *technology* to *business:*

From information technology management to business performance;

From enterprise and corporate backbone services to the lines of business;

From information technology and applications development to architecture and utility development; and

From information technology services to business leadership.

That these perspective shifts are difficult is not surprising. We have noted that many companies for which IS leadership has taken on these views rely on *business* managers as IS directors, not information technology managers. We've also noted that the degree of business perspective reflected in the IS staff appears inversely proportional to the amount of emphasis the IS staff devotes to advanced technologies; that is, IS groups that take great pride in the information technology accomplishments of their enterprise (such as the latest release of the advanced relational database to be acclaimed) tend not to exhibit the shifts in perspective necessary.

4–2 SHIFTING PERSPECTIVES FROM TECHNOLOGY TO BUSINESS

We can safely assert that information technology is mostly managed as a *technology* matter, not a *business* matter. For example, in most companies the information technology organization is led by an IS director or a chief information officer (CIO). To them are delegated most decisions about computing. Hardware and software investment decisions are largely made by information technology managers, and priority decisions are largely made on technology management factors. For example, the technology managers give high priorities to developing the service delivery capability such as time-sharing or personal computing; they place value on developing the information technology infrastructure, and this emphasis can dominate investment decisions. The IS director may target database and data communications investments or transaction-level application development to complete the enterprise database. This isn't bad; indeed, we will talk about architectures as an important perspective shift. Our emphasis here is the perspective on justification (technology vs. business impact).

Decisions to invest in technologies made for technology reasons tend not to support improved business performance. An example is standardized personal computer workstations. Typically the information technology managers work toward a standard with substantial capabilities and common software and hardware for ease of support and training. These are significant objectives, but have little direct bearing on the business success of the information technology. Certainly standards and common software by themselves do not assure that their users actually accomplish applications that improve their business performance. Yet the decision factors when initially considered by technology management, appeared necessary and prudent. They show what happens when information technology managers are the primary managers involved in evaluating (from a business impact perspective) basic information technology decisions. They are made on technology issues.

The dominance of the information technology perspective is reflected in studies of information technology managers. The Center for the Study of Data Processing studied 1500 IS managers and their views of the important issues facing them. The topics of greatest concern demonstrated interest in linking information technology planning with business planning. However, their concerns about linking such planning with the *results* in the business area, such as profitability and strategic impact, were at the bottom of the list. In particular, *measuring productivity* was nineteenth on a list of twenty-five concerns and *strategic systems* was at the bottom (Herbert and Hartog, 1986).

Of course, information technology management issues are important in their own right. The typical IS manager has exceptionally serious challenges in creating and maintaining an appropriate computing and communications environment in which the enterprise information technology efforts can be successfully conducted.

Nevertheless, the key is to make the link between information technology investment and ultimate business performance. Remembering Strassman's comments noted in Chapter Two (high investment in information technology isn't necessarily reflected in improved business performance), we know this link isn't well defined. Merely thinking of these issues in *strategic terms* isn't enough. We stated that information technology is currently managed as a technology matter, not a business matter. Our point isn't that this is bad, for there are compelling technical management problems, and information technology infrastructure investments are needed. Our point is that information technology managed as a technology matter isn't sufficient. The perspective has to shift to the business domain and the measures of information technology values that are found there.

4–3 SHIFTING PERSPECTIVE FROM ENTERPRISE TO LINE OF BUSINESS

Most business computing grew out of financial and accounting departments. Typically, finance and accounting management recognized the cost reduction potential of automated record keeping. The controllers office installed punch card equipment as a labor saving device, and the IS organizations developed from these beginnings.

The history of information systems has created a circumstance that impedes the development of information systems in the corporation. The historic development of, and resulting alignment with, central backbone systems puts the IS organization one step removed from the LOB units that make up the basic business of the enterprise. Put another way, overhead units such as accounting and payroll have limited effect on ultimate business performance—such as sales, product development, and marketing—except in cost. So the historic alignment to overhead units tends to give a cost reduction focus to the IS perspective and, more crucially, to senior management's perceptions of the IS organization. The IS director carries two burdens: first, the perception of being a technical bigot (and therefore not a part of business management), and second, the perception that the primary value of information technology lies in the reduction of the company's central overhead costs of the company.

The IS group has to break through the limitations of the central overhead groups such as finance and payroll, and change its sense of value and contribution to the line of business. Put another way, using the university example, what is the linkage between the IS organization and the success of the LOBs of the university—the schools and departments? Can the IS organization contribute to the processes that produce quality students, first-rate faculty, new donors, or successful competition for federal research support?

4–3–1 The Backbone Systems

We're not saying that the central backbone units aren't important. Cost reduction and cost avoidance are surely as important now as before, if not more so. More crucial, however, is the perspective that the *value* of even the backbone units can be considered from the perspective of the performance of the LOBs and not solely from the perspective of cost reduction of necessary corporate functional units. That is, what is the contribution of the central units to the improved business performance of the LOBs? For example, does financial information, in the hands of LOB management, add to the potential of business performance? Of course it does, and making the linkage between these units and LOB performance is the point of Information Economics. This requires a change in perception and relationships within the IS organization and the backbone units it serves. This change hasn't occurred in many organizations, and it is reflected by the sort of de-massing that is going on in many American companies. When we read of corporate infrastructure being de-massed, it is a case of the value of those overhead units *not* being linked to improvements in the performance of the business units they serve.

IS management—and the entire IS organization—is typically unfamiliar with business performance as a concept. Old ideas of cost-benefit analysis predominate about decision support for projects. Yet the basis for business performance measurements (the same as can be applied in business strategic planning) form the basis for the information technology investment evaluation. The question isn't cost justification, but the *best* projects for the enterprise, that is, those that will cause current and future business performance to improve. Richard Nolan has said that projects that produce 10 or 20 percent return on investment in information technology are no longer sustainable; management should be looking for projects that will return ten times that much, which is possible only with a vision of the factors that make up business performance (Nolan, 1986). Therefore, the evaluation of projects and investments in information technology is to be looked at from a critical success factors perspective, a key business indicator or characteristic, and a leverage point perspective. Can IS management provide the leadership for this sort of evaluation? This **is** the question; the answer is a substantial change for technology domain management!

4–3–2 Case: The "Backbone" Perspective in IS

At Old Ivy University, the accounting services office used IBM 407 equipment in 1955 to produce financial reports and the payroll. An IBM 1401 computer was obtained in 1963 to further automate those systems; a student records and student accounting system was also an early development. Until 1968, data processing reported to the controller and treasurer of the university. Because administrative systems extended, by that time, well beyond financial areas into student records, admissions, and libraries, the data processing activities were moved from financial to general administrative reporting lines to the executive vice chancellor.

Most company IS organizations were similarly developed. What's interesting is that the LOB organizations—in the university case, the schools and departments—received almost no direct data processing services until the 1980s, except those services directly arising from the corporate backbone systems in finance, payroll, and similar activities. The IS organization specifically organized itself to serve the controller and registrar, and not the schools or departments; the IS relationship to those units was deliberately filtered through the central administrative service units. (After all, "whose data is it"? Clearly, it is the controller's financial data, and so that unit should be the one to convey financial data to the schools.)

The economic justification of computer systems, not surprisingly, has arisen from current cost reduction and future cost avoidance, which are values of the backbone units. For the university, this translates into information systems designed to reduce the unit cost of activities such as producing payroll checks and to permit the enhancement of administrative activities in response to growth or governmental requirements. To the extent the central administrative unit perceives its role as providing services to the rest of the enterprise, vehicles for providing reports, including online inquiries and information center facilities for user-developed analysis, have been developed.

4–3–3 Shifting to Line of Business Performance

When Keep-On Trucking Company acquires a computer system to improve its services to customers, value is achieved through improved business performance, in this case increased revenues through enhanced sales. When Old Ivy University introduces a system to maintain student records, the value is also achieved through improved performance, in this case reduced costs for the registrar's function. In both cases, value is measured by change in business performance. The costs of producing the value—computers, software, programmers—are largely incurred by activities in the IS organization. Companies use cost accounting methods to attribute the costs of systems development and systems maintenance to the appropriate business organization that will enjoy the benefits. Brandt Allen argues that such assignment of IS costs must be done to properly manage the overall investment of corporate resources in computer activities (Allen, 1987).

In simplest of terms, Figure 4.1 describes the **Information Economics** of the situation. The existing cost-benefit and ROI literature focuses on the measurement and computation of costs required to provide services and on cost-benefit analysis. The latter is dominated by cost reduction in the business organization as the primary benefit. If we take an Information Economics perspective on the basis of business performance rather than traditional cost-benefit analysis, we begin to see that the cost side—the IS organization and its technologies—is an investment in an infrastructure, an allocation of business resources one step removed from the business units in which the value of the investments occur. Investments that benefit an overhead unit that in turn provides services and value to line of business units are possibly two steps removed. In effect, the IS director is in competition for the allocation of resources.

The allocation of business resources may go to LOBs, corporate backbone, *or* the application systems that support them (Figure 4.1). The decision should be made on **the value (of the investment) to business performance.** The decision-making that lies behind the allocation is what we wish to influence in order to create an explicit

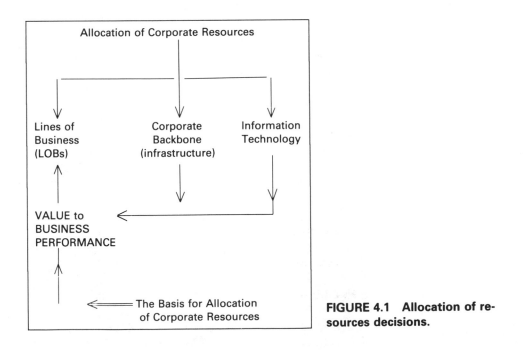

FIGURE 4.1   Allocation of resources decisions.

recognition of value provided to the infrastructure and, in turn, to the LOBs. To do this requires change in the perspective and perception of costs—the information technology and IS organization—for the technology units. This translates into various management perspectives on the appropriate financial justification for information technology investments. The allocation of corporate resources to information technology is based on justification of four kinds: (1) direct cost reduction of corporate backbone activities; (2) added value to the LOBs through enhancements to corporate backbone services to the LOBs; (3) direct cost reduction in the LOB; and (4) enhanced business performance for the LOB. Which of the four justifications is most compelling depends on the management perspective—corporate, LOB, or functional or overhead unit management.

The basic motivations and identities of the managers involved is changing. The IS organization is in the position of having to serve multiple masters. They must produce justification for investments across multiple units with varying motivations.

4–3–4 The Line of Business Perspective

In many organizations, central enterprise support units are charged out to profit centers by a "taxation" method. Each line of business contributes to the support of the overhead function. The line of business perspective and the ways in which profit centers relate to the corporate center, are characterized by Figure 4.2. There, the lines of business column summarizes all of the otherwise separate LOBs.

Figure 4.2 is a very simplified perspective on the financial relationship between corporate central activities and the several lines of business for the enterprise. Business performance is, in the end, the results for each line of business. The $2 million profit is derived from revenues over line of business expenses less the allocation of all the costs of the corporate center.

		Corporate Backbone (Central Services)	The Lines of Business(es)
REVENUES		0	$10,000,000
EXPENSES	Accounting	$ 1,000,000	0
	Finance	500,000	0
	IS Department	1,000,000	0
	President/CEO	500,000	0
	LOB Expense	0	5,000,000
	Total Expense	3,000,000	5,000,000
	Distribution to Lines of Business(es)	(3,000,000)	3,000,000
RESULTS	Profit (Loss)	$ 0	$ 2,000,000

FIGURE 4.2   Line of business perspective.

4–3–5 Case: SmallTown College and Line of Business Perspective

SmallTown College has two lines of business, undergraduate education in Arts and Sciences and graduate education in Teacher Education. All revenues are generated by activities in and from the lines of business, including alumni gifts, tuition, and fees. Figure 4.2 shows how an operating statement for SmallTown College might look; the lines of business column aggregates both undergraduate and graduate education.

If the accounting office adds staff or develops a new financial system, the cost of this addition is directly borne by the lines of business through the cost allocation. Note that whether or not SmallTown College actually does its bookkeeping in this fashion, the reality of the institution is as described. Revenues are generated by the lines of business, and costs consequently are borne there as well. So the direct relationship between central service investment and relationship to business performance in the lines of business is a critical one.

4–3–6 Taxing the Line of Business

In effect, improvements to central enterprise support units raise the tax rate. If the general counsel's office is improved, the tax increases to provide the funding for it. If information technology projects are developed to serve the support units (such as general counsel) the tax rate increases to fund the project. The justification for investing in the corporate support units should be based on the actual impact on the line of business. The line of business has to pay for it. Does it happen this way? Not often. It is the "backbone perspective" that has to change.

A corporate CIO stated it correctly: From the LOB perspective, the quality of centrally provided services should be "just good enough" (reminiscent of just-in-time in manufacturing). Anything more doesn't obviously add value to the business performance of the LOB and consequently the enterprise. The implications for the investment justification for information technology are clear. "Just good enough" is sufficient for backbone support systems that otherwise don't affect business performance.

4–4 SHIFTING PERSPECTIVE FROM TECHNOLOGY AND APPLICATIONS DEVELOPMENT TO ARCHITECTURE AND UTILITY DEVELOPMENT

In Section 3–1 we introduced a fundamental point. **To achieve real, lasting impact from information technology, the business itself must change.** To this we now add: **To make real, lasting impact possible, the IS organization will change.** The IS group has not been immune from the same forces that have been affecting the business enterprise. Certainly from an information technology perspective the pace of change has been dramatic. The evolution from IS manager to CIO (chief information officer), a current phenomenon in the profession and the professional literature, reflects the movement from a technology management dominance to a value management orientation. John Diebold noted that the IS activity is changing from a support function to a line management function, from a wholesale business to a retail business, including entrepreneurial activities (Diebold, 1985).

The value management concept (using the term benefits management) has been adopted by leading consulting firms as a way to restructure the IS organization. A related concept is the business-within-a-business idea: The IS organization provides products and services to its customers. In both cases, one consequence is a shift in view *from* application development as a process that serves user needs *to* applications as a product that is a part of the roster of facilities offered to the business domain.

The infrastructure that supports such products becomes a platform or productive facility that enables value-adding services to be created. This infrastructure view is much like a manufacturing plant and can be planned and architected to meet current and future service and product plans. Whether one adopts the business-within-a-business paradigm, a value management paradigm, or some other paradigm, the orientation to a platform (or infrastructure) with supportive architectures is valuable.

Here's a simple example of some of the dynamics involved. A material supplies firm may develop an online order entry system for its internal use. This system supports the business organization dealing with customers and order entry. The existence of the system—the information technology architecture in place for the organization—makes it possible to place order entry terminals in the offices of the businesses that purchase from the company. (This is, of course, what American Hospital Supply did.) This possibility changes the business plans of the material supplies company. It makes an aggressive growth plan possible, fueled by the unique outreach to the business's customers. The implementation of this new business strategy requires a different business organization, one that focuses on the support of ordering processes and order terminals in customer offices. In turn, this requires a different technology organization and architecture capable of supporting many remote terminals and providing new types of data to the support organization. The IS organization becomes a customer service organization rather than just a back-office support group.

The role of information technology management is to create the organization to enable, catalyze, and support the changes in the business domain. A primary lever and major tool of information technology management is the control and planning over **allocation of IS resources.** In effect, the IS director has to allocate resources consistent with the opportunities in the business domain, and then work to make the opportunities happen. This is Information Economics— investing the controllable information technology resources effectively to enable business change.

This idea of *business leadership* has received more attention this decade. It is a substantial challenge to more traditionally inclined IS leaders and their staffs. Managing the information technology seems less threatening. This outlook has to change; IS has to manage—and lead—the application of its information technology in the business and create the necessary partnership with business management in the process. The essence is linking information technology to business performance. What does the IS organization have to do to accomplish this?

The main requirement is the shift in perception from applications development to a utility and architectures focus. This shift separates the technology perspective of the computer room from the applications perspective of the staff supporting individual users. We've previously mentioned the **business-within-a-business** perspective for the IS organi-

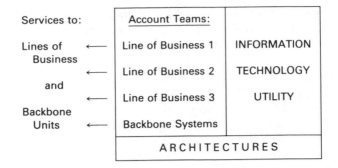

FIGURE 4.3 Technology domain organization.

zation. This encourages viewing *each* business user as a customer; further, this creates an organizational requirement to recognize each business unit's needs and requirements with a discrete support unit. For example, a university computer organization separates the machine room organization from the several application and operations groups that support each of the lines of businesses of the university (undergraduate units, graduate units, research units, and health care units). In this orientation a fifth business unit is the corporate infrastructure, such as accounting and payroll.

This perception is portrayed in Figure 4.3. The organization is built on architectures: data, function, and network architectures on which the computer utility is built. Individual account teams serve each discrete line of business and the backbone units. Such an organization makes possible planning and organization of projects and support for the many lines of business for the organization.

This perspective of the technology domain separates the computer room utility—providing programming, analysis, systems support, and operational facilities—from the staff responsible for satisfying the LOB and backbone units. Zachman's three component description of architectures, based on data, functions, and networks, is a helpful way to visualize the foundation architectures (Zachman, 1986).

4–5 ARCHITECTURES AND UTILITIES AND IS ORGANIZATION

Leading consulting groups are applying these ideas. Current strategic planning for information technology is based on the development of strategic architectures for the enterprise. These are founded on data architectures. Data dictionaries and modeling systems assist the IS staff in such planning. For example, a telephone operating company is undertaking an enterprise-wide strategic data architecture plan. A common view of data among many separate but overlapping systems is considered crucial to the future development of the business. The company was able to find twenty-four consulting groups willing to undertake the project, each with well-developed methodologies and practices to support them. The decision to go forward with the project, including the commitment to undertake major systems renewals to adopt the resulting data architecture, represented a major business-based decision. The supporting data architecture was in fact crucial to the business because the business could not grow and adapt to changing conditions without a sound technology foundation.

Similarly, an air freight company has had a year's experience in applying a strategic architecture approach to planning both technology domain investments and information systems priorities. The process provided explicit economic recognition of projects that create the underlying infrastructure for the systems important to their LOBs. This idea—infrastructure and architectural underpinning for the business—is what lies behind the current interest in strategic architectures. Leading IS organizations are working to develop their enterprise-wide comprehensive architectures. **Information systems strategic planning** is now thought to result in such architectures. The problem is that management may not understand the payoff from the investments necessary. Traditional cost-benefit approaches don't work well in areas of investment unrelated to specific development projects.

The focus on architectures and utilities represents a significant shift in perspective for the IS staff. It lays the groundwork for the effective linkage between the business and technology domains.

4–6 SHIFTING PERSPECTIVE FROM TECHNOLOGY LEADERSHIP TO BUSINESS LEADERSHIP

John Diebold poses some hard questions for the technology domain manager:

1. Does my current staff contain people with the know-how and the outlook necessary to contribute to business strategic areas, and do these people have proper visibility and incentives?

2. How can I develop properly focused strategic suggestions for top management with adequate credibility?

3. And how can I develop management consensus on the proper allocation of scarce resources, between strategic and operational needs (Diebold, 1985, p. 135)?
How indeed?

In the mid 1970s Richard Nolan wrote an article about IS leadership. This article used the terminology *architect* and *insider* to characterize two, in his view divergent, IS management styles (Nolan, 1976). The insider characteristics match the management role in the business domain. Each business unit—and particularly each line of business—requires a management role that focuses full attention on the current and future consumption of information technology. The insider is a business manager responsible for business domain exploitation of information technology. This role makes the linkage to business performance possible. Balanced with this is an account management role in the technology domain that mobilizes the technology domain resources in response to business domain requirements. The partnership of the account manager and the insider is what makes the linkage work between the domains.

The purpose is to move the leadership for the consumption of information technology to the business domain. This runs counter to the traditional view of IS (and the CIO): In their view *they* provide such leadership. Rather, the crucial IS management role is to cause leadership to occur in the business domain and support that leadership, not exercise the leadership directly. IS leadership is catalytic, encouraging, and evocative of business domain leadership. This, of course, *is* leadership in the best possible sense.

The need to assure good communications, and the strategy of assigning responsibility for it, is equally applicable to decentralized information technology. Even with personal computers, the problem of separating technology management from business management exists. One symptom is the tendency for an enthusiastic personal computer user to dive headfirst into the technical details and forget all about addressing the business requirements. The *means* rapidly becomes the *ends* for the individual involved. This occurs because the same manager or staff individual is attempting to accomplish both technology-sector and business-sector responsibilities with no checks or balances clearly defined. (This certainly happens in smaller business units that have no central data processing organization.) It is no wonder that communications problems exist and that resulting information technologies do not meet the standards for success.

Managers are sometimes lulled into failing to provide for effective communication with their own technical staff. This can be a major inhibitor at the enterprise level: Senior management assumes that the technical leadership is capable of handling all needed communication and management tasks. Many senior IS executives do not communicate well with their peers or their superiors. In a decentralized computer environment—where business management has personal computers or small departmental information technologies under its control—the same failure of communication is likely if the business side has not assigned the specific responsibility keeping communications lines open.

4–6–1 Business Domain Innovation

The 1980s collective wisdom in IS management is to serve the users, gain a consensus for development projects from an IS steering committee and deploy IS assets to maximize agreement among the senior managers of the enterprise. Kanter's *The Change Masters* (1983) tends to cast some doubt on an unquestioning acceptance of these principles. The steering committee has a tendency to become a consensus building process for the benefit of the overhead and support organizational units, and *not* the LOBs. For example, at Old Ivy University the steering committee consists of the controller, registrar, personnel director, and the (nonacademic) business manager. It is not a great surprise that the application backlog for the university consists solely of applications to increase the effectiveness of the overhead units. Not one application in support of a school is on the list. Is this the best investment of university resources in information technology?

Kanter's thoughts are crystallized in ten "Rules for Stifling Innovation," which include these five, restated in terms of information systems planning processes:

Insist that people who need approval go first through other levels of review and approval process.

Ask departments or individuals to challenge and criticize each others' proposals.

Treat identification of problems as signs of failure, to discourage people from letting you know when systems aren't working.

Control everything carefully. Make sure people count anything that can be counted, frequently.

Make sure that requests for information are fully justified, and make sure that it is not given out to managers freely (you don't want data to fall into the wrong hands) (Kanter, 1983, p. 101).

Unfortunately, these are the characteristics of traditional IS planning approaches. Change in these mindsets and these attitudes represent the change in the technology domain needed to link its activities to business performance.

4–6–2 Leadership from the Technology Domain

The character of the IS job has changed. Technology domain management should develop the leadership to: (1) develop the business domain leadership; (2) develop a partnership with the business domain leadership; and (3) create the appropriate management environment to promote effective business decision-making about information technology and effective business planning of information technology in the business domain.

There *is* urgency. We were impressed with this as we discussed the use of information technology with the executive of the cement company mentioned earlier. He had no doubt: his future was completely dependent on information technology, and his competition was going to get hurt. Reading the current trade magazines articles and news reports will only add to the sense of urgency. Information technology is at hand. What remains is the organizational capacity to adopt it successfully, and this requires the leadership and linkages among and between business and technology managers. It is these problems—and the organizational development required—toward which planning linkages are focused.

QUESTIONS

1. Why does technology management drive out business management, as in Gresham's Law?

2. What difficulty do you imagine exists for an IS professional who is making a transition from a technical perspective to a business perspective?

3. What are the shortcomings of an ROI approach to project justification? What are the strengths?

4. Why can computers remain unused by the staff in whose office they are installed?

5. Give an example of a critical success factor for a large metropolitan hospital. For a large automobile manufacturer such as General Motors.

6. Do you agree that IS organizations are managed as technology matters and not business matters? Give reasons in support of your opinion.

7. What are the challenges faced by an IS manager?

8. Give an example of a backbone application for a company you know.

9. How does an IS director lose credibility with senior management?

10. Do you agree with the idea of "just good enough" for backbone and overhead computer applications such as finance and payroll?

11. How does an IS organization exhibit characteristics described by Kanter?

12. Describe the value management concept.

13. Describe the business-within-a-business concept.

5

Information Economics and Organizational Planning

The successful development of innovative, effective information technology is a partnership between the technology domain and the business domain. The partnership is based on linkages: organizational links between the LOBs and the supporting IS organization, and planning linkages between technology domain strategic planning and business strategic planning. With both linkages in place, Information Economics can provide guidance about the best allocation of resources.

5–1 LINKING TO BUSINESS PLANNING

We have reviewed planning approaches used by many leading companies. We were interested in learning specifically how they linked their information technology planning to business planning. The linkage doesn't occur by a process (meaning specific planning steps and formal organizational decision-making activities). Rather, linkages depend on a continuing relationship with the business domain and their own approach to strategic planning. The model one company used, in simplified terms, recognized the corporate processes for support and investment in individual lines of business.

5–1–1 Case: Riki Tiki Travel

Company management recognized its business had two basic components: sales to corporate travel departments consisting of executive travel and lodging, and sales to individuals consisting of vacation and leisure travel and lodging. Several years ago these businesses were organized into separate lines of business, with separate division presidents and organizations. Corporate departments retained several important service roles including accounting, information systems, and purchasing, meaning the vendor relationships to airlines and hotel organizations.

Corporate management became used to the idea of investment in either line of business as a financial return matter. The question was simple: in which line of business can the corporation anticipate the best performance and hence financial return?

The IS director, consequently, found it appropriate to organize his efforts around three application groups, one for each line of business, and the corporate service backbone. The key element was a relationship that developed between the IS manager of the respective IS organizational unit and the line of business manager. Planning for MIS applications operated at that level, and the allocation of resources into the three application groups became a part of the overall corporate investment decisions. The result was a planning relationship built around line of business, introduced in Figure 4.3, and implemented as shown for Riki Tiki Travel in Figure 5.1.

The arrangement for Riki Tiki works because IS management is linked to business management, by line of business, for purposes of planning for MIS applications. One important innovation is the treatment of the corporate services (or corporate backbone) as a line of business for purposes of IS planning and organization. A second innovation is the formalization of the insider management role within each LOB.

We can restate these innovations in an overall Information Economics corporate planning model in Figure 5.2. This figure embodies the insider management. In it, each discrete line of business has a line management role for the development of computing within the line of business. In response, the IS organization creates the account teams to serve each line of business. This overall structure makes possible the effective practice of Information Economics through planning processes that link the IS account teams with the line of business insiders.

The planning processes focus on the LOBs. For each LOB the IS group has a designated management team with specific responsibility to match their efforts to the

Planning for MIS Applications	Information Systems Groups	
Corporate Travel Division →	Corporate Travel	INFORMATION TECHNOLOGY UTILITY
Individual Travel Division →	Individual Travel	
Corporate Services →	Backbone Systems	

FIGURE 5.1 Information technology planning for Riki Tiki Travel.

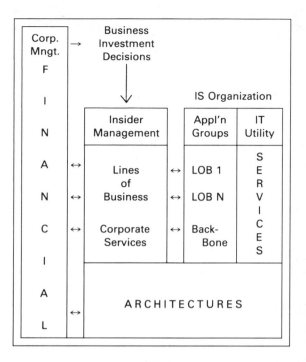

FIGURE 5.2 Corporate planning model.

LOB plan and key objectives. Behind this account team is the information technology service utility that supports the team and its LOB with technology services. These include programming, analysis and design, and online systems support. The backbone administrative units are treated as a separate LOB, though the economic justification for their projects is based on the value of the corporate services supported by information technology to the lines of business, rather than the value of the information technology application itself.

For Riki Tiki Travel, each business unit, through a planning procedure, defined the key areas for improvement. The outcome was a list of critical issues (critical success factors) that had to be resolved by each unit during the year. Some of these represented opportunities for new information technology applications. The IS group then prepared its operating plan and objectives based on the sum of all the LOB requirements. The information technology issues were subordinated to the achievement of the business issues.

At Riki Tiki, a continuing concern is the possibility that an application system can and should cross line of businesses. For example, the use of airline reservation systems in both corporate and individual travel suggested that a common communications system and perhaps a common backoffice system would be beneficial.

For similar reasons, both planning methods and the Information Economics decision models must consider the possibilities of multiple line of business delivery system architectures and corporate-wide systems. In many companies, for example, the acquisition of a corporate-wide network transcends individual LOB concerns. Similarly, providing adequate service to a particular LOB can require considerable infrastructure investment.

For these purposes the information technology area is considered a LOB in its own right.

5–2 LINKAGE THROUGH PLANNING PROCESSES

A research colloquium reported several serious issues in strategic planning: "The basic notion that corporate strategy and information systems (IS) strategy should be linked closely is an old, powerful, and enduring one. . . . For better or worse, corporations have strategies (either explicit or implicit). Likewise, IS groups within these corporations have strategies. The importance of understanding how these two sets of strategies can evolve in a way that is mutually supportive and contributes to the overall cannot be overstated." (McFarlan, 1984, 274).

Highly detailed planning processes focusing on data, processes, and current application portfolios often overburden the planners and obscure basic insights and conclusions. Business management usually loses interest in technology-based details. Another framework or planning methodology appears of limited value unless its objectives include linking technology planning to business performance.

5–3 A LOOK BACK AT DEVELOPMENT METHODOLOGIES

Technology dominated the early years of computing. Anyone active in a data processing shop in the 1960s remembers the programming and systems design projects. In most cases systems were designed to replace manual, non-automated processes. Major design tasks dealt with programs and files, most often card-oriented or tape-oriented. Whether individual programs and multiple program job streams would work at all worried everyone. System and program specifications were based on report formats and file formats with a stray systems flowchart around to show how the programs would fit together. Occasionally, and increasingly, systems did work, though not necessarily in ways the users expected or wanted.

Systems development methodologies (SDM) emerged in the 1970s with two central objectives: first, to make a much stronger connection—a linkage—between user needs and the resulting system; second, to "break the big ones into little ones" to assure successful design and implementation of users systems. Systems development methodologies solved problems of process—the step-by-step approach to analysis and design of systems—and problems of tools—the methods applied to describe proposed systems accurately from the users perspective and for the technical perspective. The systems development process and the step-by-step tasks ensured that the system conception matched the user needs by proper analysis of the problem and by effective decision-making about alternative solutions to the problem. The systems development tools (for example, data flow diagrams) ensured that the technical system design matched the user understanding of problems and solutions and posed decisions for the users in effective, understandable ways (Orr, 1986).

Information Economics has analogous objectives. Overall, enterprises plan for information technology applications in ways similar to systems development. Identification of business needs and opportunities defines future applications of computing that result in investment in hardware, software, and perhaps staff and facilities. Information Economics at one level provides tools to define the economic characteristics of the opportunity and the economic feasibility of the solutions proposed to address the opportunity. At another level, Information Economics supports the decision-making process intended to ensure that, much like systems development methodologies, the information technology conception matches the business needs. Information Economics accomplishes this with decision support tools that force thorough consideration of the project's true economic impact, both cost and benefit, of the proposal.

5–4 A LOOK FORWARD TO CHANGE AND IMPLEMENTATION

Information technology (IT) implementations, representing change in the business organization or methods, are successfully introduced into the enterprise when four distinct things occur. A vision of the possibilities develops in the organization. This vision becomes specific ideas and a proposal. The ideas are transformed into a detailed plan, which is then successfully implemented. If applied to an application system, say, a payroll system, the process is initiated with the controller's vision: A better payroll is needed and is possible with the available information technology. This vision is transformed through feasibility studies into ideas about specific opportunities; these ideas become data flow diagrams and data models supported with economic justification and organizational implications defined. Once approved, the project is implemented. This simple set of processes occurs with a simple application system and with the largest, most complex application of information technology in the enterprise.

What isn't so clear, perhaps, is that the four phases occur in both the technology and business domains, as pictured in Figure 5.3. Vision is needed in both business and technology: the business vision of opportunity and purpose, and the technology vision of what is possible and how to go about making it happen. What also isn't so clear is the centrality of decision-making at all steps of the process. There isn't just one vision, but many, and there isn't just one idea, there are multitudes. Viewed from the enterprise perspective, decision-making is complicated by the occurrence of many, perhaps hundreds of ideas that are all proposed as good ideas; the enterprise cannot do all of them, and which should proceed?

Business Domain	VISION	IDEA	PLANNING	EXECUTION	A Successful Information
Technology Domain	VISION	IDEA	PLANNING	EXECUTION	Technology Implementation

FIGURE 5.3 Phases for successful information technology implementation.

5–5 PLANNING PROCESSES

Leading corporations became interested in applying strategic planning to information systems in the 1970s. Planning the technology domain resources to cope with increasing demand for information systems has simply become too hard. McLean and Soden wrote the first book on the subject in 1977. It laid out planning methods to be used and described what companies were actually doing (McLean and Soden, 1977).

The key objective was to put the business domain requirements in the driver's seat rather than the technology domain technical requirements. The perception was that prior computer planning started from technology implementation requirements; the computer managers were more interested in the latest information technology and latest hardware and software systems. Alignment planning seeks to reverse this and make the technology domain the servant of the business domain. This is reminiscent, of course, of the circumstances in applications systems development that led to the emergence of systems development methodologies; that is, application systems did not accurately reflect user requirements; the solution was the development of a systems development methodology that started from user requirements and molded a technology system that met them.

Alignment planning is based on the same idea (Figure 5.4). The heart of the process is much like a global systems development methodology. IBM's business systems planning (BSP) methodology captures the essential characteristic. BSP's primary outcomes include an enterprise perspective of the corporate database and information systems and the expectation that decisions can be made to rank the projects necessary to bring about the full set of needed applications.

Many planning processes have emerged that work toward the enterprise perspective in systems planning. Enterprise-wide data flow diagrams and data models are tools of planning methods. More recently concepts of architectures that include data, communications networks, and application systems have emerged. From the perspective of the IS organization, laying out a long-range view of such architectures is crucial to the development of information systems because the current emphasis is on enterprise-wide sharing of information and widespread access to the corporation's data. This can be accomplished only with the planning and guidance that an enterprise-wide plan and architecture can provide.

5–5–1 Alignment Planning

Alignment planning is consistent with the way computing has always been planned. It isn't much of an intellectual move from single-system systems development methodologies to an enterprise-wide methodology. Often the same essential tools are used: data flows and data models. The implementation process from the corporate data model to individual systems appears straightforward. Many of the automated systems development tools

THE BUSINESS ORGANIZATION and PROCESSES	Alignment ——Planning——→ Processes	INFORMATION SYSTEMS ARCHITECTURE, ORGANIZATION

FIGURE 5.4   Alignment planning.

now emerging are based on an enterprise model, with an application system as a subset to the model or as a packaging of portions of the model. So alignment is an easy planning idea to articulate and sell to both business domain management and technology domain IS management.

Keep-On Trucking faced the conversion of its application portfolio from an older batch computer to a collection of minicomputers. Company management determined that this was an opportune time to look at the overall set of systems serving the company. A strategic planning process was undertaken, beginning with the business domain managers. The questions asked: What did each functional area require? What did the major functions have in common that would produce common systems needs and a common database? The process produced a five-year systems implementation plan beginning with the key customer-oriented systems. This was alignment planning: The entire process focused on what the overall company required and produced a company-wide plan and set of implementation priorities.

A railroad undertook a similar project. The motivating problem was the relative age and insularity of the existing application portfolio. A consultant was engaged to assist the company in developing the planning process to align overall data and system architecture to meet corporate-wide requirements. The result was a blueprint that described the data, processing, and applications architectures with relevant implementation priorities.

Early in the development of alignment planning concepts, it was recognized that successful planning could not be done without going beyond the needs of individual organizational units to the needs of the enterprise as a whole. That is, alignment planning has to be responsive to the strategic plan of the enterprise and the organizational units that make up the corporation. This appears obvious, but not in the context of the early 1970s when the emphasis was on serving the needs of the user organizations. As horizons expanded to visualize the enterprise-wide database and systems architectures, the need for multi-user perspectives became apparent; ultimately, the overall enterprise strategic plan ought to provide basic guidance.

The relationship between the enterprise strategic plan and the supporting technology domain systems and organization is key (Figure 5.5). Yet one experienced consultant said:

> In my experience over fifteen years of dealing with customers, my readings on the matter, and in the opinions of the leading scholars on strategic planning, the major problem confronting business today is the *lack of both a strategic planning process* and *the lack of an integrated plan which should include the IS function as its nerve center*.

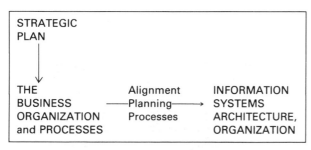

FIGURE 5.5 Link to strategic plan.

The first level solution should be aimed at convincing top management that they should implement a well-designed, integrated planning process with the active involvement of both top management and the IS Department. Once management is convinced, then let us get on with the larger problem of developing an enterprise plan.

We've heard many variations of this theme. ''Our top management isn't interested'' is common, as is ''I'm the wrong person to be hearing all this; my boss, or his boss, or our chief users should.'' In some sense this simply reflects the difference among enterprises. No two are alike, and any attempt at general discussion of planning perhaps needs to cover too broad a spectrum of possible action. Often these comments reflect the frustration a technology-oriented IS manager feels in dealing with nontechnology management.

There is, however, a more fundamental point here. How can an organization really make progress, especially in the absence of good communications between the technology and business domains? How can progress be made in the perceived absence of a reasonably well conceived business plan? The point of a comprehensive view of planning and management is that it *can* provide guidance for organizations in all these circumstances. Information technology planning is not a process of technology assimilation; rather it is a process of organizational and management development. It ultimately is a **question of leadership.**

Sometimes this leadership has to come from the technology domain. In these cases, the planning method must provide the direction for beginning to deal with the business domain management. **It is never an information technology problem.** Therefore all these initiatives are couched in business terms that are intended to identify and solve business problems. A process using simple business-related planning questions is exactly the sort of nontechnical approach that can begin to develop the appropriate dialogue between the domains.

5–5–2 Impact Planning

About 1980 a second kind of planning concept emerged. The motivating idea recognizes that alignment planning is basically a current-period snapshot of business and organization requirements. Alignment planning accurately satisfies today's business needs, but what of tomorrow? American Hospital Supply and American Airlines have become the legends for this new planning by representing the use of computing for competitive advantage in addition to alignment and support of the existing business.

The concept of strategic computing—competing with computing—has captured the attention of corporate America, or at least corporate IS directors. The idea is **impact** planning. Whereas alignment planning concentrates on serving the users and the corporate plan, impact planning is specifically intended to change the plan with information technology. American Hospital Supply did it by changing the way the company interacted with its customers; American Airlines did it by changing the basis for competing for business (such as frequent flier programs) and by creating a new LOB (for example, SABRE reservation systems sold to travel agents and other airlines). The essential questions are, if we want to, how can information technology be used to ultimately change the business plan? How can information technology be used for competitive advantage for the enterprise?

5–5–3 Enterprise-wide Information Management (EwIM)

The complete picture on planning processes is a circular one. The strategic plan is the foundation, through alignment planning, for long-range information systems planning. Information systems architecture and technology presents opportunities to change the strategic plan, which, in turn, changes the foundation for subsequent information systems support.

The EwIM view of the planning process includes four planning activities (Figure 5.6) that provides a perspective of how to approach and implement a planning activity.

Alignment starts from the existing business organization and its needs, and generates the supporting information technology plan—the information systems master plan—to satisfy the needs of the business.

Opportunity starts from the existing information technology and IS activities and defines current and future resources and assets that can be deployed to change the business plan and/or to align to business needs.

Organization starts from the line of business strategic business plan and defines the effective organizational form needed to carry it out. Works with alignment in identifying the role of information technology in carrying forward the accomplishment of the business plan.

Impact starts from technology opportunities and generates changes to the line of business business plan in terms of new products, new customers or customer interfaces, new strategies, and new markets.

These planning relationships are circular. Business planning drives business organization, which should drive the information technology planning that is intended to support it. Technology planning produces opportunities for future use of information technology in the enterprise that, through strategic planning processes, will influence business strategies and plans.

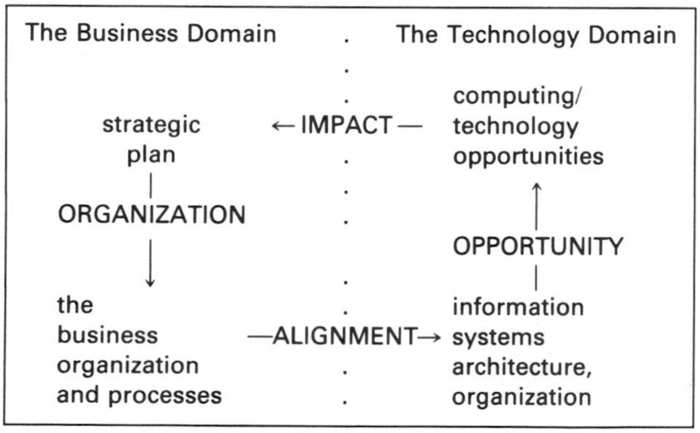

```
┌─────────────────────────────────────────────────┐
│ The Business Domain    .    The Technology Domain │
│                        .                          │
│                        .    computing/            │
│        strategic    ← IMPACT —  technology         │
│          plan          .    opportunities         │
│          |             .                          │
│     ORGANIZATION       .         ↑                │
│          |             .    OPPORTUNITY           │
│          ↓             .         |                │
│       the              .    information           │
│       business    —ALIGNMENT→ systems            │
│       organization     .    architecture,         │
│       and processes    .    organization          │
└─────────────────────────────────────────────────┘
```

FIGURE 5.6   The EwIM planning processes.

A simple example is a material supplier that may develop an online order entry system for its internal use. This system supports the business organization in dealings with customers and order entry. The existence of the system—the technology architecture in place for the organization—makes possible an initiative to place order entry terminals in the offices of the businesses that purchase from the company. This possibility changes the business plans of the material supplier company. It may make possible an aggressive growth plan, fueled by the unique outreach to the business's customers. The implementation of this new business strategy requires a different business organization, one that focuses on the support of the order terminals in the customer offices. This, in turn, requires a different technology architecture capable of supporting many remote terminals and providing new types of data to the support organization. Thus the relationship is circular.

5–6 ORGANIZATIONAL LINKAGE

Earlier we introduced the concept of the insider, a management responsibility in each business unit that matches the account team responsibility in the technology domain. Examples of the responsibilities include:

- Assuring good communication with IS organization
- Awareness of the potentials
- Justification and emphasis on business benefits (value)
- Managing the business staff and change management
- Working the partnership with IS organization
- Business standards in resulting applications

There is a parallel with information systems development methodologies. Methodologies organize the tasks to be done (for example, problem analysis and objective setting) in developing information systems applications. Methodologies are necessary to ensure the effective communication of needs and requirements *from* the business sector *to* the technology sector. The requirement for effective communications between the business unit and technology sector creates a *management* responsibility in the business unit. This management responsibility is to assure that communications among all parties occur.

In short, each side of the information project has a management responsibility. Both management roles must be in place. Both represent an accountability for the effectiveness of the respective tasks *and* the effectiveness of the communications. This dual set of responsibilities exists whether the business unit is taking on the decentralized technology responsibility.

QUESTIONS

1. What are the advantages of Ken Orr's concept of "breaking big ones into little ones?"

2. Give an example of alignment planning or an information system that is most characteristic of alignment.

3. Give an example of impact planning or an information system that is most characteristic of impact.

4. Of the four phases of innovation—vision, idea, planning, and execution, which is most important?

5. What's the difference between impact and alignment planning?

6

Costs, Benefits, and Value

Our purpose is to thoroughly explore the meaning of *value* in Information Economics. We have introduced a number of ideas throughout the first five chapters. Here we will flesh them out in some detail.

The chapter is in three parts. First, in Section 6–1 and 6–2, we re-visit the limitations of *benefits* as the concept is used as the major driver in traditional cost-benefit analysis. Second, in Section 6–7 we define each of the six classes of value: first introduced in Chapter Two: (1) return on investment, (2) strategic match, (3) competitive advantage, (4) management information, (5) competitive response, and (6) strategic IS architecture. Third, in Sections 6–3 through 6–6 we extend the two-domain definition of value first introduced in Chapter One. This will focus on the difference between technology-based value from business-based value. This has two purposes. First, to introduce a simple justification process that can be useful, and second, to set the stage for two-domain evaluations in Parts Two and Three.

6–1 THE LIMITATIONS OF BENEFIT

The management practice of justifying information systems projects is pretty well established in American companies. The logic is clear: The anticipated benefits from investments in information technology should be greater than the costs.

Several interesting problems interfere with cost-benefit analysis. One is time. Benefits are usually derived long after the costs of the project are incurred, so time-value and discounted cash flow techniques have been applied. Another problem is intangible benefits, those things that seem important but are not amenable to strict cash analysis. For example, a system that allows customers to phone in orders may have direct cash benefits in cost reduction but more likely is justified by adding attractiveness to the prospective customer's dealings with the company. What's the cash benefit of this? The analyst is reduced to making estimates of additional revenues that might be derived with the system, in effect, attempting to value something that is pretty difficult to pin down. A system that prints benefit information on payroll checks adds to employee satisfaction and loyalty. Does it give actual cash benefit? Perhaps, but it seems pretty intangible to us.

There are more fundamental problems with traditional cost-benefit approaches, including the use of return on investment (ROI) as the primary means for driving corporate decision-making for information technology. This has the effect of converting decision-making into a numbers game and shields management from having to understand the projects themselves. Just the term "hurdle rate"—the concept that projects have to have a minimum ROI to qualify for consideration—conveys the nature of the game played. If the project can achieve the rate, it's a good project; if not, it's a bad project. Worse, the character of the benefits chosen for projects that successfully compete in an ROI context, strongly tend to favor cost reduction because of its discrete and measurable character. In many cases this is appropriate, but it isn't appropriate to exclude from consideration the other important sources of value for projects.

6–2 THE LIMITATIONS OF RETURN ON INVESTMENT

In Chapter Seven we'll present a very simple example of an Information Economics planning method that uses the broader definition of value rather than traditional benefits. The project ranking, presented there, is based on value. Figure 6.1 shows a ranking based on traditional ROI.

Projects	Total Value	ROI %	Business ROI Evaluation	Tech Evaluation	Invest- ment	Ranking Level
Preventative Maintenance	35	80%	15	20	50,000	11.0
Route Scheduling	25	33%	5	20	300,000	45.0
Dispatching	22	45%	20	2	100,000	45.0
Interstate Sales System	40	20%	20	20	450,000	5.0
Customer Services	30	−35%	30	0	1,000,000	29.0
Dangerous Goods Control	36	−55%	21	15	500,000	8.0
Customer/Sales Profile	50	−80%	32	18	300,000	2.0
DB/2 Installation/Conversion	48	na	28	20	400,000	3.0

FIGURE 6.1   Simplified information economics evaluation for Keep-On Trucking Leasing line of business (*ranked by traditional ROI*).

The interesting thing in Figure 6.1 is that projects with strong business values (represented by high scores in the "Business ROI Evaluation" column), but without hard ROIs, generally were thrown to the bottom of the list. In terms of business values, the Customer/Sales Profile was evaluated by line of business management as having the largest potential effect on business performance for the line of business. It falls to the bottom in the above analysis because the project added cost and did not directly reduce other costs or contribute short-term incremental revenues. And a potentially important infrastructure project, the DB/2 conversion, has no appropriate return.

The problem is in the accounting character of cost-benefit analysis (CBA) and return on investment (ROI). David Norton comments that CBA and ROI suffer from three detriments: (1) Traditional cost-benefit and ROI approaches are microeconomic and encourage low risk investments with small returns; (2) they are a result of a manufacturing economy where labor is treated as an expense; and (3) the analysis is static and short term. (Norton, 1986). This means that potential value—the effect on business performance—from projects that have strong potential for competitive advantage and competitive response and strategic match (classes of value that we'll define in more detail in Section 6–7), can have that potential but may well be precluded from a traditional ROI analysis.

We emphasize an important point here.

We are not opposed to CBA and ROI. As will become clear in Part Two, we expend a significant amount of effort to enhance traditional CBA calculations to make it more useful when applied to information systems. And, as we will portray in Chapter Fifteen, we emphasize the role of ROI as a major component of the measure of value for information systems in a line of business. ROI is a major part of Information Economics. It's not the only part, however.

6–3 VALUE AS A SUBSTITUTE FOR BENEFIT

Throughout the book we've explored a number of ideas about *value* as a substitute for *benefit*. Here, we review a number of them as an introduction to a complete description in the next several sections.

Others have done considerable thinking about the value of information technology. The issue has gotten more attention with the competing-with-computing articles, because the *value* in many of those cases isn't the traditional cost reduction or revenue enhancement. Indeed, for example, how do we assess value to an application that raises competitive hurdles against one's competition?

The question is: What is management willing to pay for? That is, what is so valuable that it is worth investing in and paying the bill for? We offer the following starting point.

> **Value** is based on *advantage achieved over the competition,* reflected in *current and future business performance.* That which will add to the advantage over the competitors of a firm is the value in which management should be willing to invest.

Consider how one manager questioned whether his company was gaining value from information technology: "How dependent on [information technology] is my firm to

(a) improve market access, (b) provide product and company differentiation, (c) facilitate new product and service introductions, or (d) introduce operational efficiencies. . .?'' (Norton, 1986, 20). We think these four questions define value well, in terms of what management is willing to pay for. If the manager didn't have capability in each of these areas, how much would he be willing to invest to accomplish them? This seems to us to be the full meaning of value.

Consider what others have said.

> Computing augments the performance of professional and creative staff, through memory extension (e.g., access to extended libraries of materials), through computation and graphics (e.g., research), through synergistic studies (e.g., electronic mail interconnecting peer scientists geographically dispersed), through computer conferencing (Doherty and Pope, 1986).

> Inter-organizational communications systems can establish control over distribution channels and reduce distribution costs in a mature market. (This reference is excellent in terms of a strategic analysis of opportunities in the business domain (Cash and Konsynksi, 1985)).

> Information systems can provide crucial information to monitor a firm's critical success factors (Barrett, 1986).

> Information technology can provide the means for a firm to address each of the five competitive forces (Porter, 1985).

We propose a classification of value that allows us to analyze and assess value of information technology to business enterprises. This classification is based on the classes of value, presented in the next section.

6–4 CLASSES OF VALUE

In Section 2–1 we introduced *value* based on improvement to business performance. We propose the classification of value in the following categories.

Return on Investment
Strategic Match
Competitive Advantage
Management Information Support
Competitive Response
Strategic IS Architecture

Each category has particular characteristics that bear on the measurement of value.

6–4–1 Return on Investment (Cost Reduction and Performance Enhancement)

Without question the traditional view of cost-benefit remains valid for the creation of value for the company. For many firms, low cost is the basis for their basic strategy (Porter, 1980). The literature on strategic computing includes many good examples.

For example, Stephanie Barrett offers one framework that starts with a particular irony. She extensively studied the use of interorganizational communications systems (for example, the American Hospital Supply order-entry system, whereby AHS installed terminals in the purchasing offices of their customer hospitals, a famous case of the strategic effects of computing). Barrett found seventy articles written just on this one application. She discovered that the ten systems studied **all** started with productivity improvement as the pre-implementation goal; only afterwards did the strategic implications become apparent. (The irony? These systems didn't arise through competing-with-computing planning but evolved through more traditional systems planning, justified through traditional cost-benefit analysis.)

She suggests that value of information technology can be considered in groups, what we will call competitive advantage and performance improvements as represented in Figure 6.2 (Barrett, 1986).

The second category, performance improvements, is a good list of value for which return on investment can measure value. The first category reflects values not so easily measured with CBA and ROI, and fit into our other classes of value.

A second way to think about value is the Value Chain itself. The Value Chain allows description and analysis of the exact means a company uses to produce its products and interact with customers and markets. Here, the question is, What efficiencies can we introduce into the Value Chain to improve business performance? The tool offers great opportunities. For example, one might construct the following areas of opportunity for a full-service airline as in Figure 6.3.

The development of value in traditional terms, cost-benefit analysis and its focus on cost reduction justification, can be the same things that provide competitive advantage and hence true economic impact—improved profitability—and provide improved services in non-profit circumstances. In terms of Enterprise-wide Information Management (EwIM), it is the *alignment* planning process. The value sought in alignment is the improved functioning of the business organizations that make up the business, and thereby improve the overall business performance. (For special application of this idea to service businesses, see Mills, 1986.)

6–4–2 Strategic Match

Corporations have strategic goals, as do operating units and lines of business. A value of information technology is to support the achievement of these goals directly or to

Competitive Impact	competitive edge maintenance of leadership or share entry to new product/market area
Performance Improvements	reductions in staff reductions in operating locations/entities increased resource use efficiency improvements in customer services increased staff efficiency

FIGURE 6.2   Barrett's views of value. (Adapted from Barrett, 1986, 7)

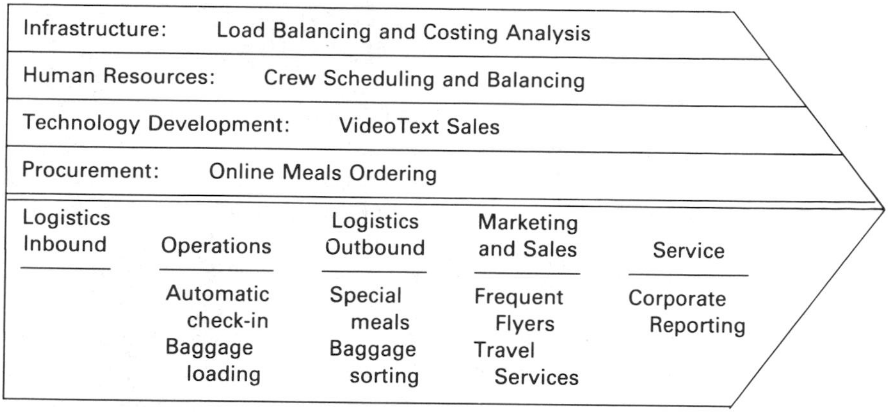

FIGURE 6.3 Full-service airline Value Chain.

support the operationalization of activities necessary to reach goals. For example, if Old Ivy University has a primary strategic goal to increase federally sponsored research support in the biomedical sciences, then the technology domain can do no better than provide the means to accomplish that goal and to support the business domain operating units whose responsibilities bear on that goal. The point here is not to change the strategic goals; rather it is to improve the organizational capacity to accomplish the goals that exist. This is the full measure of what we've previously called organization and alignment planning in Chapter Five.

Barrett discusses the various kinds of strategic goals an enterprise might have. In particular, she considers the range of alternatives adapted from Rowe and associates (1982) shown in Figure 6.4.

The value contributed by information technology is the enabling of the focus, enhancing the capacity of the business organization to achieve its roles in, ultimately, the strategic alternative. For example, Keep-On Trucking pursued a vertical integration strategic alternative in its commodities trucking business. The company acquired key suppliers in engines and engine rebuilding, a tire company, and an insurance company. As a result, those companies, previously representing expenditures (such as purchase of tires), were turned into operating subsidiaries with profit objectives. From the Informa-

Strategic Alternative	Strategic Focus
Status Quo	Stability
Concentration	Single Product Line
Horizontal Integration	Control of Competitors
Vertical Integration	Change Cost to Profit Center
Diversification	Broadening Product Line
Joint Ventures	Complementary Benefits
Retrenchment	Reduction of Activity
Divestiture	Removal non-fitting entity
Liquidation	Same
Innovation	Seizing leadership position

**FIGURE 6.4 Strategic alternatives and Focus.
(Adapted from Rowe, Mason, and Dickel, 1982)**

tion Economics perspective, it became important to the company to enable profitable operation of the subsidiaries *and* work to accomplish cross-company efficiencies in the purchase of supplies from those companies. Otherwise, the advantage of vertical integration as a strategy would not be accomplished for the company.

Strategic match may be simpler than this example suggests; the essential strategy of the firm or its lines of business is straightforward. In Porter terms, it's the generic strategies of cost focus or differentiation, applied to a broad-focus or narrow-focus market. For example, Old Ivy University may conclude that the narrow-focus market and differentiated product strategy are appropriate for its undergraduate line of business; that is, the university competes for quality eighteen-year-old students with a computer-focused arts and sciences curriculum. What can the application of information technology do to cause success in pursuing this strategy? Focused marketing systems, communications networks to the high schools in which these students are enrolled, microcomputers in the offices of selected high school counselors, and university-developed proprietary software for prospective high school students are several alternatives come to mind. Note that none of these ideas reduces nor add new revenues directly. It's *strategic match* that's important.

The value is the contribution to enabling success. Achieving it may not be easy: Robinson reminds us that day-to-day management in both domains can forget the real business value being sought as compared to the needs or requirements of the business domain organizations: "In fact, once a systems effort is begun, the original focus on business value is . . . lost. New needs arise from every quarter . . . but the basic question, 'what is this all really worth to the business' goes unasked" (Robinson, 1985, 152).

This is the real point of moving beyond cost-benefit analysis. For example, Old Ivy University business domain management may be focused on cost reduction, and so objectives for a recruitment or admissions support system is clerical cost reduction in the admissions office. "What is this all really worth to the business?" The university may benefit from cost reduction, but the significant opportunity is in enabling its strategies in the undergraduate LOB. Recognizing this, and avoiding too narrow a perspective of value, is an important result of recognizing the classes of value.

6–4–3 Competitive Advantage

A major theme of corporate strategy is the creation of barriers and hurdles against competitive inroads against the firm (Porter, 1985). Some of strategy is product and market oriented (such as creating distinctive products), but a great deal is also creating distribution and market relationships and channels that bind the firm and its customers or suppliers together in ways that make displacement of the firm more difficult for competitors.

This is one prime element of the American Hospital Supply story (see Barrett, 1986). There, the appeal of the terminal in the purchasing office of hospitals was so strong that competitors could not dislodge AHS even on the basis of product, pricing, and delivery advantages. AHS erected a formidable hurdle through its interorganizational system (IOS). Cash and Konsynski (1985) offer examples and discussion of IOS.

The potential uses of information technology to create barriers to competition can represent considerable value to the enterprise. Some possible examples are shown in Figure 6.5.

Inter-organizational systems are a primary vehicle for accomplishing competitive advantage. They aren't the only ways, as internal systems can have a similar impact. A previous example of the value chain for the airline was illustrated in Figure 6.3. The question is, How can we innovate in any aspect of the value chain to add additional value and to raise additional values for our customers to deal with us?

Normally, we think of impact planning as the vehicle for changing the strategic plan of our enterprise. This is thought of in terms of competitive use of information technology and as making major changes to fundamental strategy, for example, new products, new markets, and new LOBs. This is possible, of course, but the focus here does not require such a major and far-reaching change. In fact, such major changes may not be possible in any realistic time frame. Rather, the focus is on the contribution— the value—of information technology in altering the strategic business plan in the ways suggested above to add value to our product and our relationships to our customer. The value lies in the competitive impact, that is, the strength of the bonds we build with customers and suppliers, the values we add to our products, our modes of distribution, and the ways we interact with our customers.

6–4–4 Management Information Support

As an intangible benefit, management information is the leading example of hard-to-quantify information systems benefits. Three categories are of interest to us here: traditional management support, strategic management monitoring, and organizational performance and management support.

Competitive Force	Possible Barrier or Hurdle	Means for raising hurdle thru IOS or other systems
New competitors	Capacity or Resources needed	Extensive networks in place Extensive automation in place
Buyers moving down into our business	Efficiency of scale	Our order and delivery systems provide enhanced services
Suppliers moving up into our business	Effectiveness of experience and scale	Our order systems offer enhanced service to our customers
Substitute Products	Efficiency/pricing Quality	Our operational systems provide leading capabilities
Our existing Competitors	Bonds to our customers; Quality and Performance	IOS offer enhanced value to our customers

FIGURE 6.5 Competitive forces and hurdles. (Adapted from Cash and Konsynksi, 1985, 141)

Traditional management support. We find Anthony's management paradigm useful in specifying the value of information in providing management support. The traditional triangle defines the opportunities as illustrated in Figure 6.6.

The value of information in the three areas can be measured in traditional cost-benefit terms: cost reduction and improved performance. Beyond this, management information provides value in quality control, multiple time period planning, and consideration of alternative deployment and use of resources. For example, Old Ivy University places value on the acquisition and use of information about its admissions processes. The university uses questionnaires and in-person interviews with student applicants particularly those who choose other universities. This competitive analysis provides good insight into competitive performance and the quality of the admissions and recruitment efforts. The information systems support for the study is crucial to its success. It is valuable, but not in traditional cost-benefit terms because the study adds costs and obtains no revenues. The study does, however, result in improved supervision over current recruitment activities, guide future deployment of recruitment resources and staff, and reassure management in its basic strategies and directions. This all reflects real value and is worth something to university management (Anthony, 1965).

Strategic management monitoring. Enterprises have a fundamental strategic approach to the businesses in which they are engaged. Such strategic approaches describe the posture management has toward the business. For example, does management intend to dominate competitors with rapid product introductions or strong marketing approaches, or does management intend to protect its position in the market by conservative marketing and strong ties to distribution channels?

The way a company approaches competition and establishes its posture in its businesses creates opportunities for information technology. For example, if a company intends to be aggressive and seek to dominate its markets, then management information directed at measuring how the firm is actually doing, and how the competition is doing, may be most useful.

Companies have been described in terms of their strategy approaches to business in four basic categories: **defenders, reactors, analyzers,** and **prospectors.** *Defenders* are in narrowly defined industries with stable and predictable products in well-defined markets. *Reactors* are conservative companies that are generally averse to change except in response to what others may initiate. *Analyzers* encourage change based on careful information and broad changes in trends. *Prospectors* are in poorly defined business segments and often initiate change to obtain competitive advantages. (See Jenster, 1986).

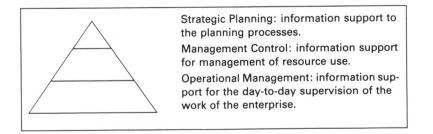

Strategic Planning: information support to the planning processes.

Management Control: information support for management of resource use.

Operational Management: information support for the day-to-day supervision of the work of the enterprise.

FIGURE 6.6 Opportunities in the enterprise.

Each of the four approaches suggests important contributions through information systems. Specifically, managers engaged in a particular approach rely on information to manage the business effectively. For example, a business with a reactor approach will do better with better information about competition and market conditions. Management willing and capable of using such information will value that information; such information will have a significant impact on business success.

Points to keep in mind: (1) There are different strategies; (2) companies differ in the degree by which management monitors the key variables that affect their business strategy approach; (3) organizational performance depends on the degree to which they are monitored; and (4) the contribution to the success of the enterprise and its strategy can be described for each of the four strategy categories, with specific value potentially provided to the enterprise.

Strategy and the management of performance. We've discussed strategy and the management of performance with several companies and organizational groups. We often include American Airlines and American Hospital Supply as examples, companies that have gained competitive advantage with information systems and have hit home runs in their businesses with information technology.

When we discuss these case examples with managers from other companies, one reaction is that "we cannot do that here; our business is an incremental business, and we don't see how we can make that much difference." For example, it is hard to see how Old Ivy University can hit the home run in undergraduate education. Information technology just isn't going to alter the basic strategy of the institution in undergraduate education. Old Ivy University can, however, do better than its competition in pursuing its strategy.

This is the point of **value** for information technology. It can make a difference in the execution of strategy, by making management better and smarter in pursuing the strategy.

One author has captured the sense of this by calling it strategy and performance *hustle.* His logic is that: (1) Everyone has computing; (2) with otherwise similar resources, some do better than others; (3) the difference appears to be management hustle as the basics of strategy or at least implementation of strategy. This leads to the idea of incremental improvements to performance as strategy, rather than a home run strategy. Home runs can also be hit by the competition once they catch on. He doesn't suggest his concept is always true: "strategic invulnerability determines all" for some. Nevertheless **a business can encourage hustle only when an information system is available to report profitability and performance** in the important areas, meaning business performance, product performance, and customers (Bhide, 1986). Real value is provided for companies that rely on hustle for their strategic differences with their competition.

The three categories of management information value link the use and availability of information to the key factors in business performance. For management control, it is information about the key resources in the business and the key operational tasks. For the basic company approach to the industry, it is the monitoring of industry conditions and competitor performance. In the case of hustle as strategy, it is the monitoring and measurement of basic business performance.

The idea is linkage to what's important for the business. In some ways this is a critical success factors orientation. What is it worth to the enterprise to do better in the business critical success factors? That is the value in management information, which gives management the tools to improve performance in those factors. It is worth a lot!

6–4–5 Competitive Risk

Gehmawat has said: ''For outstanding performance, a company has to beat the competition. The trouble is the competition has heard the same message.'' His thrust is that value is based on overcoming others' capabilities to mimic or leapfrog what we are doing now (Gehmawat, 1986, 53).

There is not any question that a company's competitors are working as hard at innovation as they are. For Old Ivy University, for example, a major problem is that the other institutions are investing in information systems and computing at a rapid pace. **Just to keep up** the university has to consider its investments in projects for administrative, teaching, and research purposes. If it does not, the risk is that other institutions will pass it by.

Cost-benefit analysis does not work at all to capture this class of value. If other universities generate a computing environment for research that significantly affects the research productivity of its faculty, then Old Ivy's faculty are not only disadvantaged, but may well be at risk by the threat they will move to some other University. For example, developments in supercomputing have the potential to make other institutions more attractive for faculty whose research interests are advanced by high-power computing.

The problem exists for everyone. So **value** is a function of keeping up with the competition and a major source of pressure for investment justification in information technology.

6–4–6 Strategic IS Architecture

We have previously made the point that the information systems business is much like a manufacturing business. There is a productive environment that must exist to make it possible to create product and to manufacture and deliver that product to customers. The IS organization has its analog ''factory'' in the computer, communications network, and software environments needed to provide services to the enterprise. It must have a plan so that incremental investments can be aligned with the long-range strategic plan.

Investment in this environment is an important value to the enterprise. Later we will present a discussion of this investment and its components.

6–5 THE LINKAGE OF COSTS AND VALUE

The application of cost-benefit analysis operates to connect business domain benefits—revenues or reduced costs—to technology domain costs—computers, hardware, software, or staff. Ideally all prospective information technology projects can be evaluated in a similar way by computing the net value produced. Assuming comparability of the numbers (for example working out the time value of money consistently), the projects with highest net value produced measured against the investment needed would be the projects chosen for implementation.

Costs have problems as well. A mature computer organization has a variety of fixed and variable cost categories that participate in a system solution. For example, a simple application system development—say, a new order entry system—typically incurs costs shown in Figure 6.7.

The terms *fixed* and *variable* refers to the direct incremental cost incurred by the IS organization because of this project. Normally a new computer is not purchased; rather, otherwise unused existing CPU time is allocated to the project. Similarly a programmer may be hired for the project. *Discrete* costs are directly attributable to the project, in cost accounting terms *direct* costs; *distributed* costs are those the project shares with other projects, in cost accounting terms *overhead* costs.

This example is meant to illustrate some of the aspects of attributing costs to a given development project. IS organizations may have different ways of treating these and other cost categories. Even without the additional benefit complexity of intangibles, *cost* can be as difficult to define accurately as *benefit*. Of course, the key word in the previous statement is *accurately*. For example, any cost distribution for distributed or overhead cost is essentially by algorithm, and algorithms are essentially arbitrary (or they would not be an algorithm).

Even more important, the technology domain can incur larger categories of costs than those directly caused by a new project. These categories are loosely characterized by two words: *infrastructure* and *architecture*. Examples of items in these categories are database management software, personal computer networking software, and data communications networks. In some ways, larger CPU capacities or disk storage devices or new operating or systems development software are in these categories. Generally, they represent an investment in the capacity of the technology domain to provide services (much like the building of a manufacturing facility) rather than explicit costs to support one specific project. The justification for these investments is crucial because they usually represent large capital amounts, and yet the return on these investments isn't substantially clear other than by attribution to the full set of projects they support. So the IS organization generally includes these costs in the cost pools to be disributed through, for example, CPU utilization in the example above. Nevertheless, these investments have to compete with other specific project investments and other corporate capital budget needs.

```
Development:
    Staff time programming              Variable / Discrete
    Staff time design and analysis      Variable / Discrete
    Computer time—programming/test      Fixed    / Distributed
    Disk Storage space for data         Fixed    / Discrete
    Software purchase price             Variable / Distributed
Operations:
    Computer time                       Fixed    / Distributed
    Disk storage space                  Fixed    / Discrete
    Forms and computer paper            Variable / Discrete
```

FIGURE 6.7   Typical costs for IS project.

From the perspective of corporate management, the problem comes down to evaluation of competing needs for funds. Consider the list of such candidates in Figure 6.8.

The difficulty in evaluation is clear. In particular, when the justification for the first four projects is partly to make the last two possible, the problem of justification, and decision-making, can become quite complex.

Fundamentally, we find cost-benefit analysis inadequate to deal with all information technology investments and business value derived from them. The traditional evaluation of a project is in business domain benefits compared to technology domain costs and investments. We recognize that there are business domain costs possible such as training, new staff, new space and facilities, and that these can be incorporated into the net value equation. Usually, however, the evaluation of projects has to deal with time value of money, intangible benefits, and short and long term elements of cost and investment.

We propose to expand the basis for economic evaluation and justification for information technology beyond cost-benefit analysis and return on investment by the ideas of *value* and *two domain analysis*. We have, of course, introduced these ideas in previous chapters, but we restate them here to emphasize our basic theme, namely, the *linkage of information technology to business performance*. First, we define a simplified Information Economics model based on a cost-distribution model. This model develops the two domain justification for projects. The first is the business economic justification based on value added to business performance. The second is an assessment of the technology factors costs and values. We will use the term *viability* to represent this concept.

The concepts of two-domain analysis and value bring clarity to difficult problems. For example, the separation of business justification from technology justification allows the separation of infrastructure investments and cost distribution of fixed costs from business justification. Similarly, difficult issues of decentralized vs. centralized computing can be treated separately from the essential justification of the business project.

6–6 TWO-DOMAIN ANALYSIS

Many IS organizations distribute the costs for services with some form of rates and/or chargeout algorithms. So a computer center may charge its users for programming time or computer CPU time. Alternatively, programming hours may be used for an after-the-fact distribution of costs to IS users. In either case the business domain departments ''pay'' for services rendered.

The chargeout practice is based on the two domains of the enterprise. Costs incurred in the technology domain (the IS organization) are charged to users in the business

$ 4 million for replacement (larger) CPU
10 million for high-speed communications network
1 million for database management software
5 million for enterprise-wide data model
5 million for strategic order entry system
1 million for customer service system improvement

FIGURE 6.8 Candidate information technology investments.

domain. Over time (usually a year) the total costs of the technology domain are expected to be balanced by cost recovery credits resulting from charges made to the business users. If the technology domain spends a million dollars in a year, the business domain will have a million dollars of costs charged to it for the year.

In Information Economics, from a chargeout perspective we can expand on the model in important ways. Two major ideas stand out. First, we substitute *value* for *benefits*, and second, we separate the the actual costs of services incurred in the technology domain from the cost distribution of costs to the business domain. Doing both accomplishes the purpose of separating business justification from technology viability, and may allow business managers to judge business domain justification and information technology managers to manage technology viability. In particular, difficult problems of investments in infrastructure and architectures can be addressed. In our view business and technology justifications are mixed in traditional cost distribution, particularly when traditional cost-benefit analysis is used.

An Information Economics model for justification is shown in Figure 6.9.

Comparison of Figure 6.9 with the traditional model shows the differences, as shown in Figure 6.10. Note that traditional cost-benefit analysis moves horizontally connecting business domain value with technology domain direct costs. Information Economics bases its justifications vertically within the domains, separating the business domain justification and feasibility from the technology domain justification and viability.

A fuller model of a two-domain Information Economics model is shown in Figure 6.11. Again, the purpose of this isn't to propose a particular way to assess individual projects. Rather, our purpose here is to set the stage for the value component of the evaluation: what is it that constitutes value in information technology applications?

The model emphasizes the difference in cost and value in the two domains. From the business domain perspective, value is created by the use of information technology

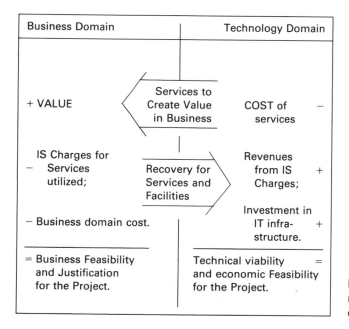

FIGURE 6.9 An information economics model derived from chargeback.

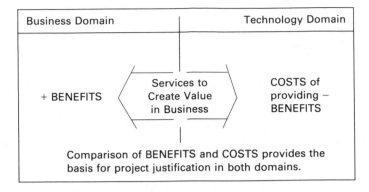

Business Domain		Technology Domain
+ BENEFITS	Services to Create Value in Business	COSTS of providing – BENEFITS

Comparison of BENEFITS and COSTS provides the basis for project justification in both domains.

FIGURE 6.10 Traditional cost justification derived from cost-benefit analysis.

to produce revenue, reduce cost, increase effectiveness or value. From the technology domain perspective, those business-domain values are the same, for the benefit of the users of information technology services. But from a service delivery standpoint, the technology domain values of those services are the costs recovered or revenues produced or investments made in the technology domain. This value is basis of support needed to create the services. Further, this value (or investment) is the basis of the technology domain infrastructure necessary to carry out these and other users' services.

In effect we return to the business-within-a-business perspective. The value in the business domain justifies the costs charges or attributed to the business domain; this is the foundation of the cost-value trade-offs in the business domain. The value in the technology domain is the proceeds from the sale of the services rendered, just as if the technology domain were a business enterprise selling its services. This perspective

Business Domain				Technology Domain	
VALUE	Created by the use of information technology to produce revenue, reduce costs, increase effectiveness or value.	Services to Create Value in Business		Defined as the true cost for resources used for services to business domain; includes risks.	COST
COST	Defined as attributable technology & business charges for resources applied to produce the value. Includes risk.	Recovery for Services and Facilities		The costs recovered or revenue produced or investment made in technology domain.	VALUE
NET VALUE PRODUCED	Business feasibility and economic JUSTIFICATION for the project . . . based on business performance			Technical feasibility and economic VIABILITY for the project . . based on technology viability	NET SUPPORT PRODUCED

FIGURE 6.11 Information economics two-domain model.

is exactly what's necessary to support management decision-making in each of the domains.

Similarly, the cost in the business domain is defined as the applicable charges for the use of technology resources applied to produce the value, including risk. Since much of information technology is a shared resource (e.g., use of a common data communications network or a main-frame computer), the actual costs are often the result of chargeback methods. Whereas in the technology domain cost is the true cost for the resources actually used to provide the services, including risk.

In the business domain, the net value produced, based on business domain value and cost, is used to determine the business feasibility and economic justification for the project, whereas the net support produced, reflecting the net of technology domain costs and values, defines the technical feasibility and economic viability of the project.

QUESTIONS

1. List the six categories of value.

2. Assume that Old Ivy University is about to install a computerized card catalog. Give an example of a value to the University the catalog represents. Give an example in each of the six categories of value.

3. What is meant by a benefit?

4. Hustle can be a company strategy. How can information technology contribute to an organization's capacity for hustle?

5. Discuss how information technology can add to the management capability of a company.

6. How can information technology erect a competitive hurdle?

7. How can information technology give a competitive advantage to a company?

7

Planning Methods: Linking Business and Information Technology

7–1 INFORMATION SYSTEMS AND BUSINESS PLANNING

Our purpose in Chapter Seven is to sketch in broad strokes the operationalization of Information Economics in an enterprise. Some years ago we recall talking to Dick Nolan about his stage theory. He was emphatic: It isn't enough to have ideas and to talk about ideas; the crucial element is the vision of how managers can actually apply the ideas in real-life conditions. We intend to sketch out such a vision here, and fill in the details in Parts Two and Three.

Until now we've focused mostly on ideas of value. We've made observations about the need for business perspective for both management and information technology managers. Chiefly this has taken the form of arguments for using business performance as the driving force behind value, management decision-making, and information technology planning. We've also looked at organizational issues surrounding business performance, with the consequence of line of business as the center for planning and decisions.

Now, we'll begin to bundle the ideas of value and decision-making into a process.

In order to simplify the discussion, the case and descriptive comments are based on several simplifying assumptions.

> *Keep-On Trucking is a single line of business company.* Consequently the planning process does not attempt to address resource allocation across multiple lines of business. Nor is a distinction made between corporate management roles and line of business management roles. The same group of managers, in a single line of business enterprise, play both roles.

> *All considerations of revenues and expenditures ignore multiple time periods.* This simplification is true also for Part Two of the book. We'll come back to time period considerations in Chapter Fifteen.

> *We continue to consider for-profit enterprises* to the apparent exclusion of not-for-profit and governmental units. We will return to this in Chapters Fifteen and Seventeen and discuss how Information Economics can be applied in those circumstances as well.

> *We overlook the specific details* of Information Economics. These will be discussed in Part Two.

We first return to themes from the first six chapters in Sections 7–2 and 7–3, as we consider how to apply them in a decision process.

Underlying the operationalization of Information Economics is a process that identifies potential projects (Figure 7.1). Bottom-up projects, generally *alignment* in character, are derived from individual user organizations. Top-down projects, often *impact* in character, are derived from an enterprise planning process, a strategic or long range planning activity.

Note that we are primarily interested here in the choices, part three of the project planning processes. Strategic planning and execution we leave to others, and we refer readers to the references for the chapter.

In previous chapters we've noted that IS managers making decisions about information technology rely heavily on some form of return-on-investment (ROI) measure to evaluate projects. With Information Economics we add evaluation methods to produce a greatly expanded measure of value in three parts: enhanced ROI reviewed briefly below, business value based on line of business performance, and technology domain value based on infrastructure investment (Figure 7.2).

In subsequent chapters we will add several cost and value assessment approaches to ROI and related cost-benefit analysis techniques. Because we intend to apply these

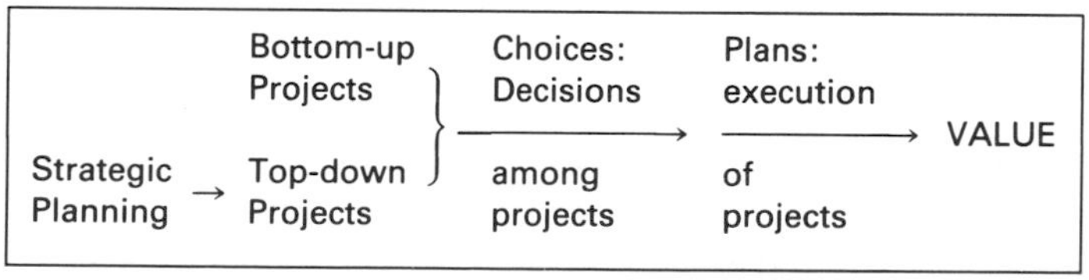

FIGURE 7.1 Project planning processes.

$$\begin{array}{ccc} \text{Enhanced} & \text{Business} & \text{Technology} \\ \text{ROI} \quad + & \text{Domain} \quad + & \text{Domain} \\ \text{Quantification} & \text{Evaluation} & \text{Evaluation} \end{array}$$

FIGURE 7.2 Value.

approaches to management decision-making about information technology, we also turn our attention to the decision processes themselves.

ROI has been popular as a valuation and assessment technique because it also matches the capital investment evaluation framework used in most companies. This match-up is one with which managers in industrial companies are comfortable. The evaluation techniques are drawn from experience and practice in business capital budgeting. In general, capital budget decisions represent the same problems and processes that we want in Information Economics, that is, a link to business performance.

We believe that capital budgeting techniques should be applied to information system projects, but that the traditional techniques are incomplete and inadequate when applied to information technology. The reverse of this assertion is that the additional techniques we introduce, although under the heading of Information Economics, should be largely applicable to the capital budgeting process itself. This may question the effectiveness of traditional approaches as now practiced in most companies. Exploring this idea is beyond the scope of this book, but the reader may wish to reflect on the possibility of applying these concepts to non-information technology projects and decision processes.

Part Two considers the valuation and assessment measures themselves. There we will look in detail at ROI and enhancements we propose, for to compound the problem of inadequacy of traditional techniques, even the commonly used ROI calculations may require special enhancements when applied to information systems projects. For example, the usual difficulties in ROI—choosing an appropriate discount rate and evaluating correctly all relevant investment alternatives—apply with special force to the consideration of such projects as computer-integrated manufacturing (CIM) or electronic mail networks. MIS application projects of this nature typically have a longer useful life than non-MIS application projects, and provide many additional values that require special consideration. These can include improved quality, organizational flexibility, and learning curves with advanced technology applicable to other strategic investments for competitive advantage. The typical capital justification processes do not begin to quantify these concepts.

We are also beginning to see MIS application projects that can extend ideas of efficiency and effectiveness beyond the boundaries of individual firms. Interorganizational systems (IOS), are a phenomenon making possible the integration of functions and activities across organizational units. A form of vertical information integration, these systems can be aligned with a firm's own strategic plans. Information Economics methods can be used to identify opportunities for these systems by viewing the unit of analysis as two or more organizations rather than just one.

Part Three considers the application of Information Economics in organizations. There we describe decision-making and decision processes—the steps that an organization can use to make resource allocation decision in information technology.

We note again some simplifications we have made here. (1) Keep-On Trucking is a single line of business company. Consequently the planning process described in the next section does not include decision processes across multiple lines of business, nor does the organizational process provide for management participation from corporate units as distinct from lines of business. (2) All considerations of revenues and expenditures ignore multiple time periods. (3) We discuss Keep-On Trucking as a for-profit enterprise.

7–2 CASE: APPLYING INFORMATION ECONOMICS TO KEEP-ON TRUCKING (KOT)

Keep-On Trucking is a mid-sized leasing company with one central IS organization. Headquarters numbers about 500 employees, with some 6000 vehicles on the road in the continental forty eight states. The IS organization operates three medium scale computers. A staff of fifty application development professionals design and install application systems.

Potential information systems projects cover the full range of possibilities. Some support the corporate headquarters, the backbone units such as accounting and customer services. Others support the various lines of business. One, for example, is an advanced maintenance support system for the hazardous materials division, one that will reduce on-the-road expenses by providing vehicle status information to dispatchers and drivers. Still others are in response to competitive pressures. For example, Keep-On Trucking's major Midwest competitor has installed in-cab computers to monitor and support drivers with information ranging from shortest routings to service locations to truck performance. This has given them a distinct advantage in certain leasing business areas, and Keep-On Trucking has to match the improvements or get out of the particular business segment.

So management is constantly faced with all sorts of potential ways to invest in information technology. These are handled as projects, with a specific assessment of each project about the value provided and the costs involved. The purpose of the Information Economics decision method is to make the wisest assignment of scarce corporate resources, which are money and people (for example, the limited IS systems development resources).

Projects come to the attention of management and are included in the decision process, in a variety of ways (Figure 7.3).

The decision process involves three levels of participants for the leasing line of business, which is a single line of business. The steering committee represents the line of business management. In simplified terms, how decisions are made is shown on Figure 7.4.

The case expands on these descriptions as actually applied at Keep-On Trucking. The emphasis here is on a simplified view of how the process functions. Essentially, each project is evaluated according to Information Economics concepts, including values and costs. The result is a simple ranking of projects.

We show an example of the outcome in Figure 7.5. We do not explain here the basis on which the evaluations are done. That is, we do not describe the actual values that enter in to the assignment of business domain and technology domain rankings. The point, rather, is that the rankings do occur, and make it possible for management to decide which projects to undertake. In the specific case presented here, Keep-On

Source of Projects	Types of these Projects
A strategic plan for the development of Keep-On Trucking's major businesses	Large systems projects, with considerable hardware and software (e.g., terminals, CPUs)
An information systems plan that has been prepared for each major business unit.	Same as above
Annual project planning, chiefly for the overhead and backbone units	Same as above
User management requirements for maintenance to existing systems	Relatively small, single department projects
End user requests for new tools for accessing company information and databases.	User staff projects or small IS supported projects

FIGURE 7.3   MIS application projects for Keep-On Trucking.

Trucking can afford to invest in about half the proposed projects, so we'd expect management to approve about the top half or so. Figure 7.5 shows each project with a ranking based on Information Economics. This figure is a subset from about 100 projects; the top one here was second out of 100, and so forth.

The reader should note that the projects are ranked based on total value, based on enhanced ROI plus business domain evaluation plus technology domain evaluation. The ranking is determined by the degree of importance placed on value compared, for example, by level of investment. An attribute of the Information Economics decision process is the capability to tailor the ranking process according to the character of the line of business. For example, if Keep-On Trucking management preferred to focus on a value-return measure rather than value alone, the projects would be ranked in a quite different sequence and, presumably, produce a different management result. Figure 7.6 shows how this might occur as a result of re-ordering Figure 7.5.

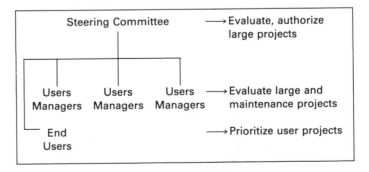

FIGURE 7.4   Evaluation participants.

Projects	Total Value	Value Return	Business ROI Evaluation	Technical Evaluation	Invest- ment	Ranking Level
Customer/Sales Profile	50	1.6	32	18	300,000	2.0
DB/2 Installation/Conversion	48	1.2	28	20	400,000	3.0
Interstate Sales System	40	.9	20	20	450,000	5.0
Dangerous Goods Control	36	.8	21	15	500,000	8.0
Preventative Maintenance	35	7.0	15	20	50,000	11.0
Customer Services	30	.3	30	0	1,000,000	29.0
Route Scheduling	25	1.1	5	20	300,000	45.0
Dispatching	22	2.2	20	2	100,000	45.0

FIGURE 7.5 Simplified information economics evaluation Keep-On Trucking leasing line of business.

The reader should note the basic difference between Figure 7.5 and Figure 7.6. Reading the latter it seems apparent that the projects that have strong strategic values to the line of business, such as the Customer Services Project which has the highest business domain value, drops to the bottom in the value-return ranking. We don't offer a theology on this—but offer the observation that the management of the line of business is confronted with the real issues in this process. Should the enterprise focus on strategic (business) values, or on a more conservative return-based value assessment? Information Economics will support both. In either event, the *value* part of the evaluation is based on the enhanced ROI plus business values.

The Information Economics process we are describing here is a logical additional step in sophistication to the information system planning process. However, the elements of a decision process, and evaluation process, must be in place for the process to be successful. We use the Information Economics process as a simple case study. Keep-On Trucking is based on our observations, over an extended period, of the experience of a large single-product international corporation.

Projects	Total Value	Value Return	Business ROI Evaluation	Technical Evaluation	Invest- ment	Ranking Level
Preventative Maintenance	35	7.0	15	20	50,000	1.0
Dispatching	22	2.2	20	2	100,000	2.0
Customer/Sales Profile	50	1.6	32	18	300,000	3.0
DB/2 Installation/Conversion	48	1.2	28	20	400,000	4.0
Route Scheduling	25	1.1	5	20	300,000	5.0
Interstate Sales System	40	.9	20	20	450,000	6.0
Dangerous Goods Control	36	.8	21	15	500,000	7.0
Customer Services	30	.3	30	0	1,000,000	8.0

FIGURE 7.6 Simplified information economics evaluation Keep-On Trucking Leasing line of business.

We believe that a project's contribution to the corporate purposes must be measured across several dimensions, only one of which is traditional ROI. These dimensions may vary by firm, but the dimensions we will suggest should be considered as the normative model. Although the dimensions of the normative model will apply to most firms, there will be considerable differences among firms in the importance attached to the various dimensions.

7–3 CASE: KEEP-ON TRUCKING (KOT)—A SINGLE LINE OF BUSINESS

It was generally acknowledged that Keep-On Trucking was not well served by the information systems department. These problems were generally well understood by senior management at KOT, and the corporation actively sought solutions. As is probably typical, its first step was to replace the head of the information systems department. They decided that the new department head should possess both technical and business expertise, with emphasis on the latter characteristics. They then looked to him to assess the situation and provide leadership and direction to senior management. After he had an opportunity to review the situation, he prepared a white paper at the request of senior management.

KOT's steering committee adopted a decision-making policy that committed them to a policy of decentralizing systems functions wherever doing so make sense. This implied several categories of systems:

1. Global systems are centrally designed, managed, and processed, usually for a uniform company-wide activity.

2. Shared systems are centrally designed and supported, but with management and processing split between headquarters and field locations. An example would be a centralized accounts receivable system operating as an aggregation of locally managed accounts receivable systems.

3. Local systems are locally developed systems, either stand-alone or interfaced to global or shared systems.

Successfully implementing this philosophy, while putting as much emphasis as possible on end-user computing tools and access to corporate data, required a well-developed strategic information systems plan, definition of responsibilities, and a user-driven decision process. The mechanism critical to the success of their process consists of a system of user policy committees that serve to integrate the information systems function with the direction and priorities of the company at several levels: a policy-level steering committee for strategic direction and major project prioritization; user policy groups for smaller project prioritization and planning; and user-driven project steering groups for managing major development projects.

After agreeing on the immediate goals and objectives, the steering committee focused on its decision-making process. It adopted a formal process for identifying project candidates and making information systems decisions.

7-3-1 Identifying Project Candidates

Potential projects come to the attention of the Information Systems Department from four user-driven sources (see Figure 7.4).

Information Systems Plan (Development Projects). The key to the long-term development effort is a well-developed strategic plan that serves as an architecture or blueprint for development. The policy-level steering committee participates in this planning process and establishes a strategy for information resources. The approved plan provides the top-down direction that ties the systems and data together in a logical fashion. Projects are identified that are needed to achieve the desired plan.

Annual Project Call (Development Projects). This bottom-up portion of the project identification process gives users an opportunity to identify major development opportunities. It is important to direct these project proposals into an annual resource allocation process so that the steering committee can see the relative priority of individual projects and authorize the most deserving projects within available resources.

User or System Requirements (Maintenance and Enhancement Projects). User requirements for changes and enhancements to existing systems, and requirements to maintain existing systems, are reviewed and authorized by applications user policy groups.

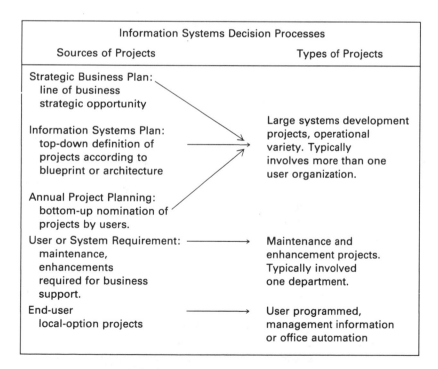

FIGURE 7.7 Decision processes.

End-user Computing (Local Option). This category encompasses personal computing, office automation, and other computing activities that are managed and processed locally. Projects in this category are generally authorized solely by users and are undertaken by the user within the integrating standards set by information systems. The IS group may provide training opportunities and general assistance, but the end-user actually completes the project.

The user groups drive the information systems process at all levels of the line of business:

1. The policy-level steering committee for the line of business serves as the board of directors for the IS function for the line of business. An effective steering committee will involve senior management in planning the overall strategic direction for MIS, allocating financial resources, and authorizing investment in major development projects.

2. User policy groups operate within the overall resources approved by the steering committee rank the smaller (that is, non-development) projects, monitor progress, and participate in the overall planning process. User groups are formed around the operations, administration, and other major systems, participants are the members of middle management most affected by systems decisions in the areas.

A different kind of user group advises and ranks resource allocation in the area of end-user computing, and generally helps the IS organization carry out the philosophy of shifting elements of data processing to the end-user by overseeing the provision of tools, training, standards, and access to corporate data.

3. The project steering committees provide user-driven direction to individual development (i.e., major system) projects. Each steering committee is chaired by the eventual system owner, normally the head of the primary department where the system will be installed. The project manager acts as secretary. The committees may be large or small, but include a management representative from every area that will be affected by the system.

4. End-user projects are initiated, managed, and carried out by users, within agreed standards, and call on IS organization personnel for assistance only on an as-needed basis.

MIS application projects come from several sources and fall into different categories. Each source and category has a user-driven mechanism associated with it. Building a computer system is analogous to a construction project, and a comprehensive information systems plan (blueprint) coupled with user management of the process helps to deliver projects that satisfy requirements while being on time and within budget.

With these steps in place, KOT took two very important steps, the additional levels of sophistication we referenced earlier in this chapter. First, they constructed the blueprint, or long range plan, that outlined their strategic data and systems architecture. The methodological steps they used to construct their blueprint are not significant here; the important point is that they saw a need to provide this top-down direction to the process. The next step they took was to introduce the tools of Information Economics to evaluate the bottom-up project candidates that were identified through their project approval

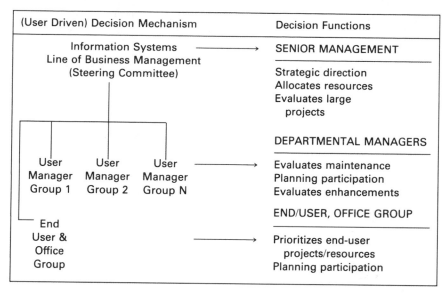

(User Driven) Decision Mechanism	Decision Functions

Information Systems ⟶ SENIOR MANAGEMENT
Line of Business Management
(Steering Committee)

Strategic direction
Allocates resources
Evaluates large
   projects

DEPARTMENTAL MANAGERS

User   User   User ⟶ Evaluates maintenance
Manager Manager Manager Planning participation
Group 1 Group 2 Group N Evaluates enhancements

END/USER, OFFICE GROUP

End
User & ⟶ Prioritizes end-user
Office   projects/resources
Group Planning participation

FIGURE 7.8 Decision participation.

process. An overview of the principles they adopted is provided in this chapter. Subsequent chapters develop these concepts more fully (see Figure 7.8).

7–3–2 Approval Process (For Large Development Projects)

The resulting planning and decision process is described in detail.

Project Initiation. An annual project plan for large systems development projects is prepared with the corporation's annual business planning and budgeting process and as part of the overall information systems plan. Each year a call memo will be sent to all departments requesting proposed project initiatives requiring computer resources. The IS department will work with the requesting departments to develop complete and accurate project requests to include labor, operating and capital costs, and a reasonable statement of value. Projects identified as necessary by the blueprint of the information systems plan may be added to the candidates.

Planning. The finance department will review value statements for accuracy and consistency, and corporate planning will assist in reviewing and ranking the proposed projects against corporate goals. Based on the ranked list of projects, and available resources, the steering committee will be asked to endorse a project plan which authorizes the most worthy projects. This approved project plan represents the first step of a two-step approval process and authorizes information systems to commit resources for an in-depth study of the user's requirements.

Requirements. During this stage, the specific user requirements are determined and alternatives for meeting them are considered. A summary document outlining the result of the requirements phase will be prepared on completion of this phase. This summary documentation will be approved by the requesting department and the steering committee, thus authorizing the project for development. This is the second step of the two-step approval process.

On closer examination in the requirements phase, a project may also fall below the cut-off point for approved projects due to higher costs and/or lower benefits than previously estimated. In that case, the project may be tabled and the next most beneficial project authorized for a requirements study.

Development and Implementation. User-driven project steering committees will monitor the progress of approved development projects against its milestones. Periodic progress reports will be made to the policy-level steering committee.

Evaluation. Evaluation reviews will be conducted on selected projects as part of the postimplementation process.

7–3–3 KOT Establishes the Link

With this approach, Keep-On Trucking established a link between business and information technology planning. As part of its corporate culture, the vision of top-down architecture definition and bottom-up project initiation was put in place. The process of developing a consensus through scoring projects on characteristics besides ROI created a dialogue among management that had been previously absent. They were explicitly recognizing that factors besides ROI were being considered in making resource allocation business decisions. Finally, they expressly wanted to consider these factors in a consistent manner.

In Part Two we describe the evaluation tools applied in the process Keep-On Trucking followed. In Part Three we describe how an enterprise can establish such a process within the organization.

QUESTIONS

1. Are Keep-On Trucking middle managers likely to believe they are a part of the planning for information systems in their organizations? Explain why or why not.

2. What is the role of a blueprint in the planning for information technology?

3. What is the role of a steering committee in the planning for information technology?

PART 2
ELEMENTS OF INFORMATION ECONOMICS

8

Cost-Benefit Analysis

Traditional cost-benefit analysis techniques support cost-displacement and cost-avoidance applications of information technology. Traditional cost-benefit techniques are the starting point for examining a truer economic impact, the goal of Information Economics. The advanced techniques, covered in following chapters, enhance the traditional cost-benefit analysis techniques and do not replace them. Therefore, understanding traditional cost-benefit techniques is prerequisite to understanding the advanced techniques of Information Economics.

8–1 COST-BENEFIT ANALYSIS

In the early 1900s, Pareto theorized that, when evaluating the worth of alternative choices (public projects), one project was superior to another when the net benefits were maximized (Wolfe, 1973). Pareto's work was the basis for original cost-benefit analysis development. Those in management science, economics, accounting, operations research, and other disciplines refined and reworked the original Pareto optimality criterion to suit their needs.

Accounting practices developed and emerged as a discipline in business schools after World War II. Accounting practices focus on measuring and reporting after-the-fact financial performance in a standard way. Assessing future impact on financial performance requires different tools than those for measuring financial performance. Translating

LOB or enterprise strategic direction into financial goals and balancing the supply and demand for corporate funds is a question of *assessing alternatives*, which is different from *measuring outcomes*. However inadequate, traditional cost-benefit analysis techniques are the common financial bridge or language between assessing alternatives and measuring outcomes. For this reason, traditional cost-benefit analysis is our starting point for Information Economics.

During the development of strategic and tactical plans of the LOB or enterprise, evaluation of alternatives takes place through optimizing the contribution to business performance. Criteria include resources required, length of time for accomplishment, and expected (potential) benefits. To do cost-benefit analysis, we determine what costs and benefits are appropriate to include. We must also determine how these costs and benefits are valued and what constraints exist in obtaining them.

8–2 COST-BENEFIT ATTRIBUTES

A *cost* is a measurement of the amount of resources required to obtain a product. Costs are expressed in quantitative dollars required. *Benefits* take the form of cost saving, cost avoidance, generation of new revenues, and intangibles. Cost saving and cost avoidance examples of benefits are obvious. Assigning a monetary value takes little effort. They represent the types of benefits traditionally included in cost-benefit analyses for data processing stand-alone and backbone systems. Generation of new or additional revenues requires the consensus of many managers before representative estimates are included in the analysis.

The less obvious, less tangible *value* is more elusive to the analyst. Defining and determining a value and obtaining agreement that the value assigned does, in fact, represent a contribution to improved performance of the line of business or enterprise is a formidable task. The less tangible values in business computing include such items as improved utilization of assets and improved information for management decision-making. These values, when achieved, lead to better decision-making. The former has some quantitative element of measurability, but the value of the latter is difficult to assess. Improved information grows in importance as information technology pervades the enterprise, for example, as it is extended from supporting predominately infrastructure (back-office) functions to supporting LOB (product-producing) functions.

We have alluded to limitations of cost-benefit analysis. Is there a point in doing a cost-benefit analysis if, at the outset, there seem to be insurmountable problems in obtaining accurate data? The answer is clear. Because cost-benefit analysis is the standard tool in organizations for ranking future expenditures (and past performance), it *must* be done. A project cannot get far (for very long) without some type of cost-benefit analysis. Whether a true cost-benefit analysis, given today's set of analysis tools, is even possible is another issue.

8–3 CONSISTENCY OF APPROACH

Accurate decision-making by management requires consistency in the information used. The process of obtaining the answers to the following six questions for your company will provide a common starting point for return-on-investment and cost-benefit analysis. This is the first step in Information Economics.

8–3–1 When Should a Cost-Benefit Analysis Be Done?

There are several points where a cost-benefit analysis is advisable. The size and nature of the effort will determine the selection of the points for a specific project. However, the primary rule is to do cost-benefit analysis whenever the relationship between costs and benefits becomes input to the decision-making process.

The first point to consider a cost-benefit analysis is the feasibility study for the project. The relationship between cost, benefits, and strategy determines its investment priority and whether the request for service is accepted. (This initial analysis is unnecessary if there is a consensus between major departments that the project is mandatory because of corporate management decisions or regulatory agency requirements. It is not it necessarily required for a sponsored system when the sponsor identifies the change as mandatory.) Although it isn't necessary to financially justify the mandatory project, it is recommended. From a management perspective, **committed projects reduce resources available** for other potential projects.

The next point for cost-benefit analysis is at the end of the analysis phase of the project. Here, all of the requirements will have been identified and a clearer picture of the change to the user's environment is available. The cost-benefit analysis findings chart a course to select alternative implementation strategies. It is of particular importance if there is a small window of opportunity for strategic applications. Here decision-making about inclusion of certain features and the sequence of implementation of multiple phases occurs.

The third point to analyze costs and benefits is particularly important for large projects. It is also important when either the expected costs or the benefits are questionable. This analysis happens during the prototype stage to verify that benefits (of the proper magnitude) are actually being realized. It is also used to determine whether additional prototype development is necessary before actual implementation.

In addition, analysis of costs and benefits occurs after implementation to assess the financial success of the project. Postimplementation analysis may or may not directly involve the information systems department personnel.

The investment dollars available are always limited. An optimized balance between growth (maximization of ROI and new ventures) and renovating and refurbishing (infrastructure, backbone, and architecture) investments must reflect the LOB or enterprise strategy. This is, in effect, a modified zero-based budgeting view. Zero-based budgeting links to long-range planning. It allows *each* project and *each* planning and budgeting cycle to compete on an equal footing for limited budget dollars. Zero-based budgets don't start with last year's budget as a base. They start from scratch (hence, zero-based) and require justification for any financial allocations (Cheek, 1977).

Today, few enterprises do multiple cost-benefit analyses of the same project. Once an information technology project is funded, it seems to take on a life of its own. We advocate a review of cost-benefit analyses and the related Information Economics issues of all projects on at least a yearly basis, including projects in maintenance, in development, and in the proposal stage.

8-3-2 Who Estimates the Benefits?

On all project efforts, the user or sponsor has the initial responsibility to identify and quantify the benefits. This occurs (ideally) with the finance function to gain consensus on benefits. The information systems department determines the development costs, and the affected enterprise organizations determine any organizational costs.

8-3-3 Who Will Use the Analysis?

During the feasibility evaluation, various levels of management review the cost-benefit evaluation. This effort results in the prioritization of the project with other investment alternatives. This determines if the proposed project or enhancement is approved. On each effort, a consensus should develop among the user or sponsor, the development organization, and finance.

At the end of the analysis stage, the user or sponsor and the development organization review the revised cost-benefit analysis. The purpose is to identify the features for implementation, deferral, or discarding. When planning phased implementation, the priorities establish the schedules for implementation. During the prototype stage, the actual benefits realized update the cost-benefit analysis. Reviews of the new findings by the user or sponsor determine whether implementation takes place, or, alternatively, they determine whether additional work is necessary to improve or guarantee the benefits before implementation.

Internal auditors usually do the postimplementation analysis. The sponsor or user management uses the audit to verify attainment of the benefits and identify areas for future work. This is perhaps the greatest area of vulnerability for information technology. All too often development time and costs, ongoing maintenance costs, and needed incremental improvements are underestimated. As a result, the information technology management loses credibility with the rest of the management team.

8-3-4 How are Benefits Measured?

There are three types of benefits: (1) tangible benefits; (2) quasi-tangible benefits, focusing most often on improving the efficiency of the already existing organization; and (3) intangible benefits, focusing most often on improving the effectiveness of the organization.

Of the three types of benefits, only tangible benefits have a known dollar impact on cash flow. However, difficult- (or impossible-) to-measure values may override the tangible benefits or costs. An example would be a change in the service procedure of a company due to a ruling by a regulatory agency. The company must conform to the ruling or refrain from certain business activities, resulting in some minimal loss of revenue. We could probably estimate the cost of changing the procedure and the potential loss of revenue for this operating cycle. What of future periods? Is this a rapidly growing market segment? Is this a market segment that once the company withdraws, it cannot effectively re-enter later? Will this change hinder a long-term marketing strategy? The sponsors or users of the project have the responsibility to identify the intangible value of the project in their request for services if it is to be considered in the decision-making process.

These steps determine the tangible benefits:

1. Break down the effort on the basis of the work functions affected by implementation.

2. For each function affected, identify alterations, additions, or eliminations associated with the specific job processes.

3. Determine the cost of performing the job process affected. Cost categories include labor, contract, equipment, facilities, material, and supplies. Cost sources include organization and function budgets or projections on the basis of time, volume, and labor rates.

4. Determine the effects on indirect costs caused by the change, such as inventory carrying costs and property taxes.

5. Determine the changes to the job processes because of the new project, system, or enhancement.

6. Determine the cost of performing the process after modification.

7. Determine where additional costs will occur in the future if no change occurs in the job process. Categories include additional volume resulting in more labor, equipment, and material or supplies; new or modified facilities; and additional indirect costs.

8. Calculate the difference between performing the process the old way and the new way. The result of this calculation will be the expected tangible benefit or an added cost of doing business.

These are the elements of the costs and benefits reflected in the worksheets introduced later in this chapter.

8–3–5 How Are Benefits Related to the Costs of Obtaining Them?

After determining the expected benefits and costs of project implementation, the relationship of benefits to costs needs definition. There are several approaches for developing the cost-benefit relationship; however, it requires a common method for the decision-making process. At a minimum, a common approach (at the LOB level) is necessary to maintain equity among project investment priorities. (See Appendix A for a glossary of additional accounting terms.)

Simple Return on Investment (ROI). This technique is also called the accounting rate of return. Simple ROI is the ratio of the average annual net income of the project divided by the internal investment in the project. This method is typical for data processing or information systems projects. The implementation and operating costs and the expected benefits are charted for the year anticipated. The point at which accumulated benefits exceed accumulated costs establishes the point where the base ROI occurs.

Use of this method assumes that funds *are* available within the organization to support implementation and any other cost-justified project. Unfortunately, unconstrained resources is a theoretical and not a realistic state. This method is not viable as a stand-alone justification method when competing for investment dollars.

Discounted Rate of Return (IRR).   IRR is also called the *discounted cash flow method* or *internal rate of return.* Discounted rate of return is probably the most widely used of all the analytical techniques. It determines the discount rate at which the present value of cash receipts equals the present value of cash expenditures.

Net Present Value.   This method uses a discount rate determined from the company's cost of capital to establish the present dollar value of a project. The discount rate is then used to determine the present value of both cash receipts and cash outlays. The discount rate may be adjusted to reflect other criteria set by management, such as an adjustment to compensate for perceived risk.

Profitability Index.   The profitability index is also called the present value index. The profitability index creates a ratio, which results from dividing the present value of cash receipts by the present value of cash outlay. A discount rate is used to determine the present value of the cash flow and outflow. It is not as widely used as IRR or NPV.

Payback Period.   A commonly used but technically deficient method, payback period determines the amount of time required for the cumulative cash inflow from a project to equal the initial investment.

Present Worth.   Many businesses use this method because it provides an accurate picture of profitability. This method assumes that the funding required to support some or all of the cost justified activities is borrowed or acquired through the sale of stock. The costs and benefits are charted over time as in the simple return on investment calculation. Then we discount the cash flow for future periods on the basis of the enterprise's cost of acquiring funds. (A current factor for the cost of acquiring funds is available from the treasurer in the enterprise.)

Probability of Attainment.   This method is an expansion of either simple return on investment or present worth. It describes varying levels of confidence within the expected benefits. Using this technique results in three sets of benefit values. The first set of numbers represents the benefits that are certain of achievement (80 percent confidence level and above). The second set of numbers represents the benefits that are probably achievable (50 percent confidence level and above). The third set of numbers represents any benefits realized if all goes well. Determination of probability is identified for the benefits related to each job process and to indirect costs and is summarized. The middle figure is the generally used basis for return on investment and present worth calculations.

Other Methods.   Other methods of developing a cost-benefit analysis use techniques that require more sophistication. These include decision analysis, structural models, and break-even analysis. Decision analysis applies game theory to business decisions. Structural models use models for the line of business and impact of change. Break-even analysis applies subjective assessments of benefits to objective assessments of costs (Sassone, 1986).

A significant problem associated with any of the above methods is the concept of risk. The methods by themselves (with the exception of Probability of Attainment) do not take risk into consideration. Other factors ignored by these methods include definitional uncertainty (the lack of specificity of scope of definition by the project proponents) and strategic match (the degree to which the proposed project is consistent with the strategy of the corporation). Other critical factors that may result as project benefits but that are not apparent to the typical financial analyst are similarly ignored. Information Economics applies traditional capital budgeting techniques to the evaluation of management information systems projects, including qualitative measures of project risk, definitional uncertainty, and strategic match. We also advocate a measure of the degree to which the proposed project aligns itself with the strategy for information systems architecture (if one exists).

8–3–6 How are Intangible Benefits Included in the Analysis?

Intangible benefits are the reasons for doing things that measurable benefits can't justify. The sponsor or user has the responsibility to relate intangible benefits (that create value) to costs. They must convince the decision-makers that other factors are more important than measurable cost. These motivating groups may include regulatory agencies, shareholders, customers, employees, and the financial community.

As you attempt to answer the six questions and measure the benefits, you will find that each enterprise has its own norm of financial analysis. There may be little to no choice (on your part) between simple ROI, net present value, or internal rate of return. We use the simple ROI calculation for our examples because the calculations are easily demonstrated.

8–4 THE WORKSHEETS FOR CALCULATING SIMPLE ROI

To calculate simple ROI, we use a set of three worksheets: (1) a development costs worksheet; (2) an ongoing expenses worksheet; and (3) an economic impact worksheet.

8–4–1 Development Costs Worksheet

The development costs worksheet (Figure 8.1) consists of five categories: (1) development effort; (2) new hardware; (3) new purchased software; (4) user training; and (5) other costs. Development effort consists of incremental systems and programming costs, and incremental staff support, such as data administration. New hardware reflects additional costs for terminals, printers, and communications. New software includes any purchased software or new software leases, and user training reflects education and learning curve costs. All other costs, including testing, are in the final category. A worksheet must be developed for each year in which development costs are incurred.

8–4–2 Ongoing Expenses Worksheet

The ongoing expenses (Figure 8.2) fall into six categories: they are (1) application software maintenance; (2) incremental data storage expenses; (3) incremental communications; (4) new software and hardware leases; (5) supplies; and (6) other.

Application software maintenance cost is obtained by estimating the number of development days (from the development costs worksheet). Apply the ratio of maintenance

```
                                              Year 1

A. Development effort
   1. Incremental systems and programming
      (e.g., estimated days times $xxx/day)      _____
   2. Incremental staff support
      (e.g., data administration at $xxx/day)     _____
B. New hardware
   1. Terminals, printers, communications         _____
   2. Other_____           _____
C. New (purchased) software, if any
   1. Packaged applications software              _____
   2. Other_____           _____
D. User training                                  _____
E. Other: _____              _____
TOTAL                                             _____
```

FIGURE 8.1 Development costs worksheet.

to development (days) and multiply by the daily maintenance rate. The product is the cost of application software maintenance. Cost of incremental data storage is the product of the estimated number of megabytes by the estimated megabyte cost. Incremental communications costs are those costs associated with lines, messages, and the like. Costs associated with new software leases or hardware leases are identified, along with supplies and other expenses. Like the development costs worksheet, an ongoing expenses worksheet should be developed for each year that expenses are expected to be incurred. (For ease of calculation, gigobytes, rather than megabytes, may be used in the calculation.)

```
                                                          Year 1-x

A. Application software maintenance                        _____
   Development effort days                    _____
   Ratio of Maintenance to development        _____
   (based on experience, e.g., 10 to 1)       _____
   Resulting annual maintenance days          _____
   Daily maintenance rate                     _____
   TOTAL application software maintenance  _____
B. Incremental data storage required: ___ MB x ___         _____
   (e.g., estimated MB at $xx.xx)
C. Incremental communications (lines, messages, etc.)      _____
D. New software leases or hardware leases                  _____
E. Supplies                                                _____
F. Other                                                   _____

TOTAL ongoing expenses                                     _____
```

FIGURE 8.2 Ongoing expense worksheet.

8–4–3 Economic Impact Worksheet

The third worksheet (Figure 8.3) summarizes the economic impact of the project. The economic impact scoring is based upon a straight-line relationship to calculate simple return on investment (ROI) of the periodic net cash flows of the proposed project over a five-year period. First, the net investment required is established. This is obtained from the development costs worksheet. Second, the yearly cash flow is established. This is obtained by establishing the net economic benefit through the users or sponsors, and then subtracting operating cost. The difference, pretax income, is reduced by the ongoing expenses, providing the net cash flow by year. Simple ROI is calculated by dividing the five-year average net cash flow by the net investment required. The economic impact score is then determined.

These three worksheets (development costs, ongoing expenses, and economic impact) are used throughout the remainder of the book to develop simple ROI for cost-benefit analysis. This traditional approach of cost-benefit analysis is compatible with targets, budgets, and quotas used for business performance measurements. The incentive at the functional level is to minimize cost (investment) and maximize the efficiency of the asset. This also holds true for the investment in strategic systems for the LOB. We use the techniques of traditional cost-benefit analysis as the base for Information Economics.

A. Net Investment Required (From Development Costs Worksheet)

B. Yearly Cash Flows: based on five 12-month periods following implementation of the proposed system. Cash flow can be negative.

	YEARS					TOTAL
	YEAR 1	YEAR 2	YEAR 3	YEAR 4	YEAR 5	
Net economic benefit	0	0	0	0	0	
Operating Cost Reduction	xxxxxx	xxxxxx	xxxxxx	xxxxxx	xxxxxx	
= Pre-tax income	xxxxxx	xxxxxx	xxxxxx	xxxxxx	xxxxxx	
(−) On-going expense from Worksheet	xxxxx	xxxxx	xxxxx	xxxxx	xxxxx	
= Net cash flow	xxxxxx	xxxxxx	xxxxxx	xxxxxx	xxxxxx	xxxxxx

C. Simple ROI, calculated as B / # YRS / A   xxx%

D. Scoring, Economic Impact

Score	Simple Return on Investment
0	zero or less
1	1% to 299%
2	300% to 499%
3	500% to 699%
4	700% to 899%
5	over

FIGURE 8.3   Economic impact worksheet.

Costs and values derived from applying the new techniques are added to the traditionally derived costs and benefits.

QUESTIONS

1. What are the methods used for financial justification for an information systems project?

2. Assume a large metropolitan hospital. How would you answer the following six questions?

   When should a cost-benefit analysis be done?

   Who estimates the benefits?

   Who will use the results of the benefits?

   How are benefits measured?

   How are benefits related to the costs of obtaining them?

   How are intangible benefits considered in the analysis?

3. Assume the Internal Revenue Service. How would you answer the same six questions?

Chap. 8: Cost-Benefit Analysis

9

Information Economics Tools

Long-range planning for the line of business (LOB) or enterprise and for the information technologies to support it is a subject of importance. Executives in the enterprise (business domain) have found that, on the one hand, long-range planning has become increasingly difficult because of the accelerated rate of change in the business environment. The information systems executives have, on the other hand, had trouble in responding rapidly to changes in the day-to-day business environment. This is due to the requirement to balance ongoing maintenance activities with developing an information architecture implementation strategy in support of near-term business strategies and conditions.

9-1 COMPETITIVE ADVANTAGE AND BACKBONE SYSTEMS

Two new concepts have emerged and are being used as descriptors by the information technology professional: *competitive advantage* and *backbone architectures*. Competitive advantage (Porter, 1985) focuses on the competitive value of computing and information technology to the line of business and enterprise. Senior business managers are pressing their information systems managers to plan for and accomplish computer implementations that will gain competitive advantage. At the same time, emphasis is also being placed on the backbone systems of the organization. Backbone systems are that set of central information systems critical to the operation of the enterprise, for example payroll or billing. Strategic planning grids became the tools to identify the character of the critical backbone systems (McFarlan, McKenney, and Pyburn, 1983). Assessing and planning information technology applications require focus on both competitive advantage and backbone systems.

How does one balance the maintenance of the current systems with the support of new LOB or enterprise functions, or balance the investment in information architectures and the creation of competitive advantage applications for the line of business? How does one conduct planning for computing that supports the business planning of the enterprise? How can one address the many associated problems in information technology *and* business in a cost-effective, financially justifiable way? The key is to enhance current techniques for financial justification. This expands the notion of tangible costs and benefits and addresses truly intangible costs and values through the development of management consensus.

Nolan (1985) suggests a set of eight computer-based competitive edges of leading companies: (1) client- or supplier-direct electronic communication; (2) global reach; (3) investing in the company's professionals; (4) reorganizing on the basis of information flows; (5) leveraging managers; (6) computer-based education; (7) creating new products and services; and (8) enhancing market responsiveness. Each focuses on improving the performance of the line of business through improved productivity and market expansion. Intelligent trade-offs between a never-ending list of potential information technology applications are mandatory in the current environment. Applications of information technology must support both the short- and the long-term strategies of the enterprise. Today, the financial justifications for new information technology applications providing competitive edge *and* backbone or architecture support are tenuous at best.

9–2 THE PROBLEM

CEOs and financial officers show little interest in whether their information technologies are state of the art unless the answer translates into improved financial performance for the LOB or enterprise. Justification of an information technology application *must* link to one of two conditions. It must improve the performance of the already existing organization (alignment), or it must improve the chances of success for new business opportunities and strategies (impact) (Benson and Parker, 1985).

The CEO is not comfortable with the current set of tools and techniques used to justify the investment in information technology. They lack definitive implementation procedures and do not yield the results expected by the CEO. And technology management isn't comfortable dealing with the business risks associated with creating competitive advantage for a LOB product.

A new view of the costs and values of information availability within the enterprise must be taken. The new view must assess the values previously thought not to be quantifiable. The assessment must be demonstrable. It must be accepted by executives in the business domain and (most especially) by the CEO of the enterprise. The assessment is developed by *communication* and *consensus* between the business and technology domains of the enterprise.

9–3 THE DIFFICULT-TO-MEASURE VALUES

Simple ROI calculations represent an attempt to quantify as much as possible. However, simple ROI alone cannot represent all of the factors that management must consider in the investment decision-making process. Some of the most cited benefits (Parker, 1982) of information technology fall into two groups. The quasi-tangible group has some directly measurable elements in the benefits. The intangible group has only indirectly measurable values.

Some examples of quasitangible benefits are: mandatory information needs, information processing efficiency, improved asset utilization, improved resource control, and increased accuracy in clerical operations. These benefits focus on making organizational assets more productive through leveraging information systems applications. They occur primarily in the organization infrastructure and are targeted toward the efficient use of resources to carry out the mission. These applications substitute for or complement already existing functions. Jobs and functions within the organization may also be restructured. They move from lower- to higher-value activities. These important benefits must be assessed and included in order to develop truer economic justifications.

Examples of intangible values are: more timely information (providing early warnings of change in the environment); improved organizational planning (making the organization more adaptive to change); increased organizational flexibility (allowing the organization to change more quickly); promotion of organizational learning and understanding (improving the organizational skills required to successfully initiate change); availability of new, better or more information (providing opportunity to compete more effectively); ability to investigate an increased number of alternatives (increasing the ability to make the best decision among alternatives); and faster decision-making (creating competitive advantage through timely action).

These values are oriented toward the line of business. They link to the effectiveness of the LOB in carrying out its mission or objectives. The applications are most likely to be of a complementary nature, such as enhancing an existing function, or of an innovative nature, such as creating a new function.

The line of business must survive in an environment of constant change—the marketplace. The ability to be flexible and to anticipate change before it occurs is part of the innovation process. The values associated with innovation and investment in the enterprise infrastructure must also be a part of the investment decision-making process.

9–4 THE SCOPE OF INFORMATION ECONOMICS

Information Economics is the structure for evaluating alternatives of information technology investment in the enterprise. Information Economics consists of costs and values tools and measurements. They are coupled with risk evaluation and other investment issues in a consensus-building, decision-making process. Information Economics addresses investment decisions concerning specific application projects and information systems architectures.

Simple return on investment (ROI) calculations are based on traditional cost-benefit

Traditional Cost-Benefit	+	Value Link-ing	+	Value Accel-eration	+	Value Restruc-turing	+	Innovation Valuation	=	Input to Simple ROI Calculations

FIGURE 9.1 Information Economics Techniques for Developing Simple ROI Calculations

analysis and addresses cost avoidance and cost displacement. The new analysis techniques described in this book extend the quantifiable costs and benefits to include value. These new techniques are additive (Figure 9.1). They use value linking, value acceleration, value restructuring, and innovation valuation. Value linking and value acceleration assist in identifying and quantifying the ripple effect of technology change in the enterprise. Value restructuring assists in quantifying changes in productivity because of technology change. Innovation valuation assists in quantifying alternatives of investment in new and innovative technology applications.

The simple ROI calculation and the assessments of other factors beyond cost-benefit factors in the business and technology domain, for example assessments of values and risks, are weighted (Figure 9.2). Business domain weighted factors (values or risks) include assessments relating to strategic match, competitive advantage, management information, competitive response, and organizational risk. Technology domain weighted factors include assessments of values or risks for strategic IS architecture, definitional uncertainty, technology uncertainty, and IS infrastructure risk. The sum of these factors become the basis for ranking alternative information technology projects.

In this chapter we will discuss the simple ROI calculations and apply them to a real business case. In succeeding chapters we describe and apply the new assessment techniques. These new techniques supplement the traditional cost-benefit approach and focus on quantification. The combination of old and new techniques ranges from traditional cost displacement to evaluating risk and uncertainty associated with gaining and sustaining competitive edge. They support alignment-oriented applications and impact-oriented applications. However, the decision about which analytical technique to apply depends on the type of information technology application. Before applying any technique, let's look at the types of information technology applications and how they map with the new assessment techniques.

9-5 TYPES OF INFORMATION TECHNOLOGY APPLICATIONS

Information technology applications are of three types for financial justification: substitutive, complementary, and innovative.

Weighted SImple ROI (Quantification)	+	Weighted Business Domain (Assessment)	+	Weighted Technology Domain (Assessment)	=	PROJECT SCORE

FIGURE 9.2 Factors for computing the project score.

9–5–1 Substitutive

Substitutive applications are those that substitute machine power for people power. Examples are payroll, accounting, and billing applications—all alignment in nature. Traditional cost-benefit analysis dealing with tangible benefits such as cost displacement and cost avoidance is effective for the ROI calculations. Although measurement of these benefits is easy, the size of benefits achieved will be low in mature enterprises.

9–5–2 Complementary

Complementary applications focus on increasing productivity and employee effectiveness for existing activities. Examples of the latter are spreadsheets, graphics, and query packages. An example of an alignment application is word processing for an administrative (overhead) function. An impact example is a marketing network and terminals for order entry or query by customers in their offices. Cash and Konsynski (1985) call this an interorganizational system. Value acceleration and/or value restructuring techniques are used here. These techniques (and applications) link to the bottom-line performance of the enterprise directly (acceleration) or indirectly (restructuring). They are effective in contributing to the financial justification. Potential contributions to business performance are larger than substitutive, but both prediction and measurement are more difficult.

9–5–3 Innovative

Innovative applications are those designed to sustain or gain competitive edge. Examples include home banking and expert financial systems. Examples of impact (changing the business) include creating a new market and creating differentiation through cost reduction. Innovation valuation is the basis for the financial justification of these applications. Potential value to the business is high, but the prediction and measurement approaches are speculative. This is because of the nature of creating entry barriers and having to be both *first* and *right* at the same time.

The application of information technology occurs at the individual, the group or department, and the LOB or enterprise levels. The application will be primarily substitutive, complementary, or innovative in nature. As a result, the combination of analyses used for financial justification will be different.

9–6 THE NEW TECHNIQUES

Five financial justification techniques are used for measuring and assessing potential information technology applications: (1) traditional cost-benefit analysis; (2) value linking; (3) value acceleration; (4) value restructuring; and (5) innovation valuation. These techniques represent the financial justification techniques that are applied in Information Economics for ROI calculations.

Traditional cost-benefit analysis fits most easily with the views of the financial planners. It supports the traditional views of the business domain for capital investment and consumption. It is good for supporting tactical plans. The technology manager may be able to apply the enterprise's method of justifying long-term capital investment to the architecture-based projects. (This is successful if the technology management is aware of the business strategy. Technology management should have an information systems strategy and master plan in place to support the business.)

Value linking and value acceleration analysis are techniques of assessing costs as they relate to enabling benefits to be achieved by other departments. This occurs via the ripple effect (value linking), or it occurs more quickly (value acceleration), accelerating a measurable effect on the bottom-line performance of the line of business or enterprise.

The assumption underlying value restructuring analysis is that because a function exists within an organization, it has some recognized value. The analysis assists in estimating the effects of modifying an existing job function. By restructuring employee and/or department efforts and moving them from lower- to higher-value activities, the value of the employee and/or department contribution increases. Although value restructuring can occur anywhere in the organization, it is a particularly useful technique when direct linkage to bottom-line performance is obscure or not established. Research and development, legal, and personnel departments are examples. These are support functions of the LOB or enterprise.

Innovation valuation techniques are used to assess alternatives among new applications of information technology. Figure 9.3 is used to determine a fast path choice of quantitative techniques to develop simple ROI.

Before applying extensions to traditional cost-benefit analysis, we will develop an analysis on the basis of current techniques as they were applied in a company called BEAM Parcels. Although the corporate structure and name are fictitious, all of the information technology projects attributed to BEAM are real, as are the decisions related to establishing investment priorities.

9–7 CASE: AUTOMATED RATING, CODING AND BILLING FOR BEAM PARCELS

BEAM Parcels is a delivery service operating primarily in Southern California and the Sun Belt region. Its main office is in Los Angeles County. BEAM specializes in overnight pickup and delivery from wholesaler or distributor to retail outlets. Its customers range from pharmaceutical distributors shipping small, lightweight packages to a refrigerator parts distributor shipping heavy, bulky cartons.

Description. BEAM Parcels rates and codes their waybills (based on size, weight, and distance shipped) manually. (Waybills are detailed invoices.) This process requires sending accounting copies to the main office. They are then sorted into appropriate categories and distributed to assigned clerks for processing. By automating these functions, manual processing is eliminated.

Objectives. The company will realize substantial labor savings through automation. They will eliminate handling hardcopy waybills and provide more accurate and timely rating and coding services.

Preliminary Benefits. Tangible benefits identified amounted to $125,000 in labor cost reduction (two coding clerks and three rating clerks).

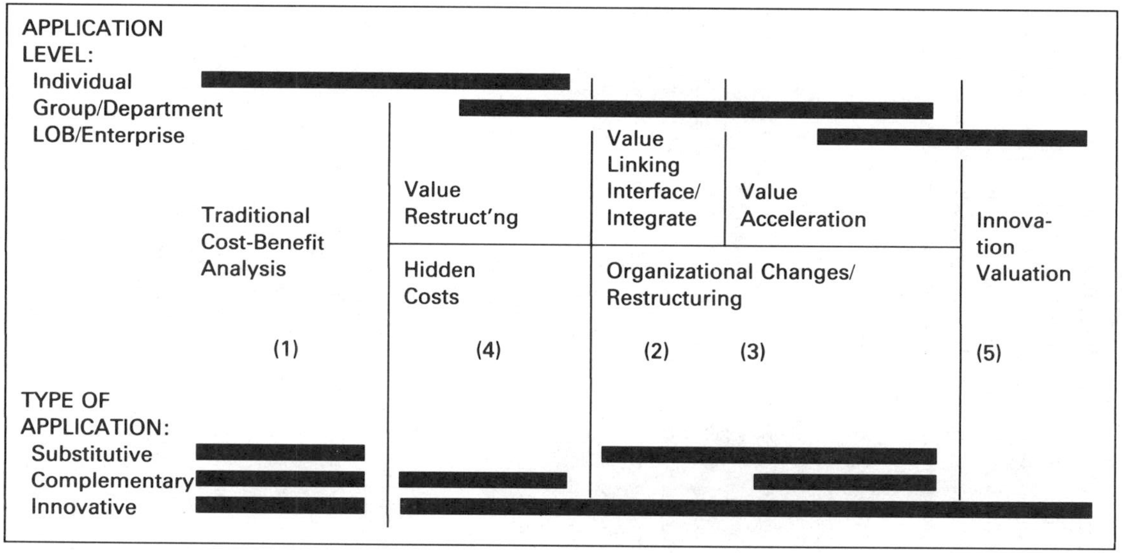

FIGURE 9.3 Mapping application types, application levels, and analysis techniques and causes. (Adapted from work by Dr. M. Schumann, Visiting Scientist, IBM Los Angeles Scientific Center, 1987)

Preliminary Cost Estimates. Preliminary cost estimates included $170,400 for development. Estimates also show that all development costs occur within one calendar year. Costs of testing the new systems will be incurred over the last six months of the year. They are half the yearly ongoing expenses.

The company had standard project justification worksheets that were completed and endorsed by the user or sponsor and development organizations before undertaking any work on a project. The information systems department completed the development costs worksheet and the ongoing expenses worksheet. The economic impact worksheet provides a summary for net investment. Included are the yearly estimated cash flows and the calculation of the simple ROI. This produced an economic impact score. The worksheet was completed by the sponsor, in this case the accounting department.

9–7–1 Development Costs Worksheet

The information systems department for BEAM Parcels completed the development costs worksheet (Figure 9.4). They estimated 852 programming days for project completion. Estimated programming days multiplied by BEAM Parcels average cost per programming day ($200) totalled $170,400. BEAM Parcels anticipates no new hardware or software costs, nor do they expect to do user training. They expect the testing costs to be half the yearly ongoing expenses ($10,456) developed in the ongoing expenses worksheet, Figure 9.5. (Unless otherwise noted, for presentation purposes, all development costs will be incurred in Year 1. Realistically, development effort can span multiple years.)

	Year 1
A. Development effort	
1. Incremental systems and programming	170400
(for example estimated days times $200/day)	
2. Incremental staff support	0
(for example data administration at $200/day)	
B. New hardware	
1. Terminals, printers, communications	0
2. Other _____	0
C. New (purchased) software, if any	
1. Packaged applications software	0
2. Other _____	0
D. User training	0
E. Other: Testing	10456
TOTAL	180856

FIGURE 9.4 Development costs worksheet for BEAM Parcels automated rating, coding and billing.

		Years 1–5
A. Application software maintenance		20912
Development effort days	852	
Ratio of Maintenance to development	.12272	
Resulting annual maintenance days	104.6	
Daily maintenance rate	$200	
TOTAL application software maintenance	$20912	
B. Incremental data storage required: ____ MB x ____ (for example estimated MB at $16.80)		0
C. Incremental communications (lines, messages, etc.)		0
D. New software leases or hardware leases		0
E. Supplies		0
F. Other		0
TOTAL Ongoing Expenses		20912

FIGURE 9.5 Ongoing expenses worksheet for BEAM Parcels automated rating, coding and billing.

9–7–2 Ongoing Expenses Worksheet

Ongoing expenses worksheet (Figure 9.5) consists of costs for application software maintenance, incremental data storage, incremental communications, and new software or hardware leases. Application software maintenance costs are based on an estimated 852 development days. Development days are multiplied by a ratio of maintenance to development (based on BEAM Parcels' previous experience with a similar project) of .12272, producing 104.55744 annual maintenance days. The annual maintenance days of 104.55744 are multiplied by the daily maintenance rate of $200, resulting in $20,911.50, rounding to $20,912.

BEAM Parcels anticipated no additional project costs for incremental data storage, communications, or new software or hardware leases. Ongoing expenses are assumed to be flat over a five year period. Note that the foregoing may be dependent on the methods of charging for services for the central information systems group.

In some circumstances utilizing the chargeout rates charged by the IS group to the user may be suitable. This will occur in circumstances where the user is treated as a separate unit financially (for example, a subsidiary). In such cases, a worksheet showing the range of chargeout rates, estimated annual usage, and annual costs to the users should be substituted or appended. The purpose here is to estimate the incremental costs as incurred by the IS group, and hence the enterprise as a whole, and not the user through chargeout.

9–7–3 Economic Impact Worksheet

The economic impact worksheet (Figure 9.6) consists of net investment required and the yearly cash flow calculations to produce simple ROI. Net investment required is $180,856, which is obtained from the development costs worksheet. Yearly cash flows are on the basis of five twelve-month periods following implementation of the proposed system. Here, BEAM Parcels is reducing its operating expenses by $125,000 per year because of reduced labor requirements.

The economic impact scoring is based on a straight-line relationship to the calculated simple ROI of the periodic net cash flows of the proposed project over a five-year period. Because the maximum practical value is 999 percent, the scoring values are calculated as follows: A $520,440 net cash flow for the five-year period divided by 5 provides $104,088 average annual net income. This average ($104,088) divided by the net investment required ($180,856) produces a 58 percent simple ROI. The resulting score for this project is 1.

9–7–4 The Proposal and the Results

The proposal was submitted. It did not rank high on the implementation priority list. Other competing projects had much higher return ratios. Resources were not assigned to the project.

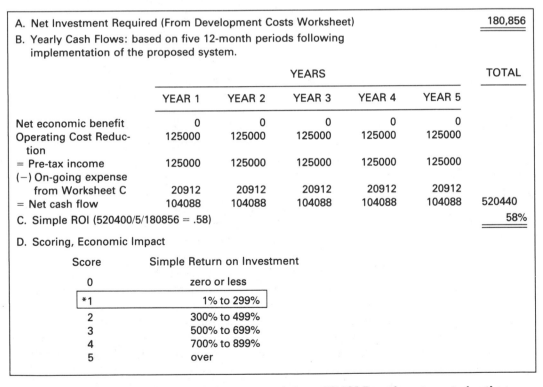

FIGURE 9.6 Economic impact worksheet BEAM Parcels automated rating, coding and billing.

Chap. 9: Information Economics Tools

CASH FLOW

DISCOUNT RATES/ 4.5   5   6   6.5   7   7

BEAM Parcels
ANALYSIS PERIOD 1/YR1 THROUGH 12/YR6
REPORT PERIOD 1/YR1 THROUGH 12/YR6

FISCAL YR-END: DEC	YR1	YR2	YR3	YR4	YR5	YR6	TOTALS
MOS IN REPORT	12	12	12	12	12	12	
CASH OUTFLOW BEFORE TAX:							
Development	170400						170400
Testing	10456						10456
Operations		20912	20912	20912	20912	20912	104560
TOTAL CASH OUTFLOW	180856	20912	20912	20912	20912	20912	285416
Labor savings		−125000	−125000	−125000	−125000	−125000	−625000
CASH FLOW BEFORE TAX	180856	−104088	−104088	−104088	−104088	−104088	−339584
CASH FLOW AFTER TAX	180856	−104088	−104088	−104088	−104088	−104088	−339584
CUMULATIVE	180856	76768	−27320	−131408	−235496	−339584	
DISC RATES	4.50	5.00	6.00	6.50	7.00	7.00	
DISC CASH FLOW	176497	−96555	−89772	−83293	−76565	−71556	−241246
DISC CUMULATIVE			79941	−9831	−93124	−169689	−241246

IRR: 50.36

**BREAK—EVEN (PAYBACK) MONTH: 33
(CASH FLOW AFTER TAX)

FIGURE 9.7 Cash flow for BEAM Parcels automated rating, coding and billing.

Was the cost-benefit analysis incomplete, or does the cost-benefit analysis process itself not lend itself to real-world decision-making? The answer to these questions required some thought by BEAM technology management.

Technology management knew that BEAM Parcels had engaged a consultant to provide an economic forecast for use in investment planning. The consultant, they found, had projected the following discount rates:

YEAR	DISCOUNT RATE
Year 1	4.5
Year 2	5.0
Year 3	6.0
Year 4	6.5
Year 5	7.0
Year 6	7.0

Perhaps, they thought, the more sophisticated approach of using a discounted cash flow would provide a more favorable analysis. Analysis of the previous BEAM project using these estimated discount rates is illustrated in Figure 9.7. In the figure, all payments are made in arrears (at end of month). The break-even (payback) month is the month within the analysis period in which the cumulative aftertax cash outflows and cumulative aftertax cash inflows become equivalent. If more than one break-even point occurs within the analysis period, the later one is given.

Adding sophistication didn't help. Using discounted cash flow, the project remained unfunded. When the values are discounted, the ROI is reduced. It had a relatively low return ratio (50.36) and length of time to break even (33 months). (The discounted cash flow calculations are documented in Appendix B. The same appendix also contains the detail monthly cash flow.) We will examine the same project again in the next chapter, apply some additional analysis techniques, and discover how the project received conditional project funding.

QUESTIONS

1. Give an example for each of Nolan's eight computer sources of competitive edge.

2. Why does management decision-making require consistent information?

3. Should a CEO care if the company's computers are state of the art?

4. Give an example of substitutive, complementary, and innovative computer applications.

5. Give an example of an intangible benefit.

6. Why should intangible benefits be included in the assessment of a project?

7. Give an example of the ripple effect of information technology.

8. Assume the BEAM Parcels case used in the text. Rather than the $170,400 development estimates, use $140,000. Rather than the $125,000 tangible benefits, use $150,000. Produce revised worksheets. (Ongoing expenses remain $20,900.)

10

Value Linking and Value Acceleration

Value linking and value acceleration are closely tied concepts and techniques. Value linking is used to evaluate financially the combined effects of improving performance of a function and any consequential results from a separate function. It represents the ripple effect of a change (improvement) in a function or process. It is not time dependent. For example, an improved billing system for BEAM Parcels (Chapter 9) focuses on costs and benefits for the information systems department. By improving the billing system, marketing and sales could identify revenue that would otherwise be lost because of incorrect billings. This additional revenue is identified and sized through value linking.

Value acceleration is used to evaluate financially any time acceleration of benefits (and costs) because of linking two departments or functions in a cause-effect relationship. This technique addresses time-dependency issues, such as causing earlier achievement of benefits. For example, the same improved billing system for BEAM Parcels also completes billing processing one day sooner. The opportunity cost related to this interest expense savings is a one-time accelerated benefit. This additional opportunity for revenue is identified and sized through value acceleration.

These two techniques may financially justify otherwise marginal information technology applications *if* those applications trigger a sufficient one-time or sustained change in another department. This second department must have a positive effect on bottom-line performance of the LOB or enterprise. Value linking and value acceleration **requires** agreement on the benefits by both business and technology sectors.

10–1 IDENTIFYING VALUE LINKING AND VALUE ACCELERATION

Value linking and value acceleration models help quantify the ripple effect of technological change in the enterprise. The application must be directly traceable and linked to the financial performance of the LOB or enterprise. Value linking and acceleration address issues of *organizational interactions* with the cost displacement and avoidance issues of traditional analysis. They clarify the view of cost and benefit flows within and to the organization. Value linking and acceleration represents benefits that can be quantified using traditional cost-benefit analysis, but are often overlooked or not included.

Value linking ties the effects of information technology to outcome measures through sustaining increased revenues, decreased costs, and/or accelerated growth. Value acceleration ties these same factors to earlier attainment of one-time benefits (and costs). Both techniques are appropriate to apply for substitutive applications of information technology. They are less effectively used for complementary applications. Again, they require agreed on linkage to the bottom-line business performance. Figure 10.1 illustrates value linking of benefits by applying information technology to an administrative function.

This provides a view of value linking in the administrative function. For example, by making communication more efficient, normally considered an intangible benefit, a host of associated (linked) benefits become measurable. Included are reduced travel (direct savings or cost avoidance), fewer meetings (increasing productivity), reduced telephone calls (reduced cost and improved productivity), and fewer written messages (reduced cost and improved productivity). Flow examples for value linking can occur in many parts of the enterprise. By identifying these cause-effect linkages, we create new opportunities for, and awareness of, the potential impact of information technology improvements.

Appendix C provides a taxonomy of profits and gains (benefits) and damages and losses (costs) for value linking. It is translated from German and is synthesized from several authors. The appendix provides a starting point for tailoring a taxonomy of value linkages for a specific LOB or enterprise.

10–2 VALUE LINKING AND VALUE ACCELERATION PRODUCTIVITY BENEFITS

Schwartz and Sassone (1984) suggest five categories of productivity benefits. These benefits may be viewed as ones of value linking and acceleration. They are operations savings, labor savings, shorter time cycle for completion, better performance, and increased revenues. Operations savings address monies that the LOB or enterprise does not need to spend for operating expenses. Changes in maintenance contracts, floor space, power requirements, and other nonlabor costs are examples. Labor savings are reflected in the actual reduction of employees. Savings can occur through the decrease of planned new hires to do the same amount or more work by, for example, increasing the productivity

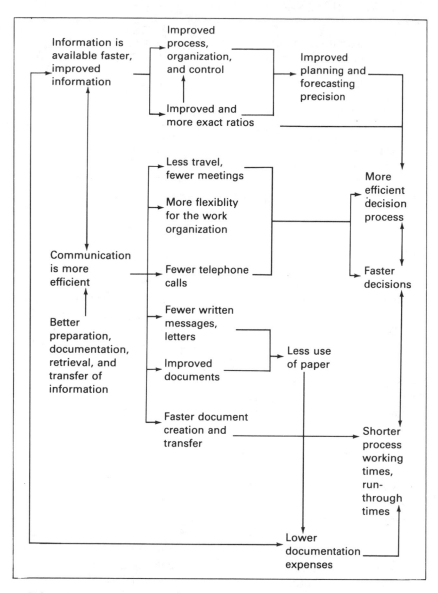

FIGURE 10.1 An example of value linking: information processing benefits in the administrative function. (Translated and adapted by Dr. M. Schumann from R. Anselstetter, Betriebswirtschaftliche Nutzeffekte der Datenverarbeitung, Anhaltspunkte fuer Nutzen-Kosten-Schaetzungen, ed2, Springer, Berlin, 1986, 44.)

of the current work force. Another view of increasing productivity is to decrease the time cycle required to complete a particular function in the LOB or enterprise, such as improving the flow of goods and communications. Better performance is the issue of quality of the product and service to the customer. Finally, increased revenues reflect

BENEFIT (Paybacks from JIT)	Per Cent Improvements	TYPE/DEPT.	TYPE/LOB
Manufacturing lead times reduced	80–90	CBA,VA	VL
Set up reduction	75–95	CBA,VA	VL
Space reduction	40–80	CBA,VA	VL
Inventory reductions—raw materials	35–75	CBA,VA	VL
Work-in-progress investment reduction	30–90	CBA,VA	VL
Purchase price reductions	5–10	CBA	VL
Finished goods investment reduction	50–90	CBA,VA	VL
Quality improvements	50–55	CBA	VL
Productivity increases	5–60	CBA	VL

FIGURE 10.2   JIT and financial justification.

the LOB or enterprise ability to deliver more competitive products to the marketplace and create competitive advantage.

A manufacturing enterprise can, for example, use value linking and value acceleration to develop just-in-time (JIT) financial justifications. (Just-in-time is an approach to inventory control where raw materials are stocked at their lowest possible levels, but are available "just in time" for the manufacturing process.) Donahue (1987) reported pay-backs (improvements) from using the JIT approach. At the LOB or enterprise level, JIT is a value linking application. No single package or system exists to integrate the entire JIT process. At the lower (department or LOB) level, each element of the process is viewed separately, using traditional cost-benefit analysis and value acceleration techniques. Figure 10.2 ties the Donahue work with the financial justification techniques of traditional cost-benefit analysis (CBA), value linking (VL), and value acceleration (VA).

10–3 A VALUE LINKING AND VALUE ACCELERATION EXAMPLE

We will now take a second look at BEAM Parcels automated rating, coding, and billing application, which in Chapter Nine illustrated traditional cost-benefit analysis. In that example, a recurring cost avoidance of $125,000 a year was achievable. It required a $180,856 net investment and an ongoing expense of $20,912 annually. The simple ROI was 58 percent. The proposal did not rank high on the priority list for initiating new projects because it did not meet the initial hurdle rate of 400 percent ROI for BEAM Parcels information systems investments. Resources were not assigned to the project. We posed the question of whether the cost-benefit analysis was complete. It was, when viewing costs and benefits of the project incurred by the departments directly affected (information systems development and billing). It was not complete, when viewed from the cause-effect relationship with marketing and sales.

Subsequent reviews showed that interest savings and revenue maximization would provide additional benefits. These related revenue benefits were developed in cooperation with marketing and sales. This was done to receive their concurrence and to insure accuracy and consistency with other projects. The benefits were quantified as follows:

```
Interest Expense Savings                                                    $    40,000
    Opportunity cost of money related to billings being processed 1 day
    sooner

    $200,000,000/365 × 40% × 18.25%
            a        b      c       d

    200,000,000/365 = 547,945.20
    547,945.20 × 40 % = 219,178.08
    219,178.08 × 18.25% = 39,999.99

    a = revenue billed yearly
    b = 365 days
    c = 40 percent of the bills are affected from a timeliness standpoint
    d = marginal debt rate

Revenue Maximization
    Revenue which would otherwise be lost due to inaccurate billings        $   800,000

    $200,000,000 × .004
          a            b

    a = revenue billed yearly
    b = customer loss factor resulting from inaccurate billings
                                                                           _____
                                                                            $   840,000
```

To reflect these new benefits, the BEAM Parcels economic impact worksheet (Figure 9.6) is modified as shown in Figure 10.3. The development costs worksheet (Figure 9.4) and the ongoing expenses worksheet (Figure 9.5) remain unchanged for the application.

The economic impact worksheet (Figure 10.3) shows the benefits identified through value linking and value acceleration. Net economic benefit is reflected for the first time. The $40,000 interest expense savings (opportunity cost of money) is a one-time (value acceleration) benefit. It is, therefore, reflected only in the first year. The $800,000 revenue maximization is a recurring (value linking) benefit that is otherwise lost due to inaccurate billings. Year 1, the $40,000 interest expense savings and the $800,000 revenue maximization combine to reflect a $840,000 economic benefit. The $800,000 revenue maximization is a continuing benefit in Years 2 through 5. Because of these newly identified value linking and value acceleration benefits, the simple ROI increased from 58 percent to 504 percent. The economic impact scoring is based on a straight-line relationship to the calculated simple ROI of the periodic net cash flows of the proposed project over a five-year period.

Because of this second analysis, the project received conditional implementation approval. (Anything over 500 percent ROI was put in the implementation queue for further study and prioritization.) Is this value linking and value acceleration, or is it simply the difference between an incomplete and a complete cost-benefit analysis? For this particular example, either side can put forth a coherent and persuasive argument. A clearer view of value acceleration benefits is seen by taking the BEAM Parcels example one additional step.

A. Net Investment Required:						180,856

B. Yearly Cash Flows: based on five 12-month periods following implementation of the proposed system.

	Year 1	Year 2	Year 3	Year 4	Year 5	Total
Net Economic Benefit	840,000	800,000	800,000	800,000	800,000	
Operating Cost Reduction	125,000	125,000	125,000	125,000	125,000	
= Pretax income	965,000	925,000	925,000	925,000	925,000	
(−) Ongoing Expense	20,912	20,912	20,912	20,912	20,912	
= Net Cash Flow	944,088	904,088	904,088	904,088	904,088	4,560,440

C. Simple ROI, calculated as B/# YRS/A   504%
   (4,560,440/5 = 912,088/180,856 = 5.04)

D. Scoring, Economic Impact

Score	Simple Return on Investment
0	zero or less
1	1% to 299%
2	300% to 499%
*3	500% to 699%
4	700% to 899%
5	over

FIGURE 10.3 Economic impact worksheet for the BEAM Parcels automated rating, coding, and billing.

10–4 A VALUE ACCELERATION EXAMPLE

The information systems department of BEAM Parcels proposes the purchasing of a software productivity package for $100,000. The productivity package will decrease development time by 20 percent. The purpose of this example is to see how value acceleration can add to the net economic benefit of a project. The assumptions are:

1. The current project has financial justification based on revenue enhancement or cost reduction. Here, marketing and sales increased and accelerated revenues justify the investment. Another, independent project causes the current (first) project to be accomplished earlier. The justification for the second project is based on the benefit (value) acceleration for the first project.

2. The direct benefits of the first project are measured with traditional cost-benefit, value linking and value acceleration techniques. This was accomplished with the preceding worksheet.

For this example, the project being evaluated is the second, otherwise unrelated project. The project will accelerate the accomplishment of the first project results. To begin, we complete the table shown in Figure 10.4.

Figure 10.4 shows the economic benefit for Year 1, measured from the point of implementation. This implementation will occur sometime in the future.

Our evaluation now is for the second (independent) project. This project will have the effect of accelerating the implementation date of the first project. The second project is the implementation of an advanced software development capability that will

The economic impact for the current project based on Year 1.	
Net Economic Benefit:	840,000
Operating Cost Reduction	125,000
= Pretax effect bottom line	965,000
Ongoing expense	20,912
= Net Cash Flow	944,088

Figure 10.4 Year 1 Economic impact for the current project.

increase the productivity of programmers by 20 percent. This productivity improvement will decrease the elapsed time needed for programming. For value acceleration, the latter is key. The increase in productivity is a direct benefit to the *first* project whose revenue acceleration and maximization can be realized two months earlier. An additional effect is the acceleration of the benefit from the second project. It is this benefit in which we are now interested. Here, the development cost savings is greater than the cost of the productivity package.

Figure 10.5 calculations are developed as follows:

1. The $800,000 is the one full year recurring benefit.
2. (original cost to develop) divided by (cost per development day) = (development days), or $170,400 divided by 200 = 852.
   (development days) divided by 5 =(development weeks), or 852 divided by 5 = 170.
   Assuming 170 development weeks and 4 programmers, 170 divided by 4 divided by 4.3 = 10 elapsed months.
   20 percent of 10 months = 2 months
   $800,000 divided by 12 = 66,667 per month
   $66,667 x 2 months acceleration = $133,333.
   We are, in effect, getting 14 months of benefits in a 12 month period.
3. The one-time benefit occurring the first time any benefit is achieved is $40,000.
4. $800,000 + 133,333 + 40,000 = $973,333.

Note that the second project has essentially stable net cash flows in Years 2 through 5. If those years anticipate net changes from year to year, additional value acceleration would be derived.

Net Economic Benefit (Year 1, annual rate)	$800,000
Estimated elapsed time saving due to implementation of the second project	20% or 2 months
Estimated additional benefit due to acceleration (based on annual rate)	$133,333
One-time benefit	$ 40,000
	$973,333

FIGURE 10.5 Computation of value acceleration.

A. Development Effort	
1. Incremental systems and programming	136,320
(80 percent of 170,400)	
(E.g., estimated days times $200/day)	
2. Incremental staff support	0
(E.g., data administration at $200/day)	
B. New Hardware	
1. Terminals, printers, communications	0
2. Other _____	0
C. New (Purchased) Software, if any	
1. Packaged applications software	100,000
2. Other _____	0
D. User training	0
E. Other: Testing	10,456
TOTAL	246,776

FIGURE 10.6 Development costs worksheet for the BEAM Parcels productivity package for automated rating, coding, and billing.

We can now revise the development costs, ongoing expense and economic impact worksheets for the productivity package (a refinement of Project 1).

10–4–1 Development Costs Worksheet

The development costs worksheet in the previous chapter (Figure 9.4) is modified to reflect the effects of the productivity package. The original $170,400 of incremental systems and programming costs is reduced by 20 percent using the productivity package, to $136,320. The $100,000 cost of the productivity package is added. The testing remains unchanged at $10,456. The new development costs worksheet is shown in Figure 10.6.

10–4–2 Ongoing Costs Worksheet

The ongoing costs worksheet in the previous chapter (Figure 9.5) remains unchanged. It is furnished as Figure 10.7 to provide the reader with the complete set of forms, rather than to introduce new information. The assumption is that, although the generation of the code was 20 percent faster, the maintenance requirements remain unchanged.

10–4–3 The Economic Impact Worksheet

The economic impact worksheet (Figure 10.8) represents changes to the productivity package. The net investment required ($246,776) is from the development costs worksheet (Figure 10.6). The net economic benefit for Year 1 of $973,333 is from Figure 10.5. Operating cost is reflected by 14 months of labor expense savings within a 12-month period (Year 1). Operating cost of $125,000 divided by 12 months = 10,417 x 2 months acceleration = $20,833. This results in an operating cost reduction for Year 1 of $125,000 plus $20,833 = $145,833, and a pretax income of $1,119,166. The pretax

A. Application software maintenance		20,912
such as,		
Development effort days	852	
Ratio of maintenance to development	.12272	
Resulting annual maintenance days	104.6	
Daily maintenance rate	$200	
TOTAL application software maintenance	$20,912	
B. Incremental data storage required: _____ MB × _____		0
(such as, estimated megabytes, $16.80)		
C. Incremental communications (lines, messages, etc.)		0
D. New software leases or hardware leases		0
E. Supplies		0
F. Other		0
TOTAL Ongoing expenses		20,912

FIGURE 10.7 Ongoing expenses worksheet for the BEAM Parcels productivity package for automated rating, coding, and billing.

income, reduced by the $20,912 ongoing expense, is $1,098,254. Years 2 through 5 remain unchanged from the previous example. As before, the economic impact scoring is based on a straight-line relationship to the simple ROI of the periodic net cash flows of the proposed project over a five-year period. Because the maximum practical value of the simple ROI is 999 percent, the scoring values are calculated and shown in Figure 10.8.

A. Net Investment Required (From Development Costs Worksheet)   246,776
B. Yearly Cash Flows: based on five 12-month periods following implementation of the proposed system. Cash flow can be negative.

	Year 1	Year 2	Year 3	Year 4	Year 5	Total
Net Economic Benefit	973,333	800,000	800,000	800,000	800,000	
Operating Cost Reduction	145,833	125,000	125,000	125,000	125,000	
= Pretax Income	1,119,166	925,000	925,000	925,000	925,000	
(−) Ongoing Expense	20,912	20,912	20,912	20,912	20,912	
= Net Cash Flow	1,098,254	904,088	904,088	904,088	904,088	4,714,606

C. Simple ROI, calculated as B/# YRS/A   382%
   (4,714,606/5 = 942,921/246,776 = 3.82)

D. Scoring, Economic Impact

Score	Simple Return on Investment
0	zero or less
1	1% to 299%
*2	300% to 499%
3	500% to 699%
4	700% to 899%
5	over

FIGURE 10.8 Economic impact worksheet for the BEAM Parcels productivity package for automated rating, coding, and billing.

Note that by accelerating $133,333 the simple ROI has dropped from 504 percent to 382 percent. This may be exaggerated, because the calculation assumes that the productivity package is consumable by this one project only. If true, then only $67,413 is realized during the first year. The $133,333 acceleration (plus savings in development costs of $34,080) is offset by the $100,000 expense to obtain the package. (We have accelerated both the benefits *and* the costs into the same time period.) If the productivity package can be used in other projects (and applying value linking), the value acceleration range based on the annual rate is somewhat more than $67,413 and less than $167,413.

10–5 A QUESTION OF RISK

We have not addressed the questions of risk. Will the productivity package perform as expected? Is the learning time for the programmers estimated correctly? Is the package the first step of an action plan to increase the productivity and responsiveness of the information systems department? Is there a competitive edge to be gained or sustained by getting the project implemented in the earlier time frame? To gain insight into these questions, additional criteria need evaluation.

BEAM Parcels management felt that serious consideration should be given to the project now, with multiple functions supporting the project nomination. The information systems department was particularly interested in the productivity package. They felt it could be used effectively in other projects. They did not, however, feel it necessary to apply the savings to other pending financial justifications.

The information systems department put forth a persuasive argument that this productivity package would have a much wider impact, even though it was being charged 100 percent to this project. If effective, it would be applied to future projects not included in this call for projects. It was part of the information systems department's strategy to invest and use productivity packages wherever possible to leverage its scarce resources.

After reviewing these new analyses and the information systems departments comments and strategy, BEAM Parcels management agreed that the implementation of the project (including the requested productivity package) would be recommended to the steering committee for their review and approval.

Although this decision seems inconsistent because of BEAM's preset hurdle rate of 400 percent, it was not. The conditional approval was not an act of faith by BEAM management, because the steering committee had previously reviewed and approved the information systems department blueprint and strategy. Supporting the strategy is important, even though it can't be reflected in the simple ROI calculation. The project would have met the hurdle rate of 400 percent ROI if the productivity package hadn't been included (ROI of 504 percent versus 382 percent). Although the project made the cut, the technology managers were concerned. There was no way to reflect the importance of projects that were in direct support of BEAM strategy if simple ROI drove their prioritization process.

QUESTIONS

1. What's the difference between value linking and value acceleration?

2. Give an example of value linking in a company with which you are familiar.

3. Give an example of value acceleration in a company with which you are familiar.

4. Given a company like IBM, give five examples of investments in information technology that could give value acceleration.

5. Given a robotics laboratory at General Motors, state five examples of investments in information technology that could give value acceleration and value linkage.

6. Given Old Ivy University, how can information technology be used for value linking? How can information technology be used for value acceleration?

7. Given a company with $2,350,000 revenue dollars, assume that 50 percent of the billing is affected by a time acceleration of two months. Marginal debt rate is 15 percent. Recalculate the interest expense savings.

11

Value Restructuring

Value restructuring addresses the values **associated with restructuring** a job or department function. It measures the value of productivity increases resulting from organizational change. Like value linking and value acceleration, it supplements the cost displacement and cost avoidance techniques of traditional cost-benefit analysis. An example of value restructuring is the measurable increased productivity of a department or function because of an office automation implementation. The productivity increase is achieved by moving the efforts of the department from lower value activities to higher value activities.

11–1 VALUE RESTRUCTURING

Value restructuring ties the effects of information technology to results measured through increased productivity. It assesses the movement of job activities from lower value functions to higher value functions. It requires both *information technology* and *organizational change* to achieve its maximum effectiveness (Hampton and Norman, 1987). Value restructuring is appropriate for complementary and substitutive applications of information technology. It is less effective for innovative applications. Finally, it requires agreed-on values for productivity increases.

Value restructuring is particularly useful if no linkage to bottom-line performance of a line of business is established, or if the linkage is obscure. Infrastructure functions such as research and development, legal departments, and marketing planning (as compared to direct sales) are examples. It is appropriate for the assessment of the value of restructuring key activities.

Value restructuring assesses the economic impact of information technology in labor-intensive support organizations. The assessment approach applies to proposed organizational changes as well.

These are issues of organizational fine-tuning on the one hand and, on the other hand, issues of organizational survival. Using information technology, the existing organization can be restructured or migrated to a more productive, effective, and competitive form. Strassmann (1985) suggests that effective management will find ways to provide incentives to employees to move their lower valued tasks to those who would find the work a higher-valued task. This provides job enrichment to the recipients. He also suggests that if the lower-valued tasks can't be moved, they are candidates for automation.

The issues of restructuring are not new. However, quantifying the benefits of such restructuring and including them as a complementary assessment to objective financial justification is new. Strassmann (1985) suggests looking at the incremental change within the established level of management productivity. He asserts that the largest factor in the economics of office work is organizational expense. Thus, the focus should be on the organizational costs rather than on the technological costs and risks.

Bain (1982) and Drucker (1986) develop ratios between LOB or enterprise output and its white-collar employment. Bain argues that as the product mix of the organization changes, the comparison of ratios becomes meaningless for quantifying productivity changes. Drucker, however, uses ratios to compare past performance with the present to set future goals based on performance. He asserts that the only competitive advantage any developed country has is its ability to make its educated white-collar workers more productive. Value restructuring assists in the quantification of these necessary productivity improvements.

Sassone and Schwartz (1986) suggest a breakdown of the hierarchy of activities within a set of managerial functions. They report that managers and professionals at both junior and senior levels spend 61 percent of their working hours on higher value activities (such as managing), 21–27 percent performing their own clerical and support functions, and 12–18 percent on wasted, nonproductive time.

The managers, and junior and senior professional personnel, categorized their activities and reported on themselves. The figures, based on a study of four departments and 587 personnel, suggest a significant opportunity to examine our current organizations. We must consider the effect of restructuring professional activities. Value restructuring techniques accomplish this examination and the subsequent financial evaluation of alternatives.

Sassone and Schwartz advocate the Hedonic wage-pricing model, a technique for computing the implicit value of job functions. One of its premises is that present employees (or a class of employees) are paid what they are worth to the LOB or enterprise. A second premise is the existence of an unending supply of additional higher value tasks. The final premise is that doing the higher value tasks will contribute to improved bottom-line performance.

In the previous chapter, the BEAM Parcels rating, coding, and billing project was analyzed with traditional and value acceleration cost-benefit techniques. BEAM Parcels has many potential projects to justify and implement. Let us examine another information technology project that is being considered at BEAM Parcels. We will first apply traditional cost-benefit analysis, and then apply a model similar to the Hedonic wage-pricing model, but using standard costs rather than actual salaries.

11–2 CASE: DRIVER PAY SYSTEM FOR BEAM PARCELS

The old system no longer met the reporting requirements. The drivers show a significant lack of confidence in driver pay, due to the number of required manual adjustments in training, vacation, and sick pay. The proposed new system would meet reporting requirements by cutting manual adjustments by 95 percent. It would build confidence in driver pay via accurate data and automate training, vacation, and sick pay. Allocation of cost by product line (shipment type) would improve. Furthermore, it would cut one day from the driver pay close, that is, the length of cycle time for the payroll.

The objective of the project is to rewrite the driver pay system so that it carries out all functions of the current system plus:

1. Maintain guarantee rates

2. Automate driver assistant (driver backup) pay

3. Automate labor accrual

4. Improve various reporting functions

The preliminary tangible benefits estimated were:

1. Manpower savings by automating manual functions; reduce temporary staffing at $12,000 a year

2. Improve accuracy of the vacation accrual at $50,000 a year

The preliminary intangible benefits estimated were:

1. Greater reporting detail on driver pay activities

2. More accurate labor reporting

The preliminary cost estimates were:

- $37,000 one-time development cost (185 development days)
- $400 one-time data management support effort (2 support days)
- $2,904 ongoing support activity
- $17 incremental storage requirements

Using traditional cost-benefit techniques and the forms as in previous analyses, we calculate a simple ROI of 158 percent on the economic impact worksheet. This was as a result of development costs of $37,400 and ongoing expenses of $2,921.

11–2–1 Development Costs Worksheet

The development costs worksheet (Figure 11.1) reflects a $37,000 one-time development cost and a $400 one-time data management support effort, for a total of $37,400.

A. Development Effort		
1. Incremental systems and programming (185 Estimated days times $200/day)		37,000
2. Incremental staff support (2 days data administration at $200/day)		400
B. New Hardware		
1. Terminals, printers, communications		0
2. Other _____		0
C. New (Purchased) Software, if any		
1. Packaged applications software		0
2. Other _____		0
D. User training		0
E. Other _____		0
TOTAL		37,400

FIGURE 11.1   Development costs worksheet BEAM Parcels driver pay system.

11–2–2 Ongoing Expenses Worksheet

The ongoing expenses worksheet (Figure 11.2) reflects a total of $2,921 continuing support expenses. The 185 development days reflect a less complex project than the previous rating, coding, and billing application for BEAM Parcels. Because it is simpler and smaller, a lower ratio of maintenance to development is applied (.07849 versus the previous ratio of .12272). This results in 14.52 annual maintenance days. Multiplying the annual maintenance days by the daily rate of $200 provides $2,904 maintenance costs. One megabyte of data storage is required at an estimated $16.80 per megabyte, or $17 per year.

A. Development costs (application software maintenance)		$ 2,904
(e.g.,		
Development effort days	185	
Ratio of maintenance to development	.07849	
Resulting annual maintenance days	14.52	
Daily maintenance rate	$200	
TOTAL application software maintenance	2904	
B. Incremental data storage required: 1 MB × 16.80		17
(e.g., estimated megabytes, $16.80)		
C. Incremental communications (lines, messages, etc.)		0
D. New software leases or hardware leases		0
E. Supplies		0
F. Other		0
TOTAL Ongoing expenses		$ 2,921

FIGURE 11.2   Ongoing expenses worksheet for the BEAM Parcels driver pay system.

11–2–3 Economic Impact Worksheet

The economic impact worksheet (Figure 11.3) does not look encouraging for application funding. Net investment required of $37,400 is from the development cost worksheet. The $50,000 yearly savings due to improved vacation reporting and the $12,000 yearly savings due to reduced temporary staffing comprise the $62,000 reduction in operating cost. Ongoing expense of $2,921 is calculated in the ongoing expenses worksheet. Simple ROI for this application is the sum of the net cash flows for five years ($295,395) divided by 5 years ($59,079) divided by the net investment required ($37,400), or 158 percent.

This project analysis is similar to the initial sizing of the automated billing project for BEAM Parcels. Both show a "good" return on investment for the enterprise. Is the return high enough? Does it warrant the enterprise investment? Have any potential benefits been overlooked in the above sizing? One of the tangible benefits relates to reduced requirement for temporary labor in the payroll department. This suggests that an improved system will cause a restructuring in the management and staff activities. Getting the most out of managers, who account for the majority of white-collar labor costs, requires changing or restructuring their activities. Use of the value restructuring model seems appropriate.

A. Net Investment Required   <u>37,400</u>

B. Yearly Cash Flows: based on five 12-month periods following implementation of the proposed system. Cash flow can be negative.

	Year 1	Year 2	Year 3	Year 4	Year 5	Total
Net Economic Benefit	0	0	0	0	0	
Operating Cost Reductions	62,000	62,000	62,000	62,000	62,000	
= Pretax income	62,000	62,000	62,000	62,000	62,000	
(−) Ongoing expense	2,921	2,921	2,921	2,921	2,921	
= Net Cash Flow	59,079	59,079	59,079	59,079	59,079	−295,395

NOTE: Ongoing expense is calculated on previous worksheet

C. Simple ROI, calculated as B/# YRS/A   <u>158%</u>
($295,395/5 = 59,079/37,400 = 1.58)

D. Scoring, Economic Impact

Score	Simple Return on Investment
0	zero or less
1	1% to 299%
2	300% to 499%
3	500% to 699%
4	700% to 899%
5	over

FIGURE 11.3 Economic impact worksheet for the BEAM Parcels driver pay system.

11-3 VALUE RESTRUCTURING USING STANDARD COSTS

We will now consider three scenarios based on standard costs. *Standard costs* are those costs that internal accounting uses for transfer or chargeout. The three scenarios are:

Scenario 1. The current salary, including overhead, equals the standard chargeout rate.

Scenario 2. Current salary, including overhead, for three professional groups (each includes one member) is higher than the standard chargeout rate. This difference could be due to seniority, time in grade, and/or rebalancing the efforts and direction of the LOB or enterprise.

Scenario 3. Current salary, including overhead, for three professional groups (each including one member) is lower than the standard chargeout rate, which could be due to early retirement of senior, higher paid professionals.

These three scenarios represent situations confronted by enterprise managers when they restructure their positions or efforts. The standard costs and salary spreads for the three scenarios are shown in Figure 11.4. These costs for BEAM Parcels include overhead costs but do not include a built-in profit.

We can develop the base figures for standard costs (or chargeout rates). Figure 11.5 represents the productivity and structure of each position before the application of information technology.

For example, the manager is paid $80,000 a year. However, he is currently spending only 30 percent of his time performing management activities (30 percent x $80,000 = $24,000). He is devoting 16 percent of his time on senior professional activities. Because a senior professional is paid a $70,000 salary, the value of the time spent by the manager on the lower-value activity (16 percent) is at the senior professional rate of $70,000, or $11,200. As the manager spends more time on lower-value activities, his value or contribution to the enterprise drops. His activities range from junior professional work (13 percent) to administrative-technical (16 percent) to secretarial work (7 percent). Finally, he considers himself nonproductive 18 percent of the time. He is, then, contributing $53,800 of valued activities to the enterprise. The other members of the department (the senior and junior professionals, the administrative-technical and

Position	Standard Chargeout Cost of Function	Scenario (1) Current Salary w/Overhead	Scenario (2) Current Salary w/Overhead	Scenario (3) Current Salary w/Overhead
Manager	80,000	80,000	85,000	75,000
Senior Professional	70,000	70,000	75,000	65,000
Junior Professional	60,000	60,000	65,000	55,000
Administrative/Technical	50,000	50,000	50,000	50,000
Secretary	40,000	40,000	40,000	40,000

FIGURE 11.4   The three scenarios.

	Manager ($80,000)	Sr. Prof. ($70,000)	Jr. Prof. ($60,000)	A/T ($50,000)	Sec'y. ($40,000)	N/P ($0)	Total ($300,000)
Mgr.	.30/24,000	.16/11,200	.13/ 7,800	.16/ 8,000	.07/ 2,800	.18/0	100/53,800
Sr.P.	.02/ 1,600	.35/24,500	.26/15,600	.13/ 6,500	.12/ 4,800	.12/0	100/53,000
Jr.P.	.01/ 800	.10/ 7,000	.50/30,000	.13/ 6,500	.14/ 5,600	.12/0	100/49,900
A/T			.01/ 600	.58/29,000	.27/10,800	.14/0	100/40,400
Sec'y				.10/ 5,000	.76/30,400	.14/0	100/35,400
Total							232,500
Less Productive Time							67,500

FIGURE 11.5 Standard costs.

the secretary) have similar spreads of time. By increasing time spent in higher-value activities, the delta representing less productive time will decrease.

Standard costs have a built-in spread of activities, from highly productive to nonproductive, for each job position, because they reflect the work components actually being accomplished. Although each LOB or enterprise has its own procedure for developing and setting standard costs, they are generally based on averages. This average is computed in a variety of ways. The computation may be based on the average of all costs for a given period. The average of the highest and lowest costs (the mean) in the period preceding the standards is another approach.

BEAM Parcels management agreed that the activities of the payroll and billing department would be restructured or redistributed. The assumptions for restructuring are:

1. Employees affected are on salary (no overtime).

2. The application of information technology is the vehicle for restructuring the activities. The activities cannot be restructured through organizational change (for example, by management edict).

3. By spending more time at the activity paid for, the employee is more productive by definition (for example, a manager spending more time in management activities).

	Manager ($80,000)	Sr. Prof. ($70,000)	Jr. Prof. ($60,000)	A/T ($50,000)	Sec'y. ($40,000)	N/P ($0)	Total ($300,000)
Mgr.	.40/32,000	.25/17,500	.10/ 6,000	.10/ 5,000	0.5/ 2,000	.10/0	100/62,500
Sr.P.	.02/ 1,600	.40/28,000	.29/17,400	.11/ 5,500	.08/ 3,200	.10/0	100/55,700
Jr. P.	.01/ 800	.15/10,500	.55/33,000	.11/ 5,500	.10/ 4,000	.08/0	100/53,800
A/T			.01/ 600	.65/32,500	.25/10,000	.09/0	100/43,100
Sec'y				.12/ 6,000	.78/31,200	.10/0	100/37,200
Total							252,300
Less Productive Time (LPT)							47,700

FIGURE 11.6 Standard costs with information technology productivity improvements.

The manager, through using information technology *and* implementing structural changes would increase the time spent managing by 10 percent (40 percent in Figure 11.6 representing "after" minus 30 percent in Figure 11.5 representing "before"). Likewise, the manager increased his senior professional activities by 9 percent, and decreased junior professional activities by 3 percent, administrative and technical work by 6 percent, secretarial activities by 2 percent, and nonproductive activities by 8 percent.

In the following three scenarios, we will use the same two labor distributions across functions, before and after information technology. The salary rates, however, will change with each scenario.

11–4 SCENARIO 1 AND BEAM PARCELS DRIVER PAY SYSTEM

If current salaries plus overhead are equal to the standard costs of the function, the company is, in effect, doing two things. First, they are recognizing that the department members are, at times, nonproductive. Second, they are paying the department members to do a spread of activities. Implicit in this scenario is the LOB or enterprise decision of no direct profit objective for the function's personnel. Additionally, higher value work is always available to do.

Because the salaries are equal to the standard costs, the financial assessment of the productivity improvements can be taken directly from Figures 11.5 and 11.6.

Post IT = $252,300	—OR—	Post ($252,300 − 300,000 = −47,700)
Pre IT = 232,500		Pre ($232,500 − 300,000 = −67,500)
Total gain $ 19,800		

We can now balance the investment costs against the additional quantification of benefits—the productivity gain. This gain is in addition to the benefits quantified through traditional cost-benefit analysis, value linking, and value acceleration.

To generate this economic worksheet (Figure 11.7), we assume one department, with productivity increases across the board. In this case, the manager is represented by a standard cost to the LOB or enterprise of $80,000. Reduction in operating cost is obtained by:

$62,000	Original reduction in operating cost shown in Figure 11.3
$19,800	Original LPT of $67,500 (Figure 11.5) minus new LPT of $47,700 = $19,800.
$81,800	Total reduction in operating cost

If the decision is made to invest in the productivity improvements, Figure 11.6 is input for developing the new standard cost for BEAM Payroll and Billing department functions.

A. Net Investment Required   37,400

B. Yearly Cash Flows: based on five 12-month periods following implementation of the proposed system. Cash flow can be negative.

	Year 1	Year 2	Year 3	Year 4	Year 5	Total
Net Economic Benefit	0	0	0	0	0	
Operating Cost Reduction	81,800	81,800	81,800	81,800	81,800	
= Pretax income	81,800	81,800	81,800	81,800	81,800	
(−) Ongoing expense	2,921	2,921	2,921	2,921	2,921	
= Net cash flow	78,879	78,879	78,879	78,879	78,879	394,395

NOTE: Ongoing expense is calculated on worksheet

C. SImple ROI, calculated as B/# YRS/A   211%
   (394,395/5 = 78,879/37,400 = 2.11)

D. Scoring, Economic Impact

Score	Simple Return on Investment
0	zero or less
*1	1% to 299%
2	300% to 499%
3	500% to 699%
4	700% to 899%
5	over

FIGURE 11.7 Economic impact worksheet for the BEAM Parcels driver pay system.

11–5 SCENARIO 2

This scenario has a salary structure higher than the standard costs for the function. This could be due to an aging professional force with seniority, rebalancing the work force within the LOB or enterprise, or outside factors such as scarcity of candidates.

Figure 11.8 shows $5800 as the cost of less productive time from standards for the department. Applying the same productivity rebalancing as Scenario 1, we achieve the results shown in Figure 11.9.

	Manager ($85,000)	Sr. Prof. ($75,000)	Jr. Prof. ($65,000)	A/T ($50,000)	Sec'y. ($40,000)	N/P ($0)	Total ($315,000)
Mgr.	.30/25,500	.16/12,000	.13/ 8,450	.16/ 8,000	.07/ 2,800	.18/0	100/56,750
Sr.P.	.02/ 1,700	.35/26,250	.26/16,900	.13/ 6,500	.12/ 4,800	.12/0	100/56,150
Jr.P.	.01/ 850	.10/ 7,500	.50/32,500	.13/ 6,500	.14/ 5,600	.12/0	100/52,950
A/T			.01/ 650	.58/29,000	.27/10,800	.14/0	100/40,450
Sec'y.				.10/ 5,000	.76/30,400	.14/0	100/35,400
Total							241,700
Less Productive Time (LPT)							73,300
Less Productive Costs							5,800

FIGURE 11.8 Activity spread prior to information technology.

	Manager ($85,000)	Sr. Prof. ($75,000)	Jr. Prof. ($65,000)	A/T ($50,000)	Sec'y. ($40,000)	N/P ($0)	Total ($315,000)
Mgr.	.40/34,000	.25/18,750	.10/ 6,500	.10/ 5,000	.05/ 2,000	.10/0	100/66,250
Sr.P.	02/ 1,700	.40/30,000	.29/18,850	.11/ 5,500	.08/ 3,200	.10/0	100/59,250
Jr.P.	.01/ 850	.15/11,250	.55/35,750	.11/ 5,500	.10/ 4,000	.08/0	100/57,350
A/T			.01/ 650	.65/32,500	.25/10,000	.09/0	100/43,150
Sec'y.				.12/ 6,000	.78/31,200	.10/0	100/37,200
Total							263,200
Less Productive Time (LPT)							51,800

FIGURE 11.9 Activity spread after information technology productivity improvements.

The financial assessment of the productivity improvements are shown in Figures 11.8 and 11.9.

```
Post IT = $263,200    —OR—   Post ($263,200 − 315,000 = −51,800)
Pre  IT =  241,700            Pre  ($241,900 = 315,000 = −73,300)
Total gain $21,500, given no change in salary structure.
```

Referring to Figure 11.5, the standard cost (total salary plus overhead) is $300,000. Costs after information technology from Figure 11.9 are $315,000 salary minus $21,500 productivity gains, or $293,500. Here the $21,500 gain through productivity improvements and reducing nonproductive time effectively offsets the higher salary rate. Benefits quantified through traditional cost-benefit analysis techniques, and value restructuring can combine to provide the financial justification. This illustrates the possibility of rebalancing efforts across multiple functions within a department.

11–6 SCENARIO 3

In this scenario, the current salary (with overhead) for the three professional groups is lower than standard or chargeout costs because of early retirement of senior (higher paid) personnel, a new function staffed by junior personnel, or a time lag before salaries reach an equilibrium to the contribution to bottom-line performance.

Applying the same productivity rebalancing percentages as Scenarios 1 and 2, BEAM has the potential to achieve the productivity improvements shown in Figure 11.11 from the starting point of Figure 11.10.

The financial assessment of the productivity improvements are obtained from Figures 11.10 and 11.11.

```
Post IT = $241,400    —OR—   Post ($241,400 − 285,000 = −43,600)
Pre  IT =  223,300            Pre  ($223,300 − 285,000 = −61,700)
Gain      $ 18,100, if no change in salary structure.
```

	Manager ($75,000)	Sr. Prof. ($65,000)	Jr. Prof. ($55,000)	A/T ($50,000)	Sec'y. ($40,000)	N/P ($0)	Total ($285,000)
Mgr.	.30/22,500	.16/10,400	.13/ 7,150	.16/ 8,000	.07/ 2,800	.18/0	100/50,850
Sr.P.	.02/ 1,500	.35/22,275	.26/14,300	.13/ 6,500	.12/ 4,800	.12/0	100/49,850
Jr.P.	.01/ 750	.10/ 6,500	.50/27,500	.13/ 6,500	.14/ 5,600	.12/0	100/46,850
A/T			.01/ 550	.58/29,000	.27/10,800	.14/0	100/40,350
Sec'y.				.10/ 5,000	.76/30,400	.14/0	100/35,400
Total							223,300
Less Productive Time							61,700

FIGURE 11.10   Activity spread prior to information technology.

	Manager ($75,000)	Sr. Prof. ($65,000)	Jr. Prof. ($55,000)	A/T ($50,000)	Sec'y. ($40,000)	N/P ($0)	Total ($285,000)
Mgr.	.40/30,000	.25/16,250	.10/ 5,500	.10/ 5,000	.05/ 2,000	.10/0	100/58,750
Sr.P.	.02/ 1,500	.40/26,000	.29/15,950	.11/ 5,500	.08/ 3,200	.10/0	100/52,150
Jr.P.	.01/ 750	.15/ 9,750	.55/30,250	.11/ 5,500	.10/ 4,000	.08/0	100/50,250
A/T			.01/ 550	.65/32,500	.25/10,000	.09/0	100/43,050
Sec'y.				.12/ 6,000	.78/31,200	.10/0	100/37,200
Total							241,400
Nonproductive time							43,600

FIGURE 11.11   Activity spread after information technology productivity improvements.

Again, the standard costs for the department total are $300,000. Because the costs were running under the standard costs (by $15,000), it would be less likely for the function to trigger an increased use of information technology and its associated costs. Exceptions would occur when the increased productivity of the department (output) would have a direct and positive impact on another department that is revenue producing. This requires value linking or value acceleration. The department may itself be revenue producing. A final exception would be the attempt to balance projected increases in wages with increased productivity, to balance at the same level as standard costs.

The three scenarios show how value restructuring can contribute to the financial justification. This is done by providing a way to size increases in productivity triggered by information technology. These values can be a justification for information technology infusion with effects on other departments or functions.

The difficulty in using value restructuring is not calculation, but verification and measurement. Value restructuring is not a vehicle to track changes over time, because the base is changing with standard costs. What it can do is to give some quantification to the magnitude of the possibilities for restructuring and for assessing restructuring alternatives.

Chap. 11:   Value Restructuring

11-7 A FINAL NOTE ON THE DRIVER PAY SYSTEM PROPOSAL FOR BEAM PARCELS

What happened to the BEAM payroll proposal? Using traditional cost-benefit analysis, we achieved a simple ROI of 158 percent. By using value restructuring, we achieved ROI of 211 percent. This is well below the initial 400 percent hurdle rate for BEAM Parcels information systems investments.

What of employee morale? How many employees are affected? Does this problem reflect poorly on the enterprise image? Is the payroll application any part of the information systems strategy? Will the delay in resolving this problem affect other projects or departments?

If the payroll proposal is funded, it will be because of factors other than purely financial ones. Those less tangible factors in the preceding paragraph will require assessment (and consensus) by the business and technology domains.

QUESTIONS

1. Define value restructuring.

2. Consider how value restructuring could occur at Old Ivy University. Give an example.

3. Speculate on a corporation such as IBM. Where do you believe the largest benefit can be derived though value restructuring?

4. Would an organization benefit more by supplying computing power to its high-paid professionals or to its lower-paid support?

12

Innovation

Innovation creates new functions within the business domain. It changes the way the enterprise conducts its business. Innovative information technology applications provide the vehicle to change business strategy, LOB products and services, and business domain organization. As a result, innovation valuation techniques focus on organizational rather than technological costs and risks.

12–1 INNOVATION AND INVESTMENT

Innovation valuation techniques are applied when the financial issues move from those of measurement to those of alternative assessment (Parker and Benson, 1986). They are useful for new, unprecedented applications of information technology. They consider the value of gaining or sustaining competitive edge, the risk and cost of being first, and the risk and cost of failure or success. Innovation can occur in any function of the enterprise value chain.

Steven Jobs had an idea that, when developed, created a new product (a computer) and a new business. A later idea within the business created another new computer product. Both ideas created new products, but the former caused the creation of a new enterprise and the latter caused renewal of the existing enterprise. Both ideas had inherent values and risks that needed assessment.

12–2 THE ENTERPRISE AND CHANGE

The enterprise must constantly change to survive. These changes are both internal and external. Internal change can be characterized as fine-tuning the current enterprise to operate as efficiently and effectively as possible. External change can be characterized as those actions that the enterprise takes in reacting to external forces. Examples are social and economic trends, legal and governmental actions and regulations, competitor actions, and supplier actions (Benson and Parker, 1985). From the perspective of information systems, internal change addresses issues of alignment with the current line of business or enterprise functions. External change addresses the issues of impacting the LOB or enterprise strategy to affect more radical organizational modifications. An example is creating new services or new products that provide competitive advantage for the LOB or enterprise. Alignment applications, such as aligning the MIS support to the existing organization, are associated with low risk—and the risk is most likely to be identified. Success depends on the ability of personnel to accept and learn the new technology. These changes are managed in an incremental way. The basis of planning and managing change is prior experience.

Impact applications, on the other hand, are associated with high risk. The risk is the unidentified pivotal risk that goes unmanaged. Impact applications create situations where, for example, the LOB or enterprise is entering into a new market or is offering or expecting new services or products from their customers or suppliers.

There is a wealth of literature on new ventures, new venture management, and the entrepreneur. (See additional readings for this chapter.) What can be inferred from the literature is that, to assure success, the management of a new venture project must be significantly different from the management of an ongoing, institutionalized project. Invention can't be scheduled with a due date. Organizations discuss breakthroughs rather than measuring lines of code for an indication of progress. From the perspective of Information Economics, the differentiations were made early in the process by Parker and Benson (1986). The differences between impact and alignment planning and management include different management styles, structures, processes, and technologies (Figure 12.1).

Nolan and Kelvie (1986) characterize the two types of management as entrepreneurial management and utility management. They view the objectives, focus, techniques, organization, and theme of each as being different. Organizations—specifically the business organization—must prepare and be ready to integrate innovation into their normal activities. Customers and suppliers (if the project involves interorganizational systems) must prepare and be ready to accept the innovation into their organizations. The enterprise must view the project as a key to successful business performance. The project champion must exist in the LOB affected. These are factors for consideration in the economic justification in addition to those previously discussed.

How can an organization begin to assess the size and costs of these risks? Arnold (1986) suggests staying power analysis. He believes that the assessment cannot be too conservative, given that 80 percent of new projects (products) fail to achieve their market-share targets. Costello (1985) discusses costs, uncertainty, and integration and decision-making for new venture analysis. These concepts are readily transferable to

ALIGNMENT	IMPACT
Support generic strategy	Support generic strategy OR support overt change of generic strategy
Risks measured against sustaining competitive position	Risks measured against gaining competitive advantage
Focus on proven practices	Risk focuses primarily on technology domain; secondarily on business domain

* Focus on different kinds of management
* Processes are different
* Technology may be different
* Tools, techniques, and methodologies are different

FIGURE 12.1 Planning and management differences: alignment versus impact applications.

the evaluation of information technology applications for competitive advantage. The Rich and Gumpert Evaluation System (1985) evaluates the risk in terms of product or service maturity and management and organization maturity. Their approach can be used as a guideline for evaluating the risk in information technology and MIS projects for competitive advantage.

We must associate certain economic costs with the investment in innovative applications of information technology. Innovation valuation includes revenue assessments, cost estimates, market factors, and cost of change in the business and technology domains. *Sensitivity analysis* is a tool for evaluating specific factors to be closely monitored. Examples are growth, return on investment, counterthreats (product, technology, market), revenue protection, and leverage in the capital market. (We recommend sensitivity analysis for evaluating large investments. We do not use it in support of the typical information systems project nomination call, unless it is already a part of the particular enterprise procedure.)

Addressing these issues when estimating the economic impact of innovative projects is necessary. Innovation valuation provides a method to compare unlike projects in a common investment decision process. It does this through the quantification, wherever possible, of the organizational costs and benefits of innovation. From a strategic viewpoint, the investment in information architectures is a part of the innovation process in supporting the LOB or enterprise during restructuring and implementing new products and product lines. We will again use a potential project from BEAM Parcels to show the process of innovation valuation.

12–3 CASE: PHARMACY SHIPMENT AUTOMATION FOR BEAM PARCELS

BEAM Parcels is considering the expansion of their computer system to accept electronically prefiled manifest data from pharmaceutical manufacturers of controlled substances. Screening and processing of manufacturer and courier entries by the appropriate governmental agency's systems will occur via electronic data interchange (EDI). The results are then transmitted back to all parties, thus allowing more expeditious transfer of controlled substances. Consignments granted prerelease become available to BEAM Parcels when the flight arrives (if shipped by air) or directly from the manufacturer (if locally available).

BEAM Parcels will benefit from this system in the following ways:

- Increase productivity
- Improve overall transfers and deliveries
- Reduce fines
- Reduce service failures
- Reduce costs for airport temporary storage and handling

The preliminary tangible benefits include $700,000 per year increased revenue. The interface will allow BEAM Parcels to provide and market an enhanced product by reducing transfer times. This advantage will continue until competition develops the necessary systems to achieve parity (an estimated ten-to-twelve-month competitive advantage).

The preliminary cost estimates include:

- $106,000 development and installation
- $ 10,838 yearly maintenance
- $ 5,000 driver and systems interface training

This is an innovative use (for the local parcel delivery market) of information technology. It will involve investment in current resources and organizational change. Accordingly, an assessment of organizational risk is necessary.

12–3–1 Development Costs Worksheet

Our first worksheet is, as in previous examples, an assessment of development costs (Figure 12.2). The development costs for innovation valuation, unlike the previous examples, require an assessment of costs related to organizational change (section D). The information systems (technology domain) organization will incur certain types of organizational costs associated with the effort to introduce and institutionalize change. We estimate training of current personnel, cost of adding new personnel, and the costs associated with the learning curves of each group. Also included is the cost of lost effectiveness because of organizational restructuring of the information systems department. Technology domain benefits come about through productivity gains from restructuring or through decreased operating expenses. Although no additional details were available, BEAM Parcels management estimated the breakdown of effort, based on past experience. The estimate includes 420 days of development effort, 60 days of data administration support, and $10,000 of terminal expense, totalling $106,000.

	YR 1	YR 2	YR 3	YR 4	YR 5
A. Development Effort					
1. Incremental systems and programming (e.g., estimated days times $200/day) (420 days × $200 per day = $84K)	84K				
2. Incremental staff support (e.g., data administration at $200/day) (60 days × $200 per day = $12K)	12K				
B. New Hardware 1. Terminals, printers, communications	10K				
2. Other					
C. New (Purchased) Software, if any 1. Packaged applications software					
2. Other					
D. Costs Associated with Innovation 1. Training					
2. Cost of adding new personnel					
3. Cost of reorganization and organization dysfunction					
4. Cost due to learning curve on A.1 and A.2 above					
E. Other					
F. Total	106K				

FIGURE 12.2 Development costs worksheet for innovation valuation for the BEAM Parcels pharmacy shipment automation.

12–3–2 Business Organization Costs Worksheet

The second worksheet for innovation valuation is new (Figure 12.3). It assesses the business domain organizational costs associated with the proposed project. As in the technology domain, the business domain benefits are reflected through productivity gains via value restructuring or through decreased operating expenses. This worksheet addresses four categories of costs: organizational effort, new facilities, temporary staffing, and other innovation-associated costs. Because the form encompasses a five-year spread, recurring and one-time costs are included in a single form.

A. The category of costs associated with innovation includes learning curves, training new staff, costs of business domain reorganization, and increased personnel

	YR 1	YR 2	YR 3	YR 4	YR 5
A. Costs associated with innovation					
1. Training new staff					
2. Cost of adding new personnel					
3. Cost of reorganizing, organizational dysfunction					
4. Cost due to learning curve on A.1 and A.2 above					
B. Organizational effort 1. Incremental direct effort (new personnel to staff functions)					
2. Incremental effort (current staff retraining)	5K				
3. Incremental staff support					
C. New facilities 1. Office space					
2. Office equipment					
D. Temporary Staffing 1. Consultants					
2. Contract labor					
E. Other (enterprise specific)					
F. Total	5K				

FIGURE 12.3 Business organization costs worksheet for the BEAM Parcels pharmacy shipment automation.

costs. This category focuses on the cost to the business domain during the development of the innovative application.

B. The organizational effort category of costs includes the costs of incremental effort to support the new function, current staff retraining, and incremental staff support outside the new function (the opposite of value chaining). This category focuses on the costs to the business domain of institutionalizing the innovation after development.

C. The new facilities category includes the cost of office space, office equipment, and similar requirements.

D. Temporary staffing is typically required as organizations restructure (and downsize). Greater utilization of consultants and contract labor with specialized skills will be in evidence.

	YR 1	YR 2	YR 3	YR 4	YR 5
A. Application Software Maintenance					
Development effort (days) 420					
Ratio of Maintenace to Development .1285					
Estimated annual maintenance days 54					
Daily maintenance rate $200					
Total Software Maintenance $10,800	10.8K	10.8	10.8	10.8	10.8
B. Incremental data storage required (MB) (e.g., estimated megabytes $16.80)					
C. Incremental communications (lines, messages, etc.)					
D. New software bases or hardware bases					
E. Supplies					
F. Other					
Totals	10.8K	10.8	10.8	10.8	10.8

FIGURE 12.4 Ongoing expenses worksheet for the BEAM Parcels pharmacy shipment automation.

12–3–3 Ongoing Expenses Worksheet

The third worksheet (Figure 12.4) addresses ongoing expenses. It is identical in form to the previous analyses. We provide a five year time frame for reflecting ongoing expenses. The only estimate available to apply to this worksheet is from the information systems department.

12–3–4 Economic Benefit Worksheet

The fourth and final new worksheet (Figure 12.5) addresses the net economic benefit. In this project, there is an uninhibited increasing market share for a short time, followed by a gradual market deterioration. The planners expect that other delivery services will offer the same service about a year later, when newly acquired customers will tend to go back to their original delivery service.

Because of already existing software, the information systems department estimates that, if work begins immediately, the system can become operational in six months. Marketing and sales believe that if the system is operational within six months, BEAM Parcels will have a twelve month lead time before competition reacts. At that point, competitive advantage will deteriorate at an effective net rate of 20 percent per year. Given these assumptions, developed by consensus between the marketing and sales, finance, and information systems departments, the BEAM Parcels economic benefit worksheet is developed. It illustrates an anticipated benefit of $2,209,800.

Net Economic Benefit	YR 1	YR 2	YR 3	YR 4	YR 5
	K$	K$	K$	K$	K$
Market Potential Initial	350.0	630.0	630.0	504.0	403.2
Delta potential growth	0	0	0	0	0
Market deterioration (after competitors enter market)	0	70.0	126.0	100.8	80.6
Expected governmental action (+ or −)	0	0	0	0	0
Economic benefit per year	350.0	630.0	504.4	403.2	322.6
Total economic benefits expected over 5 years:	$2,209.8 K				

FIGURE 12.5 Economic benefit worksheet for the BEAM Parcels pharmacy shipment automation.

These figures are developed with the assumption that, starting immediately, six months will be needed to make the system operational. Therefore, for the last six months of the year, benefits can be accruing to the company ($700K divided by 2 = $350K market potential for Year 1). Economic benefit for Year 1 is $350K.

For the first six months of Year 2, BEAM Parcels assumes it will maintain its competitive lead. During the second six months, BEAM Parcels expects an effective market deterioration of 20 percent per year to commence ($700K divided by 2 = $350K for second half of full benefits, plus $350K times .8 = $280K market deterioration for second half of second year = $630K benefits for Year 2). The Year 3 increased market potential is $630K, with a market deterioration of 20 percent per year or $504K. Calculations for Years 4 though 5 are identical to Year 3. The sum of Years 1 through 5 is the expected economic gain for this innovative information technology service to enterprise clients ($2209.8K).

After computing economic benefit, we develop the economic impact worksheet.

12–3–5 Economic Impact Worksheet

The economic impact scoring is based on a projected straight-line relationship to the calculated simple ROI of the periodic net cash flows of the project over a five-year period. (see Figure 12.6.) The simple ROI, based on a five-year projection, is 388 percent.

Here, yearly cash flows were projected from the inception of systems development. This was due to a short development time and a narrow window of competitive opportunity. A more general case is to base this calculation on five twelve-month periods following

A. Net Investment Required $111K

B. Yearly Cash Flows: based on five 12-month periods beginning with inception of implementation.

	Year 1	Year 2	Year 3	Year 4	Year 5	Total
Net Economic Benefit	350.0	630.0	504.0	403.2	322.6	
Operating Cost Reduction	0	0	0	0	0	
= Pretax income	350.0	630.0	504.0	403.2	322.6	
(−) Ongoing expense	10.8	10.8	10.8	10.8	10.8	
= Net cash flow	339.2	619.2	493.2	392.4	311.4	
						$2,155.4K

C. Simple ROI, calculated as B/# YRS/A   388%
($2,155,400/5 = 431,160/111,000 = .388)

D. Scoring, Economic Impact

Score	Simple Return on Investment
0	zero or less
1	1% to 299%
*2	300% to 499%
3	500% to 699%
4	700% to 899%
5	over

FIGURE 12.6   Economic impact worksheet BEAM Parcels pharmacy shipment automation.

implementation of the proposed system. In any case, the length of time chosen must be consistent with other projects of the same type competing for funding.

Using conservative estimates and calculation methods for estimating economic impact, the project appears to be a candidate for funding. It compares favorably with other opportunities for investment and provides a competitive advantage for the line of business. The 388 percent simple ROI is quite close to the 400 percent hurdle rate imposed by BEAM Parcels. (In this case, by extending the calculations to an eight-year period, a simple ROI of 310 percent is achieved, reflecting the gradually deteriorating competitive advantage.) Pharmacy shipment automation requires special attention because the competitive window of opportunity is potentially quite narrow. In the parcel delivery business, like others, a competitive opportunity one year may become a competitive necessity the next. Others competing for the same market share may decide to offer this service.

This illustrates the basic tension within the enterprise—the competition for resources. New projects are severely limited if, as has been observed, there are cost or profit pressures within the organization (McFarlan, McKinney, and Pyburn, 1986). In reality, resources are *always* constrained, but some years the constraints are more severe. At this point, particularly, potential investments must be assessed in an even-handed manner.

QUESTIONS

1. How are investments in innovation justified?

2. What characterizes a conducive environment for innovation?

3. Give an example of an alignment information system project and the most difficult costs to estimate.

4. Give an example of an impact information system project and the most difficult costs to estimate.

5. Do you think an enterprise is better off with all alignment projects or with all impact projects?

6. Using the BEAM Parcels example, assume that the competitive advantage window is only six months. Recalculate the financial impact statement.

13

Business Domain Values and Risks

Certain values and costs are not reflected in the simple ROI calculations. Some are unique to the business domain. Others are unique to the technology domain. These factors, examined in conjunction with simple ROI, provide a more balanced view of the investment alternatives within the enterprise. New concepts of value, based on **business performance**, and of costs, based on **business and technical risk**, complement the suite of new techniques used to establish simple ROI.

13-1 ROI, BUSINESS DOMAIN, AND TECHNOLOGY DOMAIN FACTORS

We will assess five factors in the business domain that are still outside the extended simple ROI calculations. These assessments, then, ameliorate the limitations of ROI, and make the overall ranking of the project a more realistic one. The factors unique to the business domain that we assess are strategic match, competitive advantage, management information, competitive response, and project or organizational risk. The first four elements are positive and add to the desirability of the project. Project or organizational risk has a negative score and detracts from the appeal of the project.

A second set of factors, described in the next chapter, address issues unique to

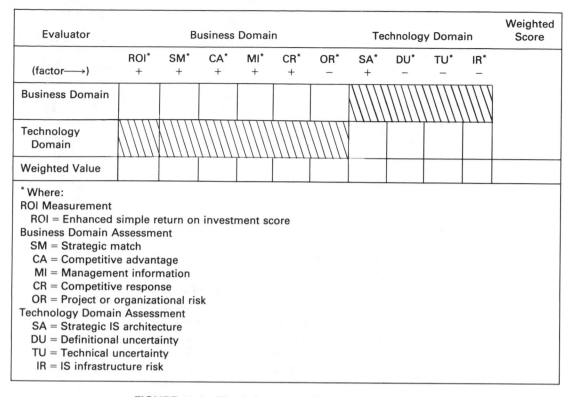

Evaluator	Business Domain						Technology Domain				Weighted Score
(factor——→)	ROI* +	SM* +	CA* +	MI* +	CR* +	OR* −	SA* +	DU* −	TU* −	IR* −	
Business Domain											
Technology Domain											
Weighted Value											

*Where:
ROI Measurement
  ROI = Enhanced simple return on investment score
Business Domain Assessment
  SM = Strategic match
  CA = Competitive advantage
  MI = Management information
  CR = Competitive response
  OR = Project or organizational risk
Technology Domain Assessment
  SA = Strategic IS architecture
  DU = Definitional uncertainty
  TU = Technical uncertainty
  IR = IS infrastructure risk

FIGURE 13.1   The Information Economics scorecard.

the technology domain. They are strategic IS architecture, definitional uncertainty, technical uncertainty, and IS infrastructure risk. Three of these elements are negative, reflecting technology risk. Only one element, strategic IS architecture, is a positive scoring value and adds to the desirability of the project.

The weight of the simple ROI calculation, combined with the assessments of the business domain and the technology domain, are then combined, using the economic scorecard (Figure 13.1). Projects can then be ordered or ranked by their scores, providing a more balanced assessment of a truer economic value to the enterprise. This provides a consistent yardstick or measurement for establishing logical investment priorities for information systems, MIS, and the enterprise. The economic scorecard will be used throughout the remainder of the text.

13–2 BUSINESS DOMAIN FACTOR #1: STRATEGIC MATCH

Strategic match focuses on the degree to which an information technology or MIS project supports or aligns with enterprise or line of business stated strategic goals. This provides an avenue for enhancing the scores of innovative or alignment applications that are in direct support of achieving *business* goals.

SCORE (0–5)

0. The project has NO direct or indirect relationship to the achievement of stated corporate (or departmental) strategic goals.

1. The project has no direct or indirect relationship to such goals, but will achieve improved operational efficiencies.

2. The project has no direct relationship to such goals, but the project is a prerequisite system (precursor) to another system that achieves a portion of a corporate strategic goal.

3. The project has no direct relationship to such goals, but the project is a prerequisite system (precursor) to another system that achieves a corporate strategic goal.

4. The project directly achieves a portion of a stated corporate strategic goal.

5. The project directly achieves a stated corporate strategic goal.

FIGURE 13.2 Strategic match worksheet.

We assume that a strategy is in place for the enterprise or LOB, and that it is clearly stated and sufficiently understood by participants in the scoring process. Participants in the scoring must work toward a consensus of understanding. The participants, for strategic match, are from the *business* domain. The scoring is not based on the interpretation of information systems management as to what is or is not in support of the business strategy. Those scoring strategic match are those who understand the nuances of the business thrust. User department management, finance management and corporate planning management (or their equivalents), although initially scoring the project from their own respective views, must negotiate with each other to develop a final value that is acceptable to each.

The scores range from zero (having no linkage to strategic goals) to five (having a direct linkage). Gradations between these two extremes can be developed for each enterprise, similar to the worksheet illustrated for strategic match (Figure 13.2). In fact, the attractiveness of the complete Information Economics structure is that it can be specifically tailored to each enterprise or LOB, and reflects the uniqueness of each.

As an example, BEAM Parcels adopted the scoring worksheet shown in Figure 13.2 for assessing strategic match by the business domain.

These represent a generic set of scoring gradations that should require little, if any, modification for an individual enterprise.

13–2–1 CASE: Driver Scheduling (Phase 2) and Strategic Match for BEAM Parcels

BEAM Parcels had produced a *statement of direction* for driver scheduling and fleet management. It noted that in previous years a significant investment of systems development resources was made in the closely related areas of driver scheduling and fleet management. Two systems were funded for development. Driver scheduling (Phase 1) maintains records on all drivers scheduled and their actual activities. The second system, fleet management (Phase 1), establishes schedules and routes and provides operating and reliability information. Future development direction includes driver scheduling (Phase 2) related to maintenance. Optimization of the driver assignments will be calculated during the month to react to schedule interruptions or the addition of routes to the planned schedule. Fleet management (Phase 2) provides communications linkages with field locations for direct update of delivery activity. Finally, fleet management (Phase 3) will provide modeling techniques to optimize delivery scheduling and to assist in operating decisions.

We focus on driver scheduling (Phase 2). This project is the next phase of the integrated driver management systems. It will expand on the scheduling capabilities and include the ability to do trip repairs in the event of revisions, disruptions, and the like. The objectives of the system are to provide online real-time access to driver schedule data and online real-time update capability. Tangible benefits amounted to $3,000,000 in labor savings over a five-year period and $144,000 cost avoidance each year due to decreased utilization of reserve driver time. Intangible benefits included more efficient use of driver crews during periods of disrupted delivery activities and continued effort to achieve a fully integrated driver management system. Preliminary cost estimates were $96,000 for development and $11,000 for ongoing expenses.

This project, as well as the other three projects listed as Phase 2 development efforts, are authorized and have resources allocated for development. However, resources are scarce at BEAM Parcels. The management steering committee has requested that all previously approved (but not yet initiated) projects go through a second approval cycle. This second approval cycle will add business domain and technology domain values and costs to ROI measurements.

The user department and the corporate planning department were requested to rate this project on the basis of how well it supported the corporate strategy, using Figure 13.2. The user department felt that the project should be given a 5, the highest rating, because a statement of direction did exist, and it was accepted by corporate management the previous year. They felt that the project matched the description of the 5 level in the strategic match worksheet. The corporate planning group scored the project a 4, because it was not included in the top tier. Having a more conservative view, they felt the project most matched the description of the 4 level in the strategic match worksheet. The two departments negotiated a value for strategic match and the other factors in the business domain. (Economic scorecards for this project and all other project examples are included at the end of the chapter.)

13–3 BUSINESS DOMAIN FACTOR #2: COMPETITIVE ADVANTAGE

The assessment for competitive advantage considers the major strategy being followed by the business. In Porter's (1985) terms, this would be an implementation of cost leadership, differentiation, or focus. The set of scoring gradations would obviously be different for each type of strategy.

The scoring mechanism to support cost leadership converges around cost avoidance, cost reduction, and identification and exploitation of any and all sources of cost advantage. Differentiation strategy scoring must be constructed around a scale that converges on those factors that would make the product **unique**. Additionally, the unique factor must be **valued** by the customer. Finally, focus strategy rests on the enterprise' target segments

SCORE (0–5)

0. The project does not create data access or interchange between this enterprise and its customers, suppliers, and collaborative unit.

1. The project does not create data access or interchange, per above, but does improve the competitive position of the enterprise by improving operating efficiencies that bear on competitive performance.

2. The project does not create data access or interchange, per above, but does improve the competitive position of the enterprise by improving operating efficiencies in a key strategic area.

3. The project provides some degree of outside access or data exchange and moderately improves the competitive position of the enterprise.

4. The project provides a moderate degree of outside access or data exchange and substantially improves the competitive position of the enterprise by providing a level of service beyond most competitors.

5. The project provides a high degree of outside access or data exchange and greatly improves the competitive position of the enterprise by providing a level of service unmatched by competitors.

FIGURE 13.3 Competitive advantage (through interorganizational communication) worksheet.

as a subset of the total market potential. Each enterprise must develop a rating gradation that will accurately reflect its chosen strategy implementation.

For example, BEAM Parcels has adopted a strategy of differentiation. Its particular emphasis is interorganizational systems (IOS) as a vehicle for sustaining their strategy and increasing their market share. They adopted the scoring worksheet shown in Figure 13.3. (Note that each enterprise will have a unique strategy, resulting in a different advantage worksheet.)

Figure 13.3 addresses data interchange between organizations as a strategy for competitive advantage. Note that, in this case, other forms of competitive advantage are subsumed in the strategic match scoring. If the industry is to a degree providing similar facilities, a value greater than 3 is unlikely. Competitive risk is increased in such cases.

For BEAM Parcels, this assessment focuses on data interchange between organizations as a strategy for competitive advantage. This particular rating provides an avenue for positively influencing the scoring of innovative or alignment applications that are in direct support of interorganizational systems, thus tying the enterprise more clearly to either its suppliers or customers and creating competitive advantage. Both data exchange *and* competitive advantage are necessary here. This element directly links to Nolan's taxonomy of eight computer-based competitive edges of leading companies (Nolan, 1985), covered in Chapter Nine.

13–3–1 BEAM Parcels and Competitive Advantage

The president of BEAM Parcels decided that the major objectives of any long-term market strategy adopted would include:

1. Increasing the value of BEAM's products in their markets to obtain higher yields and margins

2. Differentiating BEAM's products from those of the competition so that BEAM can obtain both an expanded and more stable customer base

3. Emphasizing interstate products, services, markets, and customers

4. Minimizing the labor expense in any product enhancements. BEAM is not among the low-cost producers, and must therefore constantly be sensitive to even small cost differences.

The movement of freight is both information and labor intensive for shippers, carriers, agents or consolidators, and governments. The reasons for such intensity are due to taxes (inspection and/or duties collection), goods movement control (licensing and inspection), and trade balancing (information). A normal domestic shipment most often involves the shipper, the consignee, one carrier, and state and local inspections for controlled substances and perishable goods.

Service change that will increase the value of BEAM products and differentiate them from competition will, it is believed by management, involve the exchange of more information between BEAM and shippers, consignees, state and local governments, agents or consolidators, and other middlemen. Some examples would be:

1. Faster overall times than the competition. Electronic transmission of shipment information between customer, shipper, and necessary legal authorities would speed deliveries.

2. Improved shipment tracking, reporting, and control information. This service feature would be used by customers to assure themselves of the shipment's location, condition, and progress.

3. Combined with a BEAM booking system, shippers could book and/or reserve their own space and order pickups. Customers could be electronically informed about pickup time and space confirmation or status.

BEAM Parcels had developed a **statement of direction** for customer-support linkages through interorganizational systems (IOS), the exchange of data in machine-readable form between organizations, particularly between independent companies. BEAM is currently looking at three general groups of IOS applications:

1. Customer linkages represent an array of electronic services that can be marketed to increase the value of BEAM's product in the marketplace.

2. Broker-forwarder interfaces represent an opportunity to automate this portion of the distribution cycle—primarily for BEAM's business purpose, but also as a possible supplemental source of revenue.

3. Linkages to state and local government inspection represent a particularly important opportunity, as they offer the potential to expedite the movement of freight through inspection. To the extent that BEAM can achieve these interfaces ahead of the competition, they offer the potential for significant competitive advantage.

Efforts in all three of these areas represent a very real opportunity to tie the customer closer to BEAM Parcels and to add value to the product in the marketplace.

In the future, the ability to communicate via IOS may represent not just market share, but survival.

BEAM is aware of significant investment in this area by competitors. Complete systems are being planned by both air and surface freight competitors. Marketing management recommends that BEAM fund the development of the array of services grouped together as customer-support linkages and broker-forwarder interfaces. These products are strategically important and a fundamental element of BEAM Parcels' long-term strategy.

In Chapter Twelve, we introduced a BEAM Parcels project in support of pharmacy shipment automation. In that project, the plan was to accept electronically prefiled manifest data from pharmaceutical manufacturers of controlled substances. Screening and processing of manufacturer and courier entries were to occur via IOS. The results were then to be transmitted back to all parties, thus allowing a more expeditious transfer of controlled substances. The project was innovative in nature and would provide a new service to both the shipper and governmental agency. This service is not currently available from other carriers.

Pharmacy shipment automation had a simple ROI of 388 percent. From an ROI perspective, it made the project a good contender for funding. However, the cash flows were based on market projections that showed few hedges for contingencies. What makes pharmacy shipment automation a viable project is the additional business factors discussed here. It does have a *statement of direction* in support of the project. The project is a prerequisite to another IOS. It supports the strategy of the company (it was scored a 2 for strategic match), and it provides competitive advantage. It builds on the IOS strategy of the company to differentiate the company from its competitors, and it contributes to the long-term strategy of tying customers closer to BEAM. From the perspective of competitive advantage, the system was scored a 5 by business domain management using Figure 13.3 as the scale of reference.

13–4 BUSINESS DOMAIN FACTOR #3: MANAGEMENT INFORMATION

The third factor assessed in the business domain depends on the degree to which the project provides management information on the core activities of the enterprise or line of business. Examples of management information about core activities include:

- Strategic Planning: Services, Marketing, Product Planning Capacity, Facility Forecasting
- Management Control: Budget, Sales Target, Service Performance, Capacity, Facility Utilization
- Operation Control: Customer Services, Information, Claims, Capacity, Facility Scheduling

The definition of the specific core activities for an enterprise or line of business is necessarily unique to each organization. As a consequence, although the defined

SCORE (0–5)

0. The project is unrelated to management information support of core activities (MISCA).

1. The project is unrelated to MISCA, but does provide some data on functions that bear on core activities in the enterprise.

2. The project is unrelated to MISCA, but does provide information on functions that directly support core activities.

3. The project is unrelated to MISCA, but provides essential information on functions identified as core activities. Such information is operational in character.

4. The project is essential to providing MISCA in the future.

5. The project is essential to providing MISCA in a current period.

FIGURE 13.4 Management information support worksheet.

core activities will be different, the scoring gradations applied against the core activities will not. Before beginning this process, the specific core activities of the enterprise or line of business must be determined. In Figure 13.4, the acronym *MISCA* means management information support of core activities.

This factor provides an avenue for positively influencing applications dealing with providing better management information and systems to support the business strategy.

13–4–1 Management Information Systems Core Activities (MISCA) for BEAM Parcels

BEAM Parcels, in the previous year, invested a significant portion of information systems resources in long-range planning to produce a strategic data and systems architecture. The resulting architecture is a blueprint, or plan, consisting of models of BEAM business processes and the data required to support them, along with the structure and relationship of systems that will be built in the future. The blueprint provides a top-down direction for long-term development efforts and is used with the BEAM annual project prioritization process to present an integrated project development approach, within available resources.

Fundamental to the blueprint architecture are certain philosophies and technologies relating to BEAM data: organizing, securing, and making them accessible to users. At the heart of the blueprint architecture is the development of a corporate-wide operational database that incorporates new software technologies for data organization and access. A priority for developing a major portion of that database is to provide management information on the core activities (MISCA) of the business. The MISCA project is the major blueprint implementation project for this year.

13–4–2 CASE: Customer Management Reporting System for BEAM Parcels

One of the projects under the MISCA umbrella is a customer management reporting system (CMRS). A number of regional discount and multinational customers have requested that BEAM provide them with various management reports and service audits. On a limited basis, BEAM provides reports that can be extracted from waybill detail contained in the marketing and service reliability databases. With the growth of door-to-door business and the expansion of a multiregional sales force, the demand for management reports is increasing. In order to be competitive in the marketplace, a system needs to be developed to provide reports that merge waybill service data by customer or by account. The preliminary assessment of benefits was $4,000,000 over a five-year period in retained net revenues attributable to this project. Intangible benefits include more reliable information on large accounts. Preliminary costs are $55,000 in one-time system development costs, and $4,640 ongoing system maintenance.

Again, a **statement of direction** provided an umbrella for this project. Besides showing a good simple ROI, this project has elements of competitive advantage. The business domain scored this project a 5 on MISCA.

13–5 BUSINESS DOMAIN FACTOR #4: COMPETITIVE RESPONSE

Competitive response measures the degree to which *failure* to do the system will cause competitive damage to the enterprise. This can occur because competitors already provide the service, product, or data exchange, or the industry requires the capability, or some authority mandates the system as a condition of continued business activity.

The measurement ranges on the low side if the project can be postponed for at least a year without affecting competitive position. On the high side, postponement of the project will result in competitive disadvantage to the enterprise, a loss of competitive opportunity, or curtailment of existing activities. Intermediate values are used for a more balanced potential.

The competitive response factor provides an avenue for expressing the window of opportunity for an innovative application in the overall economic assessment. It

---

SCORE (0–5)

0. The project can be postponed for at least twelve months without affecting competitive position, *or* existing systems and procedures can produce substantially the same result and will not affect competitive position.

1. The postponement of the project does not affect competitive position, and minimal labor costs are expected to be incurred to produce substantially the same result.

2. The postponement of the project does not affect competitive position; however, labor costs may escalate to produce substantially the same result.

3. If the project is postponed, the enterprise remains capable of responding to the needed change without affecting its competitive position; lacking the new system, the enterprise is not substantially hindered in its ability to respond rapidly and effectively to change in the competitive environment.

4. The postponement of the project may result in further competitive disadvantage to the enterprise; *or* in a loss of competitive opportunity; *or* existing successful activities in the enterprise may be curtailed because of the lack of the proposed system.

5. The postponement of the project will result in further competitive disadvantage to the enterprise; *or* in a loss of competitive opportunity; *or* existing successful activities in the enterprise must be curtailed because of the lack of the proposed system.

FIGURE 13.5 Competitive response worksheet.

Chap. 13: Business Domain Values and Risks

provides the element of time as an overriding imperative for implementing strategic applications.

In Chapter Twelve and earlier in this chapter, we reviewed the pharmacy shipment automation proposal. We noted in the last chapter that there is a gradually deteriorating competitive advantage. The competitive window of opportunity for this project is narrow. A competitive opportunity this year may become a competitive necessity next year if others competing for the same market decide to offer this service. Accordingly, BEAM business domain management rate this project high (5) on competitive response (risk), using the the scale provided in the Figure 13.5 worksheet.

13–6 BUSINESS DOMAIN FACTOR #5: PROJECT OR ORGANIZATIONAL RISK

Project or organizational risk focuses on the degree to which the organization is capable of carrying out the changes required by the project. The evaluation concerns the user or the business domain organization, not the technical organization. Components of the capacity of the organization include management support for change, maturity in the use of computing in the organization, and a realistic assessment of the tasks necessary to complete the project through understanding of the underlying business processes and functions.

This provides an avenue for expressing risk for projects that require product, customer, or market changes, for example, impact projects. The readiness of the business domain organization includes factors of marketing, industry maturity, and previous experience in similar lines of business. This is a negative factor, meaning that the higher measurements represent greater risk and may reduce the desirability of the project (see Figure 13.6).

The issue addressed in project or organizational risk (Figure 13.6) isn't risk per se. The purpose here is not to become risk averse. Rather, the issue is preparedness. Has the business domain prepared itself to undertake this project?

The BEAM customer management reporting system (CMRS), for example, has little project or organizational risk. Although the reports requested are new, the data to create them already exists. In fact, the reports can be created by hand, and this is being done for some larger clients. BEAM knows how to do it and why they are doing it, and they have a sponsoring (customer) organization and champion.

13–7 APPLYING THE SCORING SCHEMA

We can now begin to apply the scoring schema. The following five projects have been discussed in this and preceding chapters.

In Chapter Nine, we discussed BEAM Parcels' automated rating, coding, and billing project. BEAM was considering the automation of the rating, coding, and billing to eliminate handling hard-copy waybills and provide more accurate and timely rating and coding service. They expected to reduce the number of personnel currently necessary to do this function, and they also expected additional revenues because of more accurate

0. The business domain organization has a well-formulated plan for implementing the proposed system. Management is in place, and processes and procedures are documented. Contingency plans exist for the project, there is a project champion, and the product or competitive value added is well defined for a well-understood market.

1 through 4.

Values for 1–4 may be adopted for situations that blend elements of preparedness with elements of risk. The following checklist can be used for this purpose.

	Yes	No	Not Known
Well-formulated business domain plan	___	___	___
Business domain management in place	___	___	___
Contingency plans in place	___	___	___
Processes and procedures in place	___	___	___
Training for users planned	___	___	___
Management champion exists	___	___	___
Product is well defined	___	___	___
Well-understood market need	___	___	___

For each "no" or "not known," .5 point may be added.

5. The business domain organization has no plan for implementing the proposed system. Management is uncertain about responsibility. Processes and procedures have not been documented. No contingency plan is in place. There is no defined champion for the initiative. The product or competitive value added is not well defined. There is no well-understood market.

FIGURE 13.6 Project or organizational risk worksheet.

and timely billings. We saw that after applying additional information economics measurements, the simple ROI of this project increased from 58 percent to 382 percent (with the productivity package), and the economic impact score changed from 1 to 2.5. Because substantial labor savings would be realized in addition to increased billing accuracy and increased revenue, the project was rated a 4 for strategic match. Although the accounting department, the sponsoring organization, rated the competitive advantage as a 5, corporate planning saw no competitive impact whatsoever. These two departments compromised, and competitive advantage was rated a 3. The project was a precursor to other MISCA support planned for the future, and the project was rated a 4 in this category. It was perceived as a high competitive response (5) by all in the business domain due to the number and size of incorrect billings. No organizational risk was identified. These rankings are illustrated by Figure 13.7.

In Chapter Eleven, BEAM considered upgrading the driver payroll system. Simple ROI ranged from 158 percent to 211 percent, depending on the values assigned through value restructuring. This project was under the umbrella of a statement of direction for driver scheduling and fleet management. Management felt it was imperative to have both their billing and their payroll systems as accurate as possible, and scored strategic match as a 4. No link to competitive advantage could be seen. Because accounting was a core activity, the project was rated a 2 on management information support. No relationship exists for competitive response or project or organizational risk. Figure 13.8 contains the scoring of this project.

Evaluator	Business Domain					
(factor———→)	ROI* +	SM* +	CA* +	MI* +	CR* +	OR* −
Business Domain	2.5	4	3	4	5	0

* Where:
ROI Measurement
  ROI = Enhanced simple return on investment score
Business Domain Assessment
  SM = Strategic match
  CA = Competitive advantage
  MI = Management information support of core activities
  CR = Competitive response
  OR = Project or organizational risk

FIGURE 13.7 1# BEAM Parcels automated rating, coding, and billing.

Earlier in this chapter we discussed BEAM driver scheduling (Phase 2). Illustrated in Figure 13.9, ROI was scored a 4.5 by the finance department, and strategic match was a 5 as negotiated between corporate planning and the user department. Other business domain ratings were negotiated between the project sponsor, finance, and corporate planning.

In Chapter Twelve and again in this chapter, we examined BEAM pharmacy shipment automation, ranking it for strategic match and competitive advantage. Note that this is the first BEAM project recognized to have organizational risk (Figure 13.10). The BEAM organization has had no experience with this type of project. It will be the first application linking their customer or shippers and governmental agencies.

Evaluator	Business Domain					
(factor———→)	ROI* +	SM* +	CA* +	MI* +	CR* +	OR* −
Business Domain	1.5	4	0	2	0	0

* Where:
ROI Measurement
  ROI = Enhanced simple return on investment score
Business Domain Assessment
  SM = Strategic match
  CA = Competitive advantage
  MI = Management information support of core activities
  CR = Competitive response
  OR = Project or organizational risk

FIGURE 13.8 2# BEAM Parcels driver pay system.

Evaluator	Business Domain					
(factor———→)	ROI* +	SM* +	CA* +	MI* +	CR* +	OR* −
Business Domain	4.5	5	2	3	4	0

* Where:
ROI Measurement
  ROI = Enhanced simple return on investment score
Business Domain Assessment
  SM = Strategic match
  CA = Competitive advantage
  MI = Management information support of core activities
  CR = Competitive response
  OR = Project or organizational risk

FIGURE 13.9 3# BEAM Parcels driver scheduling (Phase 2).

Finally, we introduced the BEAM customer management reporting system (CMRS), illustrated in Figure 13.11. This was a project deemed of utmost urgency by all in the business domain. There was no business organizational risk.

We've examined five projects for BEAM Parcels thus far. Each has a unique set of values that contributes to the overall success of BEAM. If we can't fund all of them, how should the investment priorities be set? We've broadened the return on investment calculations. We've introduced business domain factors that should have some influence in the decision-making process. We see that although two of the five projects have high ranking ROI (driver scheduling and customer management reporting system), the customer management reporting system is deemed the highest priority by the business domain. Thus, a project ranking is beginning to emerge.

Evaluator	Business Domain					
(factor———→)	ROI* +	SM* +	CA* +	MI* +	CR* +	OR* +
Business Domain	2.5	2	5	3	5	3

* Where:
ROI Measurement
  ROI = Enhanced simple return on investment score
Business Domain Assessment
  SM = Strategic match
  CA = Competitive advantage
  MI = Management information support of core activities
  CR = Competitive response
  OR = Project or organizational risk

FIGURE 13.10 4# BEAM Parcels pharmacy shipment automation.

Evaluator	Business Domain					
(factor⟶)	ROI* +	SM* +	CA* +	MI* +	CR* +	OR* −
Business Domain	5	5	5	5	5	0

* Where:
ROI Measurement
  ROI = Enhanced simple return on investment score
Business Domain Assessment
  SM = Strategic match
  CA = Competitive advantage
  MI = Management information support of core activities
  CR = Competitive response
  OR = Project or organizational risk

FIGURE 13.11   5# BEAM Parcels customer management reporting system.

QUESTIONS

1. Develop simple ROI for BEAM Parcels driver scheduling project.

2. Develop simple ROI for BEAM Parcels customer management reporting system.

3. Name the five business domain factors other than ROI.

4. Nolan (1985) suggests a taxonomy of eight computer-based competitive edges of leading companies. They include providing client- or supplier-direct electronic communication, global reach, investing in the company's professionals, reorganizing based on information flows, leveraging managers, computer-based education, creating new products and services, and enhancing market responsiveness. Each focuses on improving the performance of the line of business through improved productivity and market expansion.

5. Take each and define to which of the six classes of value each applies.

6. Take "creating new products and services" and create a new scoring set of descriptions for the **competitive advantage** scoring matrix. The text example is for interorganizational communication.

14

Technology Domain Values and Risks

Many important values and risks are not reflected in financial quantifications such as simple ROI and net present value. Some of these values and risks are unique to the technology domain: strategic IS architecture, definitional uncertainty, technical uncertainty, and IS infrastructure risk. These factors provide a technology strategy context within which information technology investment alternatives can be viewed.

14–1 TECHNOLOGY DOMAIN FACTOR #1: STRATEGIC IS ARCHITECTURE

Until now, implementation projects have been treated and evaluated independently. However, the technology domain, by its very nature, may impose an ordering and urgency for projects that go beyond the business domain economic impact. Database systems, relational databases, and distributed systems may have an inherent sequence or relationship provided by the technology environment itself.

Strategic IS architecture evaluates the degree to which the project is aligned with the overall information systems strategies (Figure 14.1). This alignment is reflected in the information systems plan (blueprint). The blueprint results in systems development priorities needed to accomplish the plan. Projects that are an integral part of the plan

SCORE: (0–5)

0. The proposed project is unrelated to the blueprint.

1. The proposed project is a part of the blueprint, but its priorities are not defined.

2. The proposed project is a part of the blueprint, and has a low $ payoff; it is not a prerequisite to other blueprint projects, nor is it closely linked to other prerequisite projects.

3. The proposed project is an integral part of the blueprint and has medium $ payoff; it is not a prerequisite to other blueprint projects, but is loosely linked to other prerequisite projects.

4. The proposed project is an integral part of the blueprint and has a high $ payoff; it is not a prerequisite to other blueprint projects, but is closely linked to other prerequisite projects.

5. The proposed project is an integral part of the blueprint and is one that is to be implemented first; it is a prerequisite project to other blueprint projects.

FIGURE 14.1 Strategic IS architecture worksheet.

will be assigned a higher value on this evaluation than projects that are not, thus assuring that the viability of MIS strategy be considered at every application review. The blueprint defines the required sequence of projects necessary to implement the plan.

14–1–1 BEAM Parcels and the Blueprint Project

BEAM Parcels decided that emphasis for the current year would be given to planning for its long-term data and systems environment and determining the actions that must be taken to reach that environment. This involves determining the overall structure for applications and data—a grand design that must decide what the major data collections will be, how they should be related, what application system will draw on these collections, and how these systems should be related. The key effort that was undertaken was the blueprint project, producing the following:

1. An **information systems plan** that provides an evaluation of the current applications and technology at BEAM Parcels. It sets out an achievable target environment for databases, information systems, and technology.

2. A **blueprint for future applications development** that identifies future applications that should be implemented to realize the greatest benefit to BEAM.

3. A **preliminary requirements study for the waybill project.** The waybill project is a high-priority management information system that has been identified by senior management as needed for effective assessment of the impact of handling a given shipment from a customer under different operating scenarios. This system is seen to require information that is collected by several operational systems and to provide a decision support tool to control and project yield from a given delivery or route more effectively.

Funding for the design of the waybill project is seen as under the umbrella of the blueprint project. Preliminary system and data models for the waybill project will be prepared, and the sources, timeliness, and accuracy of currently collected information required for a system of this nature will be identified. The results of this analysis will point out potential problems with the current situation that need resolution to support the development of the waybill system.

As soon as the basic elements of the architecture are in place, the waybill project will be spun off. A project plan for the remainder of the waybill project will be prepared and submitted to management for go/no-go approval. From this point on, the waybill project becomes a separate project from the development of the overall blueprint.

4. Finally, an interface with a specially set up technology task force occurs. After the basic information systems architecture models are completed and validated by the user representatives, an interface with the BEAM technology task force will occur, using the architecture as the basis for identifying the business activities where new technology can be employed. Working with the technology task force, the blueprint will identify opportunities to apply technology in the work place.

The BEAM technology task force prepared for this interface by making an initial survey of technology that could be used by BEAM and establishing a preliminary strategy statement on the use of technology by the corporation. This strategy statement evolved into an information processing technology plan.

The charter of the information processing technology plan at BEAM was to:

1. Identify and plan opportunities to improve profitability of the parcel delivery service
2. Identify major data collections
3. Identify the systems that acquire and use the data
4. Identify where systems should be hosted
5. Identify types and location of computing and communications technology to be employed
6. Assess the current situation relative to data and systems blueprint
7. Refine the information systems organization for service delivery
8. Develop a plan to move from the current to the target environment
9. Formulate an approach for the annual planning process and,
10. Train BEAM information systems staff and key users

In summary, the information processing technology plan would first yield a long-term development plan, with projects defined and placed in sequence. Second, the preliminary study for the waybill project and a project plan for the continued development of this system will be completed. Finally, an overall architecture for BEAM's data, information processing systems, and technology will be defined and adopted.

The blueprint project required a significant commitment from BEAM Parcels— external contractors, internal information systems staff, key user support, and the involvement of top management through the steering committee.

14–1–2 CASE: Bar Code Project for BEAM Parcels

Bar codes represent one form of automatic identification and are an effective means to enter information or data into a computer for processing. Also, bar code scanners can be used to activate other processes.

A bar code is a machine-readable, self contained message encoded in the width patterns of bars and spaces. Bar codes are read by sweeping a spot of light across the printed bar code symbol and decoding the reflected light. The bar code symbol consists of an optional flag character identifying the type of information to be scanned, the information itself, and a sophisticated check digit to ensure accurate reading.

Following initial data capture, speed and accuracy of data entry are greatly increased with a bar code system. Also, the built-in error check improves reliability.

The principle application is item tracking. Standards for bar code technology have been adopted by the air freight, grocery, automotive, health care, metals, graphics, paper, recording, periodicals, machinery, and electronics industries. They have also been adopted for use by organizations such as the U.S. Government, the Department of Defense, and NATO.

At BEAM Parcels, a study team was formed to look at the feasibility of a bar code project. They were to do a feasibility analysis for implementation of an enhanced parcel-tracking and control system that would utilize bar code technology. Based on this study, they recommended that BEAM's current systems be enhanced through the addition of a bar code data capture and communications system.

Bar code technology has been identified as having the most potential for improving service reliability and productivity at BEAM. This is a proven technology that has been used in other areas of the warehousing and delivery industry to automate various data gathering functions. BEAM has the opportunity to improve service reliability and reduce operating costs at minimum risk with this technology.

The study identified a potential three-phase implementation schedule and recommended implementing only the first phase at that time. Each phase depends on the successful implementation of the preceding phase to achieve maximum benefits. Specifically, some of the operational benefits to be realized are: reduction of the information flow time lag; potential reduction of shipment processing time, particularly during critical periods; reduction of manual data collection redundancies and associated errors; increased productivity of operations personnel; improved shipment movement control through increased information reliability; and standardization of operating procedures.

The major change in BEAM Parcels' operational functions because of bar code implementation will be that the personnel who are responsible for physical package movement will also be responsible for recording that movement in the system.

The system the bar code study team proposed called for the use of scanning equipment to capture data about the movement of parcels at the following points:

Receipt of Parcels. The bar code will be used to capture the waybill number and the number of pieces received at the dock for door-to-door shipments by scanning preprinted lot labels with a bar-coded waybill number and piece identifier. For warehouse-to-warehouse shipments, it will be used only to capture the waybill number. As a part of the receipt process, lot labels with bar codes and routing information will be generated by a demand printer.

Buildup. An online scanner will be used to record the loading of pieces into a container and to alert the ramp serviceperson of any pieces that should not be put in a container on the basis of the destination of the shipment.

Destination Breakdown. The actual parcel received at destination will be verified by scanning each piece that enters the warehouse.

Delivery Truck Loading. Each piece loaded onto a door to door delivery truck will be scanned and the manifest verified.

Warehouse Check. Bar coding will be used to record loose pieces on the warehouse floor during the normal warehouse checks.

The benefits associated with the use of bar codes are seen as resulting from an improvement in service levels through better control of parcel handling. These benefits will be realized by a reduction of claims and an increase in business.

Current surveys show 15 percent of BEAM's customers stop using the company for shipping every quarter, and 35 percent of those give poor service as a reason. Traffic services at BEAM is confident that service failures will be decreased by 30 percent with the introduction of bar codes and automatic lot labeling. Here, reduced claims represent a true bottom-line increase in profits.

The bar code study team recommended an investment of more than $600,000 to implement a dock-to-dock bar code shipment movement data capture system as Phase 1 of a total bar code implementation project.

The bar code project showed exceptional promise. Simple return on investment was high (5), and the project was viewed to be highly strategic by both the business and the technology domains (5 for each). It was an integral part of the blueprint. Although bar coding did not create any data interchange, it was designed to improve the competitive position of the enterprise by improving operating efficiencies in a strategic area. Accordingly, it was rated a 2 by the business domain for competitive advantage through interorganizational communication. It provides current management information on the core activities of management control (for example, sales target and service performance) and operation control (such as claims) and was rated a 5. Competitive response was high (4) because of the constant erosion of the customer base because of poor service. Organizational risk was deemed low (2) by the business domain. The technology was proven and similar systems had been adopted by air freight industry and surface delivery personnel with few problems (Figure 14.13). (The ranking of this and other examples in the chapter are summarized at the chapter end.)

14–2 TECHNOLOGY DOMAIN FACTOR #2: DEFINITIONAL UNCERTAINTY

With change comes uncertainty. Technology change within an organization can manifest itself in many ways. The way a job is done can be restructured to be more productive; that is, the end product remains the same, but the means to that end has undergone change. The end product may also change, requiring change on the part of those inside as well as outside the enterprise. These changes involve a level of risk. The Information Economics structure allows us to assess these risks and uncertainties.

The first type of change—changing a single element within a process—involves risk that can be isolated to a single position or process. We have assessed that risk (in the business domain) through project or organization risk, and used value restructuring to assess the increased value resulting from the change.

Another type of change relates to changing many elements within the process to produce the same end product. Risk is assessed in the business domain through project or organization risk. Additional risk may be identified through examining competitive response. Value is assessed through value restructuring. Additional value may be identified through value linking and value acceleration.

A third type of change relates to adjustments and accommodations both inside and outside the organization. Any combination of all the factors we have discussed to date may be applied to assessing the value and the risk of these changes.

All of these changes have been focused on the accommodations necessary *by people* to affect the change. These people have been in the business domain of the enterprise, or in the customer set of the enterprise. The assumption has been that the technology is delivered *by the technology domain* in a timely, useable way. There are risks in the technology domain that we need to address. They stem from definitional uncertainty (DU) and technical uncertainty (TU). Definitional uncertainty is the degree to which the deliverable is a moving target. Technical uncertainty relates to the organizational readiness of the technology domain to undertake the project.

Definitional uncertainty assesses the degree to which the requirements and/or the specifications are known. Also assessed are the complexity of the area and the probability of nonroutine changes. The key here is unknown requirements. The measure is negative, in that increased uncertainty produces a higher negative measurement (see Figure 14.2).

The definitional uncertainty score provides an avenue for the technology domain to express risk associated with the project as it relates to requirements, specifications, and change.

In Chapters Twelve and Thirteen we discussed BEAM parcels pharmacy shipment automation. It was considered to be a system that would effectively support the business strategy. It involved a direct interface with BEAM customers. BEAM business managers wanted to be the first to offer this service to the marketplace. BEAM Parcels needed to be both *first* and *right* to achieve the associated sales projections. This translates into a

---

SCORE: (0–5)

0. Requirements are firm and approved. Specifications firm and approved. Investigated area is straightforward. High probability of no changes.

1. Requirements moderately firm. Specifications moderately firm. No formal approvals. Investigated area is straightforward. Low probability of nonroutine changes.

2. Requirements moderately firm. Specifications moderately firm. Investigated area is straightforward. Reasonable probability of nonroutine changes.

3. Requirements moderately firm. Specifications moderately firm. Investigated area is straightforward. Changes are almost certain almost immediately.

4. Requirements not firm. Specifications not firm. Area is quite complex. Changes are almost certain, even during the project period.

5. Requirements unknown. Specifications unknown. Area may be quite complex. Changes may be ongoing, but the key here is unknown requirements.

FIGURE 14.2 Definitional uncertainy worksheet.

significant level of definitional uncertainty. Could BEAM accurately define the requirements of this kind of offering to their customer? Probably not the first time. The technology domain scored the pharmacy shipment automation project a 4. It escaped a 5 rating only because some of the requirements were generally known (see Figure 14.11).

14–3 TECHNOLOGY DOMAIN FACTOR #3: TECHNICAL UNCERTAINTY

The other identified risk in the technology domain is technical uncertainty, which assesses the readiness of the technology domain to undertake the project. Four separate assessments are included: skills required, hardware dependencies, software dependencies, and application software. The purpose of this assessment is not to emphasize risk-averse planning. Rather, the purpose is to **recognize the risk** and **emphasize the preparedness** and preparations needed for project success. The measure is a negative one. The higher the technical uncertainty, the more negative the resulting evaluation (see Figure 14.3).

The bar code project for BEAM, introduced earlier in this chapter, was scored high on technical uncertainty by the technology domain. Extensive new skills were required by the staff and, to a lesser degree, by management. Skills required were ranked a 4 level risk by Information Systems.

There was a dependency on specific hardware. The hardware was available and in use outside BEAM, but no one within the current IS organization had had any experience with it. Accordingly, the IS organization rated the hardware dependency a 5 risk level.

New operating systems software support must be installed to support the new bar code applications. BEAM believes that the necessary software is available, but has not installed it, so they are not sure whether they will have to tailor it to their needs. This will be the first use of bar code technology within BEAM Parcels. Software dependencies were rated a 4 by Information Systems.

BEAM Parcels' management had been in contact with an air freight company that had installed bar coding. BEAM expected to be able to purchase the software that had been developed for the air freight application and modify it with a moderate effort. Applications software was scored at a 2 risk level.

The average of the ratings for skills required, hardware dependencies, software dependencies, and applications software was 3.75. It was rounded up to a 4 risk level scoring (Figure 14.13).

14–4 TECHNOLOGY DOMAIN FACTOR #4: IS INFRASTRUCTURE RISK

IS infrastructure risk assesses the degree of nonproject investment necessary to accommodate this project. It is an environmental assessment involving factors such as data administration (such as new data dictionary requirements), communications (for example, new forms of communications capabilities required), and distributed systems (such as new methods of data access required). The scoring alternatives are listed in Figure 14.4 and range from 0–5, as have all of the other factors we assessed.

SCORE: (0–5)

A. Skills required are available in the technology domain. _____

B. Dependency on specific hardware not now available. _____

C. Dependency on software capabilities not now available. _____

D. Dependency on application software development. _____

Total (A + B + C + D)/4 = Rating: _____

A. Skills required
  0. No new skills for staff, management. Both have experience.
  1. Some new skills for staff, none for management.
  2. Some new skills required for staff and management.
  3. Some new skills required for staff, extensive for management.
  4. Extensive (new) skills required for staff, some for management.
  5. Extensive (new) skills required for staff and management.

B. Hardware dependencies
  0. Hardware is in use in similar application.
  1. Hardware is in use, but this is a different application.
  2. Hardware exists and has been tested, but not operationally.
  3. Hardware exists, but not utilized yet within organization.
  4. Some key features are not tested or implemented.
  5. Key requirements are not now available in MIS configuration.

C. Software dependencies (other than application software)
  0. Standard software, or straight-forward or no programming required.
  1. Standard software is used, but complex programming is required.
  2. Some new interfaces between software are required, and complex programming may be required.
  3. Some new features are required in operating software; some complex interfaces between software may be required.
  4. Features not now supported are needed, and moderate advance in local state of the art is required.
  5. Significant advance in state of the art is required.

D. Application Software
  0. Programs exist with minimal modifications required.
  1. Programs are available commercially with minimal modifications, or programs available in-house with moderate modifications, or software will be developed in-house with minimal complexity.
  2. Programs are available commercially with moderate modifications, or in-house programs are available but modifications are extensive, or software will be developed in-house with minimal design complexity but moderate programming complexity.
  3. Software is available commercially but the complexity is high, or software will be developed in-house and the difficulty is moderate.
  4. No package or current in-house software exists. Complex design and programming are required, with moderate difficulty.
  5. No package or current in-house software exists. Complex design and programming is required, even if contracted outside.

FIGURE 14.3 Technical uncertainty worksheet.

The emphasis is on the entire IS organization, including hardware, software, and staff, in terms of the necessary investment needed to accommodate the proposed project. Some of this investment may be a prerequisite; an example is a database management system. Some of this investment may be of an integration character, that is, the investment

SCORE: (0–5)

0. The system uses existing services and facilities. No investment in IS prerequisite facilities (e.g., database management) is required; no up-front costs not directly a part of the project itself are anticipated.

1. Change in one element of the computer service delivery system is required for this project. The associated up-front investment other than direct project costs is relatively small.

2. Small changes in several elements of the computer service delivery system are required. Some up-front investment is necessary to accommodate this project. Some later investment for subsequent integration of this project into the mainstream of the IS environment may be necessary.

3. Moderate changes in several elements of the computer service delivery system are required. Some up-front investment is necessary to accommodate this project; some later investment for subsequent integration of this project into the mainstream of the IS environment will be necessary.

4. Moderate change in elements of computer service delivery is required, in multiple areas. Moderate to high up-front investment in staff, software, hardware, and management is necessary to accommodate the project. This investment is not included in the direct project cost, but represents IS facilities investment to create the needed environment for the project.

5. Substantial change in elements of computer service delivery is required, in multiple areas. Considerable up-front investment in staff, software, hardware, and management is necessary to accommodate the project. This investment is not included in the direct project cost, but represents IS facilities investment to create the needed environment for the project.

FIGURE 14.4 IS infrastructure risk worksheet.

needed to integrate this project into the mainstream IS environment and application portfolio or needed to integrate subsequent projects together with this one.

Specific elements of change may be different for individual enterprises. The assessment here is not one of capacity. Capacity per se may be stressed by a new project, but this should not reflect on the specifics of this project.

14–4–1 CASE: The Task Force on Computer Capacity at BEAM Parcels

Because of pro-active technology managers, BEAM Parcels had begun integrating technology initiatives into business strategy initiatives. With bar coding and pharmacy shipment, the successful implementation of business strategy required successful technology implementation and support. As the role of technology grew, BEAM business management realized they could not take the availability of technology capacity for granted. The investment in the blueprint project brought into focus both the requirement for planning for technology to develop and deliver the right software in the right sequence, and the requirement for planning for the appropriate hardware capacity. The steering committee chartered a task force to evaluate the investment alternatives available for insuring adequate computer capacity.

BEAM Parcels has used computer equipment for its business processes since the introduction of data processing at BEAM in the late 1970s. They currently have three computers installed in their California head office. One of the machines is a large-scale processor, installed new in the 1970s (System A). Systems B and C are intermediate-scale processors of a more recent architecture. System B is a new machine, installed last year, and does not require examination and action by the task force. System C is similar to System B; however, the capacity of it, like System A, is being stressed.

All three machines are on third-party leases. System A (production) is used in support of business systems such as finance, truck operations, maintenance and engineering, personnel, and marketing. System B (time share) supports application development and office automation systems. System C is dedicated to the parcel tracking and control system.

The task force adopted the following three guidelines suggested by BEAM IS management for considering the percentage of CPU (central processing unit) usage to measure the efficiency of BEAM's business processors:

1. A processor that primarily carries out batch (offline) work is considered to have reached effective utilization or processor saturation when the CPU is 80 percent busy. Replacement planning needs to begin around the 70 percent point to have the capacity installed before 80 percent saturation is reached. System A is partially devoted to batch work.

2. A processor that primarily does regular commercial online work is also considered to have reached effective utilization or processor saturation when the CPU is 80 percent busy. However, at 50 percent effective utilization, the response time will begin to degrade and have a negative impact on users. Replacement planning should begin within the 50 to 70 percent range, depending on desired service levels. Part of System A and all of System B are devoted to online processing.

3. A processor that is dedicated to an equipment control program such as that installed on System C is considered to have reached effective utilization or processor saturation at 90 percent CPU busy.

It was agreed that the industry-wide capacity growth rate averages about 45 percent per year. BEAM, however, has experienced an overall (that is, combined Systems A, B, and C) compound growth rate of about 35 percent annually over the past five years, for actual computing capacity installed.

As with an electric power utility, a computing utility must provide sufficient capacity to satisfy its peak periods of demands. Machine capacity measurements have been taken on BEAM's mainframe computers and are translated into average peak requirements over a period of time. If BEAM is to accommodate these requirements, it can be done by either moving usage to nonpeak times through changes in business or through provision of additional computing capacity. The task force focused on the latter course of action.

System A is the main business (production) computer. It has experienced an average annual growth rate of 37 percent over the past five years due primarily to the introduction of online database systems in support of inventory control, route planning, driver management, payroll and personnel, accounts payable, and other systems. Transaction volume resulting from these applications has increased dramatically—as much as 200 percent over the last sixteen months. Future machine capacity growth requirements are expected to be in the 20 percent to 30 percent range, with 25 percent conservatively forecasted as the most likely growth rate.

By the end of this past year, System A was approaching saturation at 74 percent utilization. As a result, response times are now varying widely and are becoming an increasing problem. For example, the inventory control system is seeing response time between five and twenty-five seconds. The desirable level for response time is three seconds. Although the lease on System A extends until July of next year, a decision is required now to either expand capacity or else curtail systems development work. The opportunity cost (loss) associated with curtailing business systems development is estimated to be about $8 million annually.

System B, the time-sharing system, has experienced an average growth rate of 48 percent annually, largely because of the introduction of interactive program development. It does online development and office automation (that is, end-user) work and is currently about 35 percent utilized. This is the least capacity constrained of the three computer systems. Future growth on this system is expected to range between 25 percent to 35 percent, with a most likely 30 percent growth rate, due primarily to projected end-user mainframe data access and analysis. This projected growth would cause the current machine to cross the 70 percent utilization planning point sometime within the next fifteen to eighteen months. No action on this system is required now.

System C, the parcel tracking and control system, has averaged growth of 14 percent annually over the last five years because of both new development and transaction volume increases. Future growth is forecast to range between 10 and 20 percent, with a most likely growth rate of 15 percent annually. The machine is currently about 76 percent utilized and is expected to have passed the point at which replacement planning should occur by the time its lease expires this year. Additional capacity will be needed to accommodate business growth and new development. The opportunity cost (loss) associated with curtailing development is estimated to be $5 million annually.

The task force considered and documented a total of ten possible alternatives, including doing nothing to provide the computer capacity BEAM needed to conduct business. The do-nothing base case and the three most promising alternatives are briefly outlined below. Primary emphasis was given to machine reliability (backup potential), capacity to meet forecast demand, and cost to provide that capacity. A measure of relative machine performance, MIPS (millions of instructions per second), will be used to show the amount of machine potential being discussed.

> *Do-Nothing* **Retain existing computers** and extend leases as they expire. Costs will decline as the market value of the machines diminishes. Not included in this analysis is the increasingly difficult task that maintenance and personnel retention will become as the machines grow progressively more outdated. Capacity will soon not be sufficient to support new development, resulting in an estimated opportunity cost (loss) of $8 million annually. Four-year operating cost (NPV @ 15 percent) of this alternative is estimated to be $2.3 million. Performance total is 11.3 MIPS.

> *Alternative 1* **Acquire three new midsized computers** to replace the currently leased, older computers. This alternative proposes to replace the System A computer with two midsized computers and to displace the System C computer with a third midsize computer. System A's lease would be terminated early, and System C would be replaced on expiration of the existing lease. The first two new machines

would be used to split System A's production work. The third new machine would be used for System C. The current System C machine would be retained to become the parcel test and backup computer. This alternative is recommended as the most cost-effective introduction of the newer computing technology necessary to position BEAM for the future. It will allow capacity for new development, reduce the amount of computer room floor space allocated to mainframes, and substantially reduce the cost of maintenance, electrical power, and cooling. It is also the most flexible alternative, allowing significant backup possibilities in the event of a machine failure or a disaster. Four-year operating cost (NPV) is estimated to be $5.9 million. Incremental cost for this year versus do-nothing is $0.8 million. Performance total is 17.4 MIPS.

Alternative 2 **This option is the same as Alternative 1,** except for timing of machine replacement. The current System A machine would be retained in place of one of the newer ones until expiration of its lease, at which time it would be replaced. Although this alternative allows completion of the almost two years remaining on the lease of the current System A machine, it does so at a higher cost. The economics of the newer technology allows significant savings that more than offset the cost of early lease termination. This alternative would also require more floor space and reduces machine backup options. Four year operating cost (NPV) is estimated to be $5.8 million. Incremental cost for this year versus do-nothing would be $0.9 million. Performance total is 17.9 MIPS (over next 18 months) and 17.4 MIPS thereafter.

Alternative 3 **differs from Alternative 1** only in that a larger machine would be substituted for the two midsized computers proposed for System A. Overall machine capacity is approximately the same under this alternative, but machine backup possibilities are significantly reduced. Four-year operating cost (NPV) is estimated to be $5.7 million. Incremental cost this year versus do-nothing would be $0.8 million. Performance total is 16.3 MIPS.

The cost of providing BEAM's main business computing capacity, for this comparison, consists of hardware lease costs plus associated maintenance, power and cooling, software, floor space, and other support costs. It also incorporates credits, where appropriate, for new equipment warranties and on-site test allowances.

BEAM's cost for this year for the three mainframe business computers is $1.2 million. This cost constitutes the do-nothing alternative and is shown in Figure 14.5 against the total cost of the equipment alternatives under consideration.

	Year 0	Year 1	Year 2	Year 3	Year 4	4-Year NPV @ 15%
Do-nothing	1.2	1.1	1.0	0.9	0.8	2.3
Alternative 1	—	1.9	2.2	2.2	2.0	5.9
Alternative 2	—	2.0	2.1	2.1	1.9	5.8
Alternative 3	—	1.9	2.1	2.1	1.9	5.7

FIGURE 14.5 Cost comparison of alternatives ($millions).

Do-nothing assumes an extension of current leases when they expire, at reduced market rates. Alternatives 1, 2 and 3 assume four-year leases.

What of the opportunity costs? Actual projects underway in Year 0 had an identifiable financial benefit of $16 million annually. New Year 1 development projects currently under consideration by the steering committee have an identifiable financial benefit forecast to be $26 million annually. Benefit estimates at approximately this level are assumed for new projects to be undertaken in future years. However, as a conservative estimate, future benefits of new development projects are assumed to be only $13 million annually —a conservative discount of 50 percent from those proposed for Year 1. This is assumed to be the opportunity cost for each year of delay in implementing future development.

The do-nothing alternative will provide the capacity to undertake only a few of the new development projects and may stop completion of some projects that are underway. Either of the other three alternatives will allow new development to proceed. The cumulative opportunity cost (loss) associated with the do-nothing alternative is outlined in Figure 14.6.

The task force believes that the three key elements in reaching the correct decision for BEAM's future business computing needs are demand, capacity, and cost.

The do-nothing alternative is the least expensive in total operating costs. However, the capacity it provides is insufficient to meet either current or projected needs and has a significant opportunity cost associated with it. Alternative 1 is the most cost effective, partially because of newer technology that allows a longer lease commitment and thus more favorable lease financing terms. Alternative 3 provides the most computing capacity, but with significant system backup difficulties.

The task force recommended Alternative 1, to acquire three midsized business computers to replace two of the current computers (Systems A and C). They felt that this was the most reasonable alternative for accommodating capacity requirements over the next several years. They also felt that long-term (three to four years) leases would be a prudent investment. Because of the task force recommendation, Alternative 1 underwent the ranking process by business and technology domain management.

Can the same process be applied to the prioritization of investments to create the computer utility and in application development? Let's look at how this hardware investment emerged from the scoring process (Figure 14.7). Simple return on investment was high, so it was rated a 5. Because any of the Alternatives 1 through 3 supported the total business strategy, the hardware investment was rated a 5. Competitive advantage was defined in BEAM Parcels' terms as supporting electronic data interchange or interor-

	Year 0	Year 1	Year 2	Year 3	Year 4	4-Year NPV @ 15%
Do nothing		<5>	<18>	<31>	<44>	<60>
Alternative 1	—	—	—	—	—	—
Alternative 2	—	—	—	—	—	—
Alternative 3	—	—	—	—	—	—

FIGURE 14.6 Opportunity cost (loss) of alternatives ($millions).

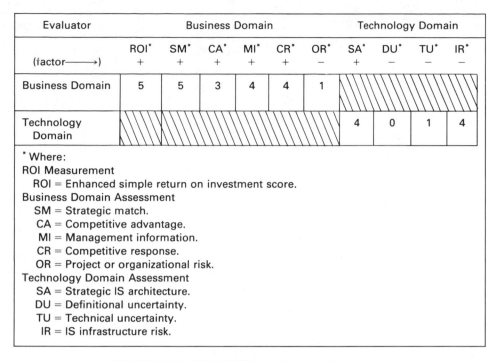

Evaluator	Business Domain						Technology Domain			
(factor ⟶)	ROI* +	SM* +	CA* +	MI* +	CR* +	OR* −	SA* +	DU* −	TU* −	IR* −
Business Domain	5	5	3	4	4	1				
Technology Domain							4	0	1	4

* Where:
ROI Measurement
  ROI = Enhanced simple return on investment score.
Business Domain Assessment
  SM = Strategic match.
  CA = Competitive advantage.
  MI = Management information.
  CR = Competitive response.
  OR = Project or organizational risk.
Technology Domain Assessment
  SA = Strategic IS architecture.
  DU = Definitional uncertainty.
  TU = Technical uncertainty.
  IR = IS infrastructure risk.

FIGURE 14.7   7# BEAM Parcels capacity project.

ganizational systems. The hardware proposal does not *create* IOS or EDI, but it does improve the operating efficiencies in *many* key areas, so was rated a 3 rather than a 2. The hardware is the delivery system for MISCA (management information systems in support of core activities) and was rated a 4. Opportunity loss and probable curtailment of new activities along with dropping some current development efforts resulted in a 4 rating for competitive response. The final business domain factor, organizational risk, was rated a 1 because there were at this point no contingency plans and no business domain plans.

The hardware proposal was rated a 4 for strategic IS architecture in the technology domain. Although it was not a prerequisite to the *next* project to be implemented, it is needed for fairly near-term future capacity.

Definitional uncertainty was scored a 0. Technology management knew what had to be done. Technical uncertainty was low, in that many of the proposed computers had already been installed in other companies. The information technology investment (IS infrastructure risk) was high (a 4). This represented the facilities investment and moderate-to-high change in both the delivery systems and the staff preparation.

14–5 RATINGS FOR THE SEVEN BEAM PROJECTS

We have just completed the ratings for the seventh, and last, BEAM project examined for this book. We will now review the previous six projects to complete their scoring.

Evaluator	Business Domain						Technology Domain			
(factor———→)	ROI +	SM +	CA +	MI +	CR +	OR −	SA +	DU −	TU −	IR −
Business Domain	2.5	4	3	4	5	0	/////	/////	/////	/////
Technology Domain	/////	/////	/////	/////	/////	/////	1	3	2	1

*Where:
ROI Measurement
  ROI = Enhanced simple return on investment score.
Business Domain Assessment
  SM = Strategic match.
  CA = Competitive advantage.
  MI = Management information.
  CR = Competitive response.
  OR = Project or organizational risk.
Technology Domain Assessment
  SA = Strategic IS architecture.
  DU = Definitional uncertainty.
  TU = Technical uncertainty.
  IR = IS infrastructure risk.

FIGURE 14.8 1# BEAM Parcels automated rating, coding, and billing.

1. BEAM Parcels'' automated rating, coding, and billing is alignment in nature. The emphasis is on more accurate and timely rating and coding of customer invoices. The image of the company could be affected adversely if the customers were concerned over too many billing errors; and BEAM was losing dollar billings because of incorrect and late waybills. Although labor reduction was the basis for calculating the ROI, the sponsoring department, which would lose the labor allocation, was a strong internal advocate of the project (see Figure 14.8).

2. The driver pay system is also an alignment project (Figure 14.9). It had to do with more accurate training and vacation reporting. From a technical perspective, it was attractive because it would replace an RPG system with a COBOL system. From a business perspective, it related to the corporate culture—the company being concerned about the morale of its employees.

3. BEAM Parcels driver scheduling (Phase 2) has a statement of direction. The project represents a part of the overall strategy of the business domain. Additionally, the project represents part of the overall strategy of information systems. It represents a move to online, real-time access to schedule data and updating capability and a move to the COBOL environment (Figure 14.10). Because BEAM had migrated most applications software to the COBOL environment, they perceived little technical risk in this isolated application.

4. Pharmacy shipment automation represents a competitive advantage for the business (Figure 14.11). It also represents a competitive risk—Are the outside users ready

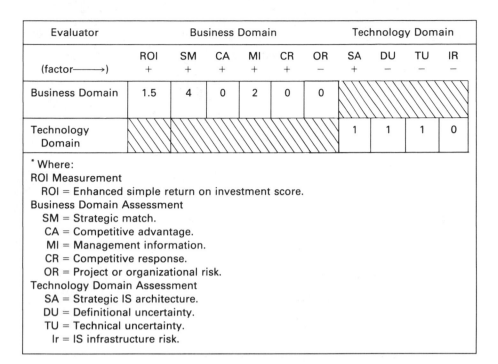

Evaluator	Business Domain						Technology Domain			
(factor——→)	ROI +	SM +	CA +	MI +	CR +	OR −	SA +	DU −	TU −	IR −
Business Domain	1.5	4	0	2	0	0				
Technology Domain							1	1	1	0

* Where:
ROI Measurement
  ROI = Enhanced simple return on investment score.
Business Domain Assessment
  SM = Strategic match.
  CA = Competitive advantage.
  MI = Management information.
  CR = Competitive response.
  OR = Project or organizational risk.
Technology Domain Assessment
  SA = Strategic IS architecture.
  DU = Definitional uncertainty.
  TU = Technical uncertainty.
  Ir = IS infrastructure risk.

FIGURE 14.9 2# BEAM Parcels driver pay system.

Evaluator	Business Domain						Technology Domain			
(factor——→)	ROI +	SM +	CA +	MI +	CR +	OR −	SA +	DU −	TU −	IR −
Business Domain	4.5	5	2	3	4	0				
Technology Domain							4	3	1	0

* Where:
ROI Measurement
  ROI = Enhanced simple return on investment score.
Business Domain Assessment
  SM = Strategic match.
  CA = Competitive advantage.
  MI = Management information.
  CR = Competitive response.
  OR = Project or organizational risk.
Technology Domain Assessment
  SA = Strategic IS architecture.
  DU = Definitional uncertainty.
  TU = Technical uncertainty.
  IR = IS infrastructure risk.

FIGURE 14.10 3# BEAM Parcels driver scheduling (Phase 2).

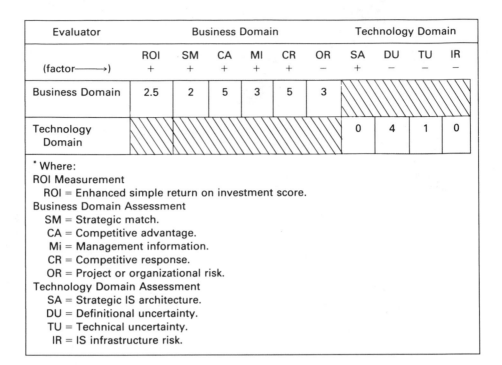

Evaluator	Business Domain						Technology Domain			
	ROI	SM	CA	MI	CR	OR	SA	DU	TU	IR
(factor——→)	+	+	+	+	+	−	+	−	−	−
Business Domain	2.5	2	5	3	5	3				
Technology Domain							0	4	1	0

* Where:
ROI Measurement
  ROI = Enhanced simple return on investment score.
Business Domain Assessment
  SM = Strategic match.
  CA = Competitive advantage.
  Mi = Management information.
  CR = Competitive response.
  OR = Project or organizational risk.
Technology Domain Assessment
  SA = Strategic IS architecture.
  DU = Definitional uncertainty.
  TU = Technical uncertainty.
  IR = IS infrastructure risk.

FIGURE 14.11   4# BEAM Parcels pharmacy shipment automation.

Evaluator	Business Domain						Technology Domain			
	ROI	SM	CA	MI	CR	OR	SA	DU	TU	IR
(factor——→)	+	+	+	+	+	−	+	−	−	−
Business Domain	5	5	5	5	5	0				
Technology Domain							0	3	2	0

* Where:
ROI Measurement
  ROI = Enhanced simple return on investment score.
Business Domain Assessment
  SM = Strategic match.
  CA = Competitive advantage.
  MI = Management information.
  CR = Competitive response.
  OR = Project or organizational risk.
Technology Domain Assessment
  SA = Strategic IS architecture.
  DU = Definitional uncertainty.
  TU = Technical uncertainty.
  IR = IS infrastructure risk.

FIGURE 14.12   5# BEAM Parcels customer management reporting system.

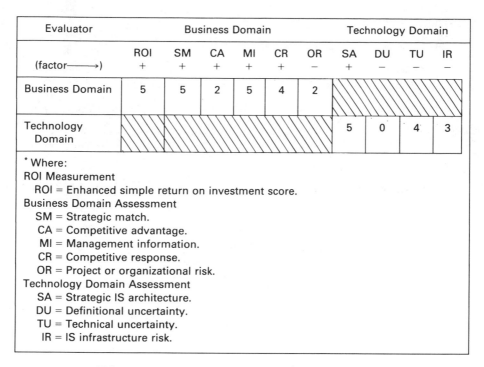

Evaluator	Business Domain						Technology Domain			
(factor———→)	ROI +	SM +	CA +	MI +	CR +	OR −	SA +	DU −	TU −	IR −
Business Domain	5	5	2	5	4	2				
Technology Domain							5	0	4	3

*Where:
ROI Measurement
  ROI = Enhanced simple return on investment score.
Business Domain Assessment
  SM = Strategic match.
  CA = Competitive advantage.
  MI = Management information.
  CR = Competitive response.
  OR = Project or organizational risk.
Technology Domain Assessment
  SA = Strategic IS architecture.
  DU = Definitional uncertainty.
  TU = Technical uncertainty.
  IR = IS infrastructure risk.

FIGURE 14.13   6# BEAM Parcels bar code project.

for this technology? It also represents definitional uncertainty in the technology domain in that the requirements could (and will) shift.

5. The customer management reporting system (Figure 14.12) is perceived by the business domain as both competitive advantage and competitive risk. It offers the needed MISCA support. Technology perceives a lack of definition and wonders what marketing *really* wants, what customers *really* want.

6. The bar code project is viewed as a strategic system by both the business and technology domains (Figure 14.13). However, there was some level of associated technology uncertainty. New skills, hardware, and software were required, as were, of course, the substantial investment in new technology.

We have calculated and rated return on investment and the business and technology domain factors. Yet we know that these elements are not equal in importance when faced with making investment decisions. We must somehow translate or weight these factors in a way that will reflect business strategy. BEAM management, through an evaluation of their corporate culture and stated corporate mission, began the development of weights for each of the factors.

QUESTIONS

1. Name the four technology domain factors.

2. Assume that Old Ivy University is undertaking a card catalog implementation using computing. Describe what you think are the largest risks the university faces in the project.

3. Give examples of definitional uncertainty from systems with which you are familiar.

4. Assume that for BEAM Parcels' bar code project the development costs are $600,000, revenue associated with the project is $5,800,000 per year, and ongoing costs are $2,000 per yr. Compute the simple ROI.

5. Consider BEAM Parcels' pharmacy system. What steps can the MIS director take to reduce the risks presented?

6. Assume that for BEAM Parcels' capacity planning project one-time development and installation costs are $750,000. Compute the simple ROI.

PART 3
APPLYING INFORMATION ECONOMICS

15

The Basis For Corporate Value

15–1 INTRODUCTION

In Chapter Seven we introduced corporate planning processes. We described them as having several steps, one of which is the point at which choices are to be made among many alternatives, shown there as Figure 7.1 and here as Figure 15.1. We recognize that top-down projects come from strategic planning processes and that bottom-up projects are a product of individual management groups and departments expressing their specific requirements. We will explore such processes in more detail in Chapter Sixteen.

These planning processes produce many projects to be considered. For example, at BEAM Parcels this year the combination of bottom-up and top-down processes produced more than one hundred projects. With limitations on available resources, this was four times the ability of BEAM to invest in systems. So our focus now is on the decisions to be made *among* the candidate projects. Certainly BEAM management had to make decisions about which projects to undertake.

In simple terms we want a method to decide which projects represent the wisest investment of scarce resources. We have already explored in Part Two how to place value on, and assign risk to, an individual project. Now we are interested in the **relative importance of each kind of value and risk** in order to select among many projects. For example, the planning activity at Old Ivy University produced seven candidate projects. In this process, Old Ivy administrators ranked the projects by applying the

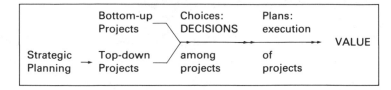

FIGURE 15.1   Project planning processes.

following value weights to each of the individual projects, thus defining their investment strategy for these projects (Figure 15.2).

The column marked *Maximum Score* is the weight multiplied by five. This is done to produce a total score representing value that will add to one hundred.

Previously in Part Two we described methods to evaluate the individual values and risks for a project. The methods produce an evaluation range (0 to 5) for each value and risk and an overall value for each project, the sum of all values and risks. Assuming we have resources sufficient for half the total projects, we can now determine which projects merit further investment.

We make this determination with an evaluation process that weights the classes of value for the enterprise. In the case of Old Ivy University, return on investment (ROI) was by far the dominant category with fifty of the hundred points assigned to it. If the university has insufficient resources to do all projects, then those that are done are selected largely on the basis of return on investment. If a series of projects for Old Ivy University were evaluated by applying the stated weights, the resulting project rankings might look something like Figure 15.3.

We now ask, Where did the weights come from? How did we decide that return on investment is the most important basis for evaluation? Why shouldn't competitive

	Evaluation Range	Weight	Maximum Score
BUSINESS DOMAIN VALUES AND RISKS			
A. Return on Investment	0 5	10	+50
B. Strategic match	0 5	2	+10
C. Competitive advantage	0 5	2	+10
D. Management information	0 5	1	+ 5
E. Competitive response	0 5	2	+10
F. Project organization risk	0 5	−1	− 5
TECHNOLOGY DOMAIN VALUES AND RISKS			
A. Definitional uncertainty	0 5	−2	−10
B. Technical uncertainty	0 5	−2	−10
C. IS strategic architecture	0 5	3	+15
D. IS infrastructure risk	0 5	−2	−10
Total Values		20	100
Total Risk and Uncertainty		−7	35

FIGURE 15.2   Old Ivy University (Undergraduate Line of Business).

Project Name	Sponsor	User Group	Cost	Annual Benefit	IRR%	Rank	Values
Library Card Catalog	Library	Provost	133	1753	1315	72	SA SA
Information Center	IS	Div 1	58	299	508	56	SM MI
New Payroll System	Finance	Admin	71	625	884	50	
Accounts Payable Upgrade	Finance	Admin	310	787	253	48	SM SA MI
Student Records Pass Fail Upgrade	Registrar	Admin	48	346	714	40	
Admissions Network	Marketing	Admin	44	360	813	38	SA
Instructional Support System	School	Provost	68	5	−27	34	SM SA

Value: SM: Strategic Match   MI: Management Information
SA: Strategic IS Architecture

FIGURE 15.3   Candidate projects for Old Ivy University.

advantage be the more important factor? Given the crucial element of student recruitment, should strategic match be really the dominant factor? Specifically, should the admissions network be higher on the priorities, and should our system of values reflect this result? The problem is that an investment in admissions will add costs to Old Ivy University. Because the number of students admitted each year is intended to be the same, doing a better job in admissions means getting better quality students to apply. There are no incremental revenues to be produced, either. So the ROI measurement will put the project at the bottom of the list. Yet it probably is the most important project of all.

In its broadest terms, we have a problem of fit. Information technology investment opportunities are fitted into the allocation of corporate resources, along with investment opportunities in corporate backbone and line of business projects. Likewise, Information Economics tools can be fitted into the decision process. This notion of a fitting problem and the thoughts on corporate culture and strategy apply to all forms of corporate decision-making. We, however, will focus on the relationship of these concepts to information technology decisions.

15–2 DEFINING CORPORATE VALUES

What we want to establish now is the *relative* values of each of the classes. That is, what is the *relative* importance of each category for a specific company?

15–2–1 Value based on Corporate Culture

We're interesting in understanding how to define the appropriate values or weights to be given to the values and risks in information technology. One possible source is the culture of the enterprise. Corporate culture is a shared belief system that consists of the organization's history, beliefs, and values. It also embodies the viewpoint and values of senior management—the predominant perspective and style of the leaders of the company. Corporate culture represents a powerful, and usually persistent, organizational element. The IS manager must understand the organization before he or she can success-fully compete for scarce corporate resources, yet the way these decisions are made rests importantly on aspects of corporate culture and a shared belief system. The prevailing corporate culture must be both understood and integrated with the IS resource allocation decision. The following are some of the more commonly recognized aspects of corporate culture (Churchman, 1971).

> *Organization.* Are reporting relationships traditional or matrix? Is the responsibility for functions required to carry out strategy centralized or decentralized?
>
> *Systems.* Are planning and budgeting processes formal or informal? Are performance monitoring and reward systems participative or dictatorial?
>
> *Resources.* Are the key resources needed to carry out tasks acquired by an entrepreneurial or bureaucratic approval process? Which resources are scarce? Is corporate philosophy one of stable employment or hire and fire?

Culture. What is the real way decisions are made? Is there conservative or risk-taking philosophy? Is the perceived way to succeed in the company via short-term or long-term results?

We said that corporate culture is a major factor in the resource allocation decision process. It may even determine whether there is an explicit process, the form the process will take if it exists, and the degree of rigor it will employ. It also determines whether an assessment of risk will be an accepted and acknowledged part of the process. More than anything else, it includes the values that will be used in the decision, that is, defined strategy, explicitness, dependency on return on investment criteria, corporate versus line of business focus, and many others.

Although we can generically define corporate culture, specifying what it is for a particular enterprise is difficult. The ideas are important but give relatively little guidance to defining the actual importance of each class of value. For Old Ivy University, for example, can we examine the list of items comprising culture (for example, Churchman's list) and extract an appropriate weighting for each value and risk? Would this process lead to an assessment of the weights assigned to return on investment? Perhaps, but it is hard to see how, exactly.

15–2–2 Value as a Function of Corporate Mission

A second source for deciding what is important and translating that into weights, is the company's stated corporate mission. BEAM Parcel's overall corporate mission statement is illustrated in Figure 15.4.

We do get some guidance from such statements. For example, we might be able to determine that financial information systems may have some importance, given the statement that business units will provide the corporate staff with financial performance

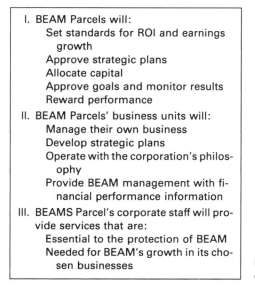

I. BEAM Parcels will:
    Set standards for ROI and earnings growth
    Approve strategic plans
    Allocate capital
    Approve goals and monitor results
    Reward performance

II. BEAM Parcels' business units will:
    Manage their own business
    Develop strategic plans
    Operate with the corporation's philosophy
    Provide BEAM management with financial performance information

III. BEAMS Parcel's corporate staff will provide services that are:
    Essential to the protection of BEAM
    Needed for BEAM's growth in its chosen businesses

FIGURE 15.4 BEAM Parcel corporate mission.

information. However, in measuring projects against these standards, it is not clear that we get the necessary guidance for selecting among competing projects.

15–2–3 An Example of Assigning Corporate Value

Consider an example from Old Ivy University. Looking at it from an undergraduate line of business perspective, Old Ivy University attracts its students based on quality and campus life. Tuition is high relative to other nearby institutions. Given this, would it seem more important to invest scarce resources in projects to save operating dollars (perhaps reduce the head count in the accounting department), or more important to invest those resources in student recruitment (strategic alignment with the goal of increased enrollment), or more important to invest in systems to improve the quality of teaching? Of course, management of the university may believe that all three should be done. Probably all three *should* be done in an ideal world where resources are unconstrained. If resources are available, they can be. If not, choices have to be made. Our point is that the weighting of the classes of value give us the tool to help make the choices.

Note that Figure 15.2 shows the actual weighting of values and risks for Old Ivy University in its undergraduate line of business. Apparently return on investment is important, and strategic alignment is not so important in spite of the implication above that student recruitment, matched to the goal of increased enrollment, might be more important. The process of weighting allowed Old Ivy administrators to thrash out the real priorities.

One experience with the technique illustrates its power. In a previous meeting, Old Ivy administrators prioritized a series of projects by a process of voting; the highest ranked project received the most number of votes. When the administrators then assessed projects and applied the weights from Figure 15.2, an interesting thing occurred. Projects that had been high on the priority list went to the bottom of the list. They had no return on investment impact (indeed, they increased cost), and yet they had no corresponding effect in the other categories. For example, a project to re-do a plant maintenance work order system added cost and presumed to influence the quality of service in grounds and building repair areas. The economic return was modest. The project added nothing in the other areas of evaluation. It dropped to the bottom of the list.

The degree of management trauma this produced was significant. The technique of weighting categories clearly **reordered the basic priorities for investment.** Administrators observed projects that had a performance impact on the university in its major areas went to the top; projects that had little business impact and only modest economic impact went to the bottom. In effect, either the weighting method was wrong (that is, the weights were improperly assigned to each category of value and risk), or prior prioritization methods gave the wrong result. The plant maintenance work order system, previously ranked highest by voting, had dropped to the bottom much to the consternation of those who voted for it.

What actually occurred at the meeting was that the operations vice president still wanted the system for—to him—good reasons. He wanted to upgrade the perceived level of service in his areas. So he argued that strategic goals of the university (*strategic match* in terms of the classes of values) should include quality of physical plant—the campus—as an important ingredient in attracting and keeping students. In effect he argued as well that strategic match should be at least as important as return on investment. He might be right. However, the tone of the argument had changed: the agenda had been recast in terms of what is important for the university. This occurred because the process of weighting placed an assessment of importance on each category of value for the undergraduate line of business. This forced administrators to decide both the weights given to each value and also whether the plant project actually possessed a value. It became possible for senior management to decide what **is** important and make resource allocation decisions accordingly.

This technique defines the politics of the decision process as well. This is the underlying point of the **consensus** discussions in Chapter Sixteen. What we want is a decision-making process that occurs in the open, involves a variety of managers in the application of (hopefully) objective measures, and shapes the underlying arguments and justifications for impact on the organization and its business performance. If we can accomplish even part of this, we have accomplished a great deal.

15–3 HOW VALUE AFFECTS DECISIONS

Let us look at three different organizations and see how corporate values should affect information technology investment decisions. We have chosen three universities. The first is a small public institution. The second is a medium-sized private institution, and the third is a large private research institution.

Institution One is a small, regional state university with mostly undergraduate programs. The institution is part of a large state educational system and is typical of an organization without a strong priority to develop new business opportunities. ROI and risk avoidance are probably most important. So little weight is given to strategic business opportunities for innovation and advantage. Institution Two is a medium-sized private institution in precarious financial circumstances. Return on investment—cost reductions, in particular—and tight management control are important. Even more impor-

Weightings	Business Domain						Technology Domain			
	ROI	SA	CA	MI	CR	OR	SA	DU	TU	IR
Institution One	H	M	L	H	L	L	M	L	M	M
Institution Two	M	M	H	H	L	M	L	M	M	M
Institution Three	M	H	H	L	H	M	H	L	L	L

Business Domain Assessment
ROI - Return on investment
SM - Strategic match
CA - Competitive advantage
MI - Management information
CR - Competitive response
OR - Project organizational risk

Technology Domain Assessment
SA - Strategic IS architecture
DU - Definitional uncertainty
TU - Technical uncertainty
IR - IS infrastructure risk

Where
H -High
M-Medium
L -Low

FIGURE 15.5   Values for each of three institutions.

tant, however, are initiatives to strengthen key instructional programs to make them more attractive within their markets. This is the real focus of the school's administration. Institution Three is a large research university with significant medical campus activity and a teaching hospital. The institution is strongly competitive with other top-ranked institutions in the world. Consequently, institutional values focus on building competitive strengths and building on its competitive advantages.

Let's look at specific examples. We have taken the same seven projects that had previously been proposed for Old Ivy University. Our purpose is to see how these projects would be ranked—and consequently selected for implementation—for each of the three quite different universities. Our premise is that the institutional *values* as reflected in the weights given to each risk and value will result in very different priorities for the projects.

In Figure 15.5 we interpret the above descriptions of the three institutions into the respective assignment of weights to each class of risk and value. We adopt a "high-medium-low" designation for clarity here. We will convert these to numeric weights in Figure 15.6.

We've shown each factor weighted by high, medium, or low. Applying the entries from Figure 15.5 we assign actual weighting factors in Figure 15.6. The first half gives the relative value assigned (for example, 2 is half the weight given to another category with 4). For each project, this number is multiplied by the project value in the category. For example, if the admissions network is judged to be a 3 in strategic advantage, and if that category is given a weight of 4 in the institution values, then the project has a resulting value of 12 in this category. We then normalize to a scale of 100 for value in the bottom half of Figure 15.6 by multiplying each weight by 5. The result in each column is the maximum value possible for value and risk and uncertainty for a given project.

Later in the chapter we will introduce a more organized way to set weights for different categories of organizations. For now, the comparative weights given to the classes of value are portrayed in Figure 15.6.

Each individual project has been ranked according to the procedures set out in previous chapters. The assignment of weights for individual projects is a process of assigning a rank from 0 to 5 in each category. Now we will apply the three different sets of weights, which characterize three very different types of institutions. By extending the results and ordering the systems accordingly, we see that very different results are obtained, as in Figure 15.7. First, Figure 15.6 shows the individual project values derived by methods described in Part Two. For this example, each project is given the same score for value and risk, for each institution. (See Appendix E for the conversion tables used.)

By applying the different set of weights for each institution, which reflect explicit decisions about the relative importance of each category, the decision process gets **very** different results. The difference means, essentially, that **different kinds of organizations should apply information technology differently** accordingly to priorities unique to them. Had we simply applied return on investment techniques alone, we would produced the *identical* ranking of projects for each institution because ROI for each project in this example was stipulated to be identical. Yet the process of defining the relative weights for each institution produced a marked difference in project rankings. Indeed,

Weights	ROI	SM	CA	MI	CR	OR	SA	DU	TU	IR	Total Value	Total Risk
Institution 1	10	2	0	6	0	0	2	0	-4	-4	20	-8
Institution 2	4	2	4	8	0	-2	2	-4	-4	-4	20	-14
Institution 3	3	4	6	0	4	-8	3	-2	-2	-4	20	-16

Maximum Score	ROI	SM	CA	MI	CR	OR	SA	DU	TU	IR	Total Value	Total Risk
Institution 1	50	10	0	30	0	0	10	0	-20	-20	100	-40
Institution 2	20	10	20	40	0	-10	10	-20	-20	-20	100	-70
Institution 3	15	20	30	0	20	-40	15	-10	-10	-20	100	-80

Business Domain Assessment
ROI - Return on investment
SM - Strategic match
CA - Competitive advantage
MI - Management information
CR - Competitive response
OR - Project organizational risk

Technology Domain Assessment
SA - Strategic IS architecture
DU - Definitional uncertainty
TU - Technical risk
IR - IS infrastructure risk

FIGURE 15.6 Weights and maximum scores for three institutions.

Projects	ROI	SA	CA	MI	CR	OR	SA	DU	TU	IR
Library Card Catalog	0	4	2	0	3	2	3	1	3	2
Information Center	0	1	0	4	0	4	4	0	2	0
New Payroll System	4	2	0	3	0	3	4	2	1	3
Accounts Payable Upgrade	3	2	1	3	0	2	4	2	1	3
Students Records P/F	3	3	2	1	3	3	0	3	1	2
Admissions Network	0	5	3	3	4	4	5	0	3	4
Instructional Support	0	5	4	0	5	3	2	4	4	4

Projects	Institution 1		Institution 2		Institution 3	
	Score	Rank	Score	Rank	Score	Rank
Library Card Catalog	−7	6	−6	6	17	1
Information Center	26	4	26	1	−20	7
New Payroll System	54	1	22	3	−10	6
Accounts Payable Upgrade	44	2	24	2	1	5
Student Records P/F	30	3	2	5	5	4
Admissions Network	10	5	20	4	15	2
Instructional Support	−18	7	−24	7	14	3

FIGURE 15.7   Project ranking and scores for each institution.

we have applied the unique business characteristics of each institution to the decision process. **This is exactly what Information Economics is about.**

15–4 ESTABLISHING CORPORATE VALUES

The method for defining corporate values is the determination of the relative weight, or importance, for each category of value and risk. We propose to carry out the weighting process in a simple way. Given the ten classes of value and risk, we wish to rank order them for our business, distribute a positive weighting factor that adds to 100 for values, and apply a negative weighting factor for risk and uncertainty. As we saw, this had already been done for Old Ivy University in Figure 15.2. But on what basis do we choose the relative importances and weights? To answer this, we propose a multi-step self-assessment a company can conduct to help decide a starting point for weights. We emphasize *starting point*. This process is the most organizationally dependent, and managerially dependent, of any. So the major point is that management must be involved in the process. All we present here are tools to assist in the thought process. The ground rule is that we are dealing, now, with individual lines of business. We will consider corporate goals and effects on weighting a bit later. Here, we will look at individual lines of business.

15–4–1 A Self Assessment to Establish Value

The initial question is whether the line of business is currently profitable and considered to be in good shape. A parallel question is whether the computer service used in the line of business is currently effective or, colloquially, broken. We combine these two questions into a small grid for analysis purposes as shown in Figure 15.8.

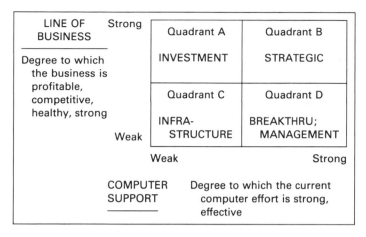

		Strong	Quadrant A INVESTMENT	Quadrant B STRATEGIC

LINE OF BUSINESS — Degree to which the business is profitable, competitive, healthy, strong — Strong / Weak

Quadrant A — INVESTMENT / Quadrant B — STRATEGIC
Quadrant C — INFRA-STRUCTURE / Quadrant D — BREAKTHRU; MANAGEMENT

Weak — Strong

COMPUTER SUPPORT — Degree to which the current computer effort is strong, effective

FIGURE 15.8 Establishing corporate (line of business) values.

Note that we do not consider the business implications of a weak business. In a diversified company, that may affect the future of the line of business itself. More commonly, this condition is a realistic one in single line of business companies. For example, Keep-On Trucking has been in the commodities transportation business, a business dramatically affected by deregulation and its customers' business conditions. The company has had little opportunity to move out of the business, so it is quite reasonable to conduct a planning and decision process despite its weak condition.

The implications for a line of business in each of the four quadrants lie in the determination of what is important, and hence the weighting of the ten classes of value and risk. For example, Von Nievelt (1986) has studied the ability of companies to successfully pursue competitive advantage. He notes that the opportunity to improve management productivity is useful only in businesses with average or superior strategic position. He observes there is little evidence that information technology applications by themselves create business opportunities. This is a helpful idea. Companies that are not now in a strong position have different things to concern themselves with than companies that are in a strong position.

On the basis of the self-assessment shown in Figure 15.8, we can give examples of the relative values individual companies are likely to have. As Von Nievelt pointed out, for example, a company can take advantage of management information if it is strong in its markets; a company in Quadrant A or B will value this more highly than one in Quadrant C or D. Similar judgments can be made for each of the quadrants.

Quadrant A: Investment.   The line of business is strong; the computer support, however, is weak. This is not an unusual circumstance in a diversified company, particularly when acquisitions bring in new divisions with poor previous computer support. What is important here? It is unlikely that substantial short-run gains can be made until the quality of computer support is increased. Generally this means investment in the infrastructure and backbone systems. In this way the foundation is laid to make later strategic contributions to the enterprise.

BUSINESS DOMAIN	LIKELY VALUE	COMMENT	RESULTING WEIGHT
A. Return on investment (ROI)	Medium		2
B. Strategic match	Low		0
C. Competitive advantage	Low		0
D. Management information	Medium	Strengthen Management	2
E. Competitive response	Highest		8
F. Project organization risk	Medium		−2
TECHNOLOGY DOMAIN			
A. Definitional uncertainty	Medium		−4
B. Technical uncertainty	Medium		−4
C. Strategic IS architecture	High		8
D. IS infrastructure risk	Low		0
		Total Value	20
		Total Risk and Uncertainty	−10

FIGURE 15.9   Investment quadrant corporate value.

The real risk, however, is falling behind competition in the deployment of computing.

Interpretation.   This line of business (Figure 15.9), with its strong business foundation, has the time and opportunity to invest in its future. Consequently, a focus on future growth and current infrastructure development is appropriate. The weights reflect this opportunity.

Quadrant B: Strategic.   The line of business is strong; the computer support is also strong (Figure 15.10). Both the systems infrastructure and the backbone systems

BUSINESS DOMAIN	LIKELY VALUE	COMMENT	RESULTING WEIGHT
A. Return on investment (ROI)	Medium		2
B. Strategic match	High		4
C. Competitive advantage	Highest		6
D. Management Information	Medium		2
E. Competitive response	High		4
F. Project organization risk	Low		−1
TECHNOLOGY DOMAIN			
A. Definitional uncertainty	Medium		−2
B. Technical uncertainty	Low		−1
C. Strategic IS architecture	Low		1
D. IS infrastructure risk	Low		1
		Total Value	20
		Total Risk and Uncertainty	−4

FIGURE 15.10   Strategic quadrant corporate value.

BUSINESS DOMAIN	LIKELY VALUE	COMMENT	RESULTING WEIGHT
A. Return on investment (ROI)	Medium		2
B. Strategic match	High	Assume Management Goals	4
C. Competitive advantage	Low		0
D. Management information	High	Strengthen Management	4
E. Competitive response	Medium		2
F. Project organization risk	High	Cannot afford risk	−4
TECHNOLOGY DOMAIN			
A. Definitional uncertainty	High	Cannot afford risk	−4
B. Technical uncertainty	Medium	Cannot afford risk	−2
C. Strategic IS architecture	Highest	A crucial element	8
D. IS infrastructure risk	Low		0
		Total Value	20
		Total Risk and Uncertainty	−10

FIGURE 15.11 Infrastructure quadrant corporate value.

are sound. So the predominant issue is future period contributions of computing to the health of the enterprise. Contributors to the bottom-line (ROI) are also important.

Interpretation.   The research departments, particularly in the sciences, at Old Ivy University are examples. A regional bank with strong ATM networks and strong back-office support systems is a second example. These strong-strong enterprises have the opportunity to invest in competitive advantage and competitive hurdle applications. The purpose of investment can be to increase the future strength of the enterprise.

Quadrant C: Infrastructure.   The line of business is weak; the computer support is also weak. The thought process to define the appropriate weights is shown in Figure 15.11.

Interpretation.   The commodity transport business of Keep-On Trucking is a prime example. The business is terrible but so are the computer services available to the business. So decisions about computer investment are tied directly to the development of the infrastructure. The issue is survival, and computing can help by firming up the capability of the business to conduct its affairs effectively and efficiently. But the investment opportunities are in the back-office and infrastructure areas first.

Quadrant D: Breakthru or Management.   The line of business is weak; the computer support however is strong. Typically this happens in divisions of companies where one of the other divisions has caused a significant computer capability to emerge (see Figure 15.12).

Interpretation.   The business objective is survival, but the existence of a strong computer capability opens the possibility of investment and development that can significantly strengthen the business potentials.

BUSINESS DOMAIN	LIKELY VALUE	COMMENT	RESULTING WEIGHT
A. Return on investment (ROI)	High		4
B. Strategic match	Highest		6
C. Competitive advantage	Low		0
D. Management information	High		4
E. Competitive response	Low		0 .
F. Project organization risk	High		−4
TECHNOLOGY DOMAIN			
A. Definitional uncertainty	Medium		−2
B. Technical uncertainty	Medium		−2
C. Strategic IS architecture	Highest		6
D. IS infrastructure risk	Medium		−2
		Total Value	20
		Total Risk and Uncertainty	−10

FIGURE 15.12 Investment quadrant corporate value.

15–4–2 Implications

Most planning models create a risk of confusing what an organization *should* be concerned with and what the organization *is* concerned with. We see this in our presentations on strategic planning. A middle manager will approach us and say, ''Good thoughts, but I sure wish my boss had been here to hear what you had to say!'' This is shorthand for ''My boss is worried about the wrong things; he really should be worried about 'strategic' things.''

Perhaps. Then again, we find that the mistake is more often made in the other direction—time and energy invested in long-range strategic considerations when the business isn't strong or hasn't established the foundation on which to move to the more strategic opportunities. We find it crucial to match the considerations of what is important to reality, which is the purpose of the examples given from the four quadrants.

Of course, we are looking at just one part of the situation, namely the application of computing to the enterprise. The larger questions of business strategy and strategic management can also be brought into the collection of issues to be considered. This, however, is beyond the scope of this current book.

15–5 ESTABLISHING THE BASIS FOR VALUE—CORPORATE VALUE SYSTEMS

Donaldson and Lorsh (1983) have explored the value systems that dominate companies. They propose that three major classes of values can be observed: values founded on financial issues, on product and market issues, and on organizational issues. The three value classes give important clues to what companies view as important.

The source of the values lies in the relationship between the company and its environment. A financial company relies on its relationships to constituencies, markets,

Financial	Product/Market	Organizational
Growth Rate of Earnings	Rank in Industry	Absolute Size
Dividend Payout	Share of Market	Growth rate of sales
Credit Limits	Growth rate of sales	Diversification
		Growth rate of earnings
		Reserves

FIGURE 15.13   General systems values.

or suppliers of funds, or regulators that are dominated by financial concerns. A bank might fall in this class. A product and market company relies on its relationships with customers, suppliers, sources of raw materials, and markets in general. A retailer might fall in this class. An organizational company relies on relationships with government, its employees, and the community. A governmental agency falls in this class; so might a university.

The representation of the values lies in the sorts of measurements that management believes reflects the health and productive status of the company. They might be compared in Figure 15.13.

Donaldson and Lorsh apply this framework to note that corporate goals may be financial in character, whereas at times lines of business have product/market or organizational characteristics. Our point is to raise two complementary ideas. First, the value system a company has may dictate what is important in Information Economics terms, and consequently be a major factor in assigning weights to the classes of value and risk. Second, the management actors in a company have personal goals; the value system at work and, as importantly, the compensation system for management may also be major factors.

Shanklin and associates (1985) have observed that unless a company sets its compen-

BUSINESS DOMAIN	Financial Values	Product/Market Values	Organization Values
Return on investment (ROI)	X		X
Strategic match		X	X
Competitive advantage		X	
Management information	X		
Competitive response		X	
Project organization risk		−X	−X
TECHNOLOGY DOMAIN			
Definitional uncertainty	−X		−X
Technical uncertainty			−X
Strategic IS architecture	X		
IS infrastructure risk			
"X" Represents Categories with High or Highest Values.			

FIGURE 15.14   Corporate values.

sation plans according to the values and the negotiated strategic missions of their strategic business units (SBUs), planning methods have little chance to work well in practice. This is the key insight in understanding planning, and, by extension, Information Economics. Management motivations and incentives are key. We call the former the value system assessment, and the latter the scorekeeping assessment. They may be the same; in fact differences in the assessments can be very disruptive.

We speculate on the consequent value and risk weighting on three value system categories in Figure 15.14.

We can, of course, convert the assessment into weights, in a fashion similar to

Weights	ROI	SM	CA	MI	CR	OR	SA	DU	TU	IR	Total Value	Risk
Financial	7			7			6		−6		20	−6
Product Market		7	7		6	−6					20	−6
Organizational	10	10				−4		−4	−4		20	−12

Maximum Score	ROI	SM	CA	MI	CR	OR	SA	DU	TU	IR	Total Value	Risk
Financial	35			35			30		−30		100	30
Product Market		35	35		30	−30					100	−30
Organizational	50	50				−20		−20	−20		100	−60

Business Domain Assessment
ROI = Return on investment
SM = Strategic match
CA = Competitive advantage
MI = Management information support
CR = Competitive response
OR = Project organizational risk

Technology Domain Assessment
SA = Strategic IS architecture
DU = Definitional uncertainty
TU = Technical Risk
IR = IS infrastructure risk

Projects	ROI	SA	CA	MI	CR	OR	SA	DU	TU	IR
Library Card Catalog	0	4	2	0	3	2	3	1	3	2
Information Center	0	1	0	4	0	4	4	0	2	0
New Payroll System	4	2	0	3	0	3	4	2	1	3
Accounts Payable Upgrade	3	2	1	3	0	2	4	2	1	3
Student Records P/F	3	3	2	1	3	3	0	3	1	2
Admissions Network	0	5	3	3	4	4	5	0	3	4
Instructional Support	0	5	4	0	5	3	2	4	4	4

Projects	Institution-1		Institution-2		Institution-3	
	Score	Rank	Score	Rank	Score	Rank
Library Card Catalog	0	6	48	3	20	4
Information Center	40	3	−17	7	−6	7
New Payroll System	67	1	−4	6	28	1
Accounts Payable Upgrade	60	2	9	5	22	2
Student Records P/F	22	5	35	5	22	2
Admissions Network	33	4	56	2	18	5
Instructional Support	−12	7	60	1	6	6

FIGURE 15.15 Corporate values reflected in project ranking.

the four quadrant process. Perhaps each "X" in Figure 15.14 should be the highest likely value and all other categories measured at zero. By considering the Old Ivy projects previously described, and by combining Figures 15.6 and 15.7, this would produce Figure 15.15 for businesses with Corporate Values defined in Figure 15.14. (See Appendix E for the conversion calculation tables.)

Since we have used the same projects from Old Ivy University, we can compare these rankings to the earlier set for the three universities. Here, when ranked for different corporations with different value systems, the contrast in priorities is striking. The differences in corporate values dramatically affects the relative importances of the projects. (Of course, the project names do not relate to a normal corporate project list, but we have left them the same as before for continuity.)

15–6 PUTTING IT TOGETHER

These then become the key concepts in the relationship of corporate culture and values to Information Economics:

- *Culture* determines whether strategy, risk and other values will be explicit or implicit.
- *Strategy and risk* become a vision of change to be brought about through the allocation of resources. Again, the vision can be explicit or implicit.
- *Strategic architecture* is the long-term vision as it applies to information technology, that is, the blueprint of future systems as data.
- *Information Economics* is the collection of tools that makes explicit those underlying values in the corporate culture that determine the allocation of resources to the information technology projects necessary to implement the blueprint.

As determined by the corporate culture, some companies' strategies are not explicitly stated. Tools such as Michael Porter's Value Chain are intended to make them explicit. Similarly, some companies' strategic systems and data architectures are not explicitly stated. The tools of Information Economics are designed to make explicit the criteria used to allocate resources to the information technology projects necessary to implement the systems and data architecture.

Information Economics will not change corporate culture; rather, Information Economics is a device for **communicating the shared beliefs** or value contained in the corporate culture. When the culture is changing, Information Economics can make clear the alternatives.

For example, we recently observed a large corporation as it underwent a change in senior management. That entailed a significant change in style and direction. As a result, the corporate culture—the values and decision-making processes—were significantly altered. Information Economics responds to these changes by making explicit the value attached to various decision dimensions. Once explicit, the weights attached to these dimensions are readily adjusted as part of the planning process.

QUESTIONS

1. Assume that Old Ivy University is weak in its undergraduate line of business but strong in its computing support. Rank the projects listed in the chapter according to the weights given.

2. How does corporate culture affect the definition of appropriate weights to the six categories of value?

3. Speculate on how corporate culture might be a factor in the assimilation of an acquisition's data processing organization.

4. Describe how the assignment of weights implements the varying importance of values to an enterprise.

5. Describe the three key concepts that link corporate culture to Information Economics.

16

The Corporate Decision Process

In previous chapters we have expanded concepts of value and risk to provide a more accurate measurement of proposed investment in information technology. We now seek to answer the question: Where should the enterprise invest in information technology?

16–1 DECISION PROCESSES IN THE ORGANIZATION

The idea is simple. Typically the IS department creates a set of proposed application systems projects. Perhaps the IS executive seeks out proposed projects from users. Perhaps users themselves come forward with needed systems. Perhaps a strategic planning process results in proposed projects to support new business initiatives. Perhaps the IS executive perceives a need for expanded hardware facilities or for advanced software facilities such as a relational database manager. The consequence of all these projects is the need to decide which are best for the enterprise; that is, assuming the enterprise cannot undertake all of them, someone must determine which merit the investment of enterprise resources.

    Assume for a moment that the president of the firm takes the responsibility to decide. The IS executive might prepare a list of all possible projects and descriptive materials about individual projects. The decision process consists of the president, using the materials presented to him, determining which projects have the best positive impact on the firm. How this is decided is the basis of Information Economics: the appropriate statements of value and the appropriate statements of cost and risk. On these the president will decide.

Most enterprises have some form of a decision process in place. Our goal is to add Information Economics to that process. Here we will explore several characteristics of this process and the ways in which Information Economics can be usefully applied. We can look at it from several perspectives.

From the enterprise perspective, **the application of Information Economics is within a planning and decision process. Its goals are to maximize the effect of IS on the enterprise and to make the best decision in allocation of corporate resources.**

As we have asked before: What is it worth to a company to create competitive distinctiveness in their products? What is it worth to strengthen a company's relationships with its customers? What is the cost of an advanced systems development tool or a relational database management system? How do managers successfully choose between alternative investments? Clearly, the ones chosen should have the most impact on the performance of the enterprise. To make the appropriate choices, we need a way to assess proposed resource allocations.

Our view of an effective decision process has these components:

- A decision process that (1) gets line of business management involved; (2) gets the senior management who makes fiscal investment decisions involved; and (3) makes decisions on the basis of value (the anticipated effect on business performance)
- A decision process that seeks out the best opportunities for information technology
- A framework for the implementation of the opportunities, which is, for example, the role of the IS blueprint and information systems architectures

We note that these requirements go beyond a decision process and specify a planning activity in which one step is making decisions about alternative projects and investments. We do not intend to describe planning for information technology in detail; rather, we focus on the interaction between planning and the decisions planning processes generate. To do this, we will develop the planning ideas. Briefly, we will look at three basic elements of planning: (1) getting the ideas for potential applications; (2) deciding which ideas are best; and (3) successfully implementing the ideas. The second element is Information Economics.

Viewed from the *IS manager's perspective,* **a technology domain result is needed. The manager needs an implementation plan, a project list, and an infrastructure to support the plan and the projects.**

At this point we note a basic conflict in the planning process for information technology.

On the one hand, a planning process needs to produce a plan for implementation. In the larger IS organizational context, often this plan needs to be shaped as data, information systems, and communications architectures. These are important ways in which information systems resources and developmental process should be organized. As we noted in Chapter Five, the need for an implementation plan is most associated with **alignment** planning. An Enterprise-wide Information Management (EwIM) idea, alignment planning produces a data or systems architecture aligned with the needs of the business domain.

On the other hand, a planning process should also produce ideas for changing the business. In EwIM terms these are **impact** applications that change the business plans and strategies and perhaps change the organizational units that carry out the business plans.

The conflict between these two outcomes is fundamental. Certainly it is important to support the existing business and, indeed, create a sound infrastructure (based on architectures) to carry out the business requirements. Yet the business has to change. The conflict has to be reconciled in the decision processes used to determine where the information systems investments are to be made.

For example, one of the Bell operating companies undertook a substantial long-range planning process for its information systems. The IS organization viewed this process as an exercise in long-range data administration and for excellent reasons. They'd been struggling with out-of-date and fragmented information systems portfolios. They needed to develop and re-do these systems and believed the key attribute of the new systems is the sharing of data among currently separated systems. To them, the approach was a strategic database approach driven by the data administration group.

At almost the same time, a large regional bank undertook almost exactly the same type of project, the re-doing of a large set of currently separate but functionally intertwined applications that service commercial organizations and other banks in their credit card operations. The same approach was taken, a data-oriented architectural approach.

In both the Bell company and the regional bank, the planning process produced systems designs created, largely, by the focus on data architectures, dominated by the need of the IS organization for an implementable result. The projects were almost exclusively *alignment* in nature. In neither case were *impact* opportunities specifically considered, although both organizations claimed to consider future business needs in the construction of the architectures and the related systems projects.

In one case the ultimate outcome was successful; in the other, a dismal failure. The failure occurred because business conditions changed (or, more accurately, continued to change), making the architecture a limit to business reaction to change rather than an enabler. The failure also occurred because the process for decision—the Information Economics of the situation—did not consider the full sets of inherent values and risks.

The point here is to demonstrate the basic conflict between getting business-based ideas and producing implementable information systems projects. A planning and decision process has to be capable of resolving the conflict. This isn't to say that the implementation and architectural ideas are not important. Together, they develop the *capacity* of the enterprise to conduct its business. For example, Old Ivy University is in the research business. Investment in the capacity of the university to conduct research—creating the infrastructure for research support such as laboratories, research technicians, research library facilities, and computing systems—may well be the most important investment the university can make. It is the same in business. The core areas of the business, those productive activities that permit the business to conduct its affairs, can be represented by architectures and backbone systems such as order entry and manufacturing control.

The idea of **capacity** to conduct business is a part of business strategic planning. For example, **strategic management** is described by Igor Ansoff (1983) as including more than just strategic planning, which is limited to considerations of the firm's strategy.

Participant in Process	Value	Investment	
Business Manager(s)	Business Domain Factors for Justification	Technology Domain Factors for Viability	
Financial Officer			
Corporate Planning			
IS Management			Agreed Ranking
Consensus: Agreed Values and Evaluations			

FIGURE 16.1   Information Economics Evaluation.

Strategic management adds consideration of a firm's organization and its capacity to carry out strategy. This idea of **capability,** including the goal of aligning the organization itself to the strategic needs of the business, leads to the concept of infrastructure. In information systems terms, this is architecture and backbone systems. In business terms, this is the alignment of information technology to support the core areas of the business.

This idea of corporate capability can be crucial. We've provided for this in two classes of value: strategic IS architectures and business strategic match. The important point, however, is that the decision process has to be capable of assigning the appropriate value to individual projects and proposed investments.

Viewed from the *business manager's perspective,* a business domain result is needed. This may be produced by an information systems architecture and infrastructure; whatever the implementation details, the result must be a vehicle for improving business performance.

Our approach to reconciling both the business and the technology manager's requirements is a decision process that explicitly recognizes the two domains—business and technology—and the evaluation of individual projects on both domain's needs. Further, our approach is to require participation in both domain evaluations by business and technology management. We introduced the two domain approach in Chapter Two and Figure 2.3, repeated here as Figure 16.1.

Our basic view is that Information Economics, in its evaluations, accomplishes the marriage of (1) change in the business as the basis of value and hence the basis of evaluation by business management; (2) a decision process causing evaluation and choice of projects on the basis of value and hence justification; (3) a planning process that introduces the necessary business vision about business opportunities; and (4) an overall process that implements this marriage.

As we know from Chapter One, Information Economics applies a decision framework that separates the *business justification* for information technology from the *technical viability* for the proposed application. Both are necessary, but the measurements and considerations are separate and should be determined separately. From the business perspective, justification is based on the project value compared to cost.

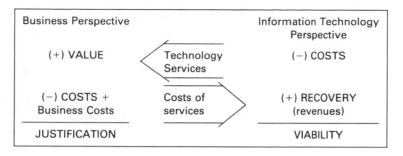

FIGURE 16.2 Basis for decisions.

Figure 16.2 demonstrates the perspectives which we more fully explored in Chapter One, Figure 1.1.

The separation into two perspectives allows evaluation of information technology value and priorities for the business distinct from the infrastructure, staff, and facilities required. The issues are different. As we noted in Chapter One, the source of **value** is the character of the business itself, which may not be so clearly definable in strict fiscal terms. True economic impact can be determined, and projects and investments considered and approved with confidence, by considering justification separately from technical viability. The objective is to assure that Information Economics in fact links business performance, the basis for value and thus justification, to the proposed information technology applications.

16–2 PLANNING AND DECISION PROCESSES

We've noted that, from all perspectives, three essential elements of planning and decision processes are needed: development ideas and projects, deciding which should be implemented, and actually implementing them. This is shown in pictorial form in Figure 16.3.

Bottom-up projects, generally alignment in character, are derived from individual user organizations. For example, the university controller's office believes it needs a new payroll system and an updated accounts payable system; the registrar believes a student records modification for pass-fail grades is necessary. The IS organization wishes to upgrade the student accounting system with a relational database. Top-down projects, often impact in character, are derived from an enterprise planning process, a strategic or long-range planning process. For example, the university has a task force on school and department productivity. This group has produced a long-range plan for administrative infrastructure which includes many systems projects intended to improve each school's management performance. Another effort is an enterprise-wide library systems project intended to integrate the ten now separated library bibliographic records systems. A third effort is an explicit attempt to modify the marketing and recruitment strategy for

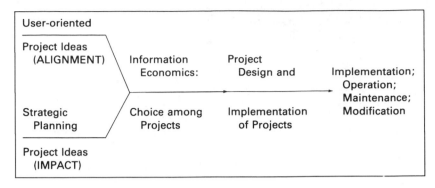

FIGURE 16.3   Planning and decision process.

the university by interconnecting the admissions office with many first-rank secondary schools. Finally, the IS department foresees the need for an information center requiring the installation of several software systems.

The examples given are typical in that several projects are identified in the various ways described. Some are bottom-up in the sense that they derive from individual user organizations; some are top-down in the sense that they derive from an enterprise-wide planning process. The result is a set of candidate projects:

> Library Card Catalog Integration
> Admissions Communications Network
> Information Center Systems
> Payroll System
> Accounts Payable System Upgrade
> Student Records Pass-Fail System
> Instructional Support System

We assume the university cannot afford to undertake all seven projects. So we have to decide which is most important for the institution. We need to rank the projects and hence choose the most important. The structure of the decision process for doing this, of course, is the issue here.

16–3 THE ADDITION OF VISION

How does the process occur? Where does **vision** come from? Through our Enterprise-wide Information Management Joint Study (Benson and Parker, 1987) we have looked at a number of institutions and companies. We have observed one overriding commonality in planning success stories—the successful application of information technology in a company is a complex process of vision through execution. In each case, four different and distinct, but related, things occurred:

Agreement on the future: business and technology VISION	→	Development of the business IDEAs for information technology application	→	Business and information technology PLANNING and DECISIONS about applications, projects	→	Successful EXECUTION of the business and information technology plans

The four elements are the basis for success in information technology planning methods to produce innovation. Articles, books, and to a large extent, consultants' practices, tend to focus on developing *either* the vision-to-idea phase *or* the planning-to-execution phase, but not both together. All four phases need careful attention and are a part of the success stories we and others have studied and reported.

The state of the art is a planning process that clearly provides **all** four planning elements. The character of planning processes can be described:

	VISION	IDEAS	PLANNING	EXECUTION
Purpose	Define Fundamental Business Direction and Priority	Create new ideas for use of information technology	Architectures; Justification Applications; Decisions	Project tasks and schedules
Typical Planning Tools	Business strategy Portfolio analysis	Critical success Factors Customer resource life cycle	Information Economics Information technology blueprints Enterprise-wide data models	Action plan; Project plans

An early Enterprise-wide Information Management report looked at twenty-five planning methodologies (Benson and Parker, 1985). Many planning methodologies use many of the tools and vocabularies represented by the four elements (vision-to-execution). The distinction is on the degree to which the planning methodology *develops* the results as compared to *describing* them. For example, critical success factors can be useful in describing the current business condition. They can also be useful in developing a new understanding of new opportunities. It is the difference between impact and alignment planning.

State of the art in planning is based on methodologies that can produce **new** insight and useful results in all four areas.

So much for the planning part. The purpose is to put in place the role of Information Economics. We emphasize that Information Economics is a decision process and not an idea process, which comes from planning. Nevertheless Information Economics depends on having a planning process in place to produce the ideas, the projects, about which decisions are to be made.

16–4 AN EXAMPLE

All this, of course, sounds pretty academic. What really matters is getting something done in a real organization. The test isn't the academic elegance of such a process, but rather whether the process produces real results. The following process summarizes what one single line of business company actually does. A simple example of a planning and decision process in use at Keep-On Trucking has previously been presented (Figure 16.4).

This is an example from a mid-sized company on how planning and decision processes can be development and applied. The success of a particular planning and decision process appears to rest on the simple question will the process derive ideas for the application of IT? Seek out IT opportunities? Make the best choices about alternatives? Get the right managers involved in decision-making?

To illustrate what happens when the process does not accomplish these objectives, one consultant wrote the following about his client's organization, Keep-On Trucking.

> An aura of indecision and uncertainty about the future course of computing exists in the organization. This aura is both of substance (what is to be done?) and of process (how will it be decided what is to be done?). This aura prevents short-term progress in making important decisions and implementing new systems. This uncertainty creates an environment that reinforces organizational perceptions about computing; the aura breeds the suspicion that no plan exists to address the many compelling needs. In part because of the uncertainties, there is a strong sense of parochialism in each organizational unit.

In a second engagement, the same consultant wrote:

> The Critical Success Factor for this company is the effective development of computer applications. To this end, the following strategy should be adopted: (1) Stimulate the line

---

Keep-On Trucking's Process for Large Projects

I. Project Initiation. An annual project plan for large systems development projects is prepared in conjunction with the corporation's annual business planning and budgeting process. A memo is sent to all departments requesting proposed project. Projects deemed necessary by the blueprint of the information systems plan may be added to the candidates.

II. Planning. The finance department reviews benefit statements for accuracy and consistency, and corporate planning assists.

III. Requirements. During this stage, the specific user requirements are determined and alternatives for meeting them are considered. Upon closer examination in the requirements phase, a project may also fall below the cut-off point for approved projects due to higher costs and/or lower benefits than previously estimated.

IV. Development/Implementation. User-driven project steering committees monitor the progress of approved projects.

V. Evaluation. Evaluation reviews are conducted on selected projects as part of the post-implementation process.

FIGURE 16.4 A simple planning and decision process.

management in all organizational units to define, recognize, and motivate application systems opportunities; and (2) communicate effectively to management the opportunities and directions for application development.

The message here is the emphasis on the critical role played by planning processes leading to the application of Information Economics.

16–5 COMPANIES *ARE* DIFFERENT

We've consistently used the term *line of business* to represent the element of the company related to strategy and performance. For example, Old Ivy University has four lines of business (undergraduate, professional education, research, and health care). The concept of line of business is helpful in describing strategy and describing the management planning and decision processes needed to carry out strategy and make effective decisions about information technology.

Many companies consist of just one core line of business. For example, a small liberal arts college (SmallTown College) is built around a core of undergraduate education. Similarly, a retail organization is built around a core of retail stores selling to similar customers. Keep-On Trucking is an example of a single line of business company; its core business is the shipment of materials for its customers.

It is useful to describe a company with multiple lines of business as a *diversified* company. Generally for such companies a corporate management provides various corporate services; for example, human resources management and payroll activities are commonly managed at the corporate management center. The term *backbone system* has grown out of such centralized administrative functions. To such a company, the single common payroll system is one such system.

Single line of business companies such as Keep-On Trucking differ among themselves insofar as strategies, products, markets, and customers are concerned. Generally, however, they are similar in that there is no essential difference between corporate management and line of business management. Plans and decisions made at the corporate level are indistinguishable from plans and decisions made at the line of business— there is only one set of individuals involved, and their perspective of the company itself and of the core line of business is identical.

In many ways, a single line of business company can be considered the same as a division or business unit in a diversified company. Keep-On Trucking, for example, could be acquired by, say, a larger company such as American Airlines and operated as a division of that company. This would add a corporate level of planning and decisions.

We note that such a company can have several layers of planning and decision processes:

- Planning leading to resource allocation among its units.
- Planning leading to adoption of strategies for a unit.
- Planning leading to the justification for investments in information technology.

Again, in a single line of business company these levels are essentially indistinguishable. For a diversified company or one with multiple divisions or units, however, we observe that business strategic planning has two quite separate elements. First, there is the sort of planning that Richard G. Hamermesh describes in *Making Strategy Work* (1986). This planning focuses on the allocation of resources—investments, really—across an enterprise's lines of business. The purpose of this level of strategic planning is to determine how best to apply the enterprise resources across the lines of business. We will follow Porter's lead and call this *corporate strategy* (see Porter, 1987). The second class of strategic planning looks at each line of business to consider *business strategy:* product, customer, market, basic competitive strategies. An important source for this class of planning is Michael Porter's book *Competitive Advantage* (1985), which introduces the concept of **line of business** (LOB) as the critical point of analysis for business strategy.

Both corporate strategy (represented, for example, by portfolio planning) and business strategy are major parts of planning for information technology. In effect, the concepts of portfolio planning, such as used at General Electric (Hamermesh, 1986), can govern the allocation of corporate resources, of which information technology is one potential claimant. Second, as we noted in Chapter Four, we have found the line of business and its Value Chain exceptionally helpful in organizing thoughts and processes in information technology planning.

16-6 HOW COMPANIES DIFFER: IS AND LINE-OF-BUSINESS SUCCESS

Companies plan, for business strategy, around lines of business (LOBs) or strategic business units (SBUs). Examples of ways in which MIS planning must be a part of the SBU strategy abound. To state that strategic responses to the current highly competitive business climate must include MIS planning is to state the obvious; however, most companies still have not adopted the means to integrate the MIS and business planning processes.

This problem of integrating, or fitting, the process is one that begins in the corporate culture. The corporate culture determines whether there will even be a formal process, its degree of rigor, and the form it will take. This issue of fit is also a function of the form of organization employed. Figure 16.5 shows that this generally takes one of several forms.

Obviously there are other possible combinations of organizations and decision-making—for example, multiple LOBs with centralized corporate decisions—but the

Decision Process as Organization Fit		
Line(s) of Business (LOB)	Location of MIS Resource	Location of MIS Decisions
Single	Corporate	Corporate
Multiple	LOB	LOB
Multiple	Corporate	LOB

FIGURE 16.5 How companies differ.

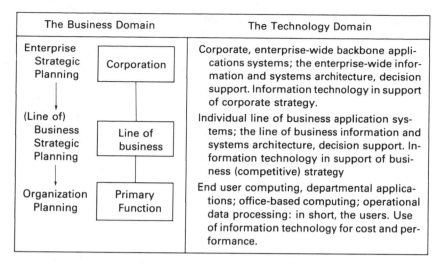

The Business Domain		The Technology Domain
Enterprise Strategic Planning	Corporation	Corporate, enterprise-wide backbone applications systems; the enterprise-wide information and systems architecture, decision support. Information technology in support of corporate strategy.
(Line of) Business Strategic Planning	Line of business	Individual line of business application systems; the line of business information and systems architecture, decision support. Information technology in support of business (competitive) strategy
Organization Planning	Primary Function	End user computing, departmental applications; office-based computing; operational data processing: in short, the users. Use of information technology for cost and performance.

FIGURE 16.6   Where companies differ.

ones shown in Figure 16.5 are predominant. The key point is that the predominant form of MIS resource allocation decisions is by the line of business, regardless of whether the company is in single or multiple lines of business, or of whether the IS resource is decentralized by LOBs or centralized at the corporate level.

By placing the business and technology domain together, we get an appreciation of the problem facing managers on both sides (Figure 16.6).

Companies differ at all levels of the enterprise. As we have previously observed, Old Ivy University with its four core lines of business has quite distinct corporate strategy and corporate-level planning as compared to SmallTown College, a liberal arts school in the Midwest. Both are quite different from Keep-On Trucking, which has one trucking-based core business, and BEAM Parcels, which also has one core business.

Yet the planning activity throughout the enterprise, at each of the three levels, is always parallel in the business domain and the technology domain. More to the point, in all enterprises, planning for each domain **requires interaction** with the management from the other domain. **Companies** differ in structure, management complexity and organization, and level of complexity in lines of business but the **planning activities** that lead up to Information Economics can be similar. In fact, we will see that a major component of Information Economics is the way in which the particular character and values of a company are reflected in the values used in the decision processes.

We will resolve the differences between companies with scorekeeping—the basis by which management places value on its activities—and not with process. We will look at weighting and values and at the ways in which a management applies values to the many lines of business involved.

Processes may be different. Planning processes don't have to be identical between companies. What planning has to accomplish, however, is always the same: *vision* to *ideas* to *planning* and *decision* to *execution*.

16-7 DEVELOPING A PLANNING AND DECISION PROCESS

We risk convincing the reader that this chapter is about planning. It isn't, but Information Economics is significant within some form of a planning activity. A method to create the alternatives among which choices have to be made is necessary, and this method is usually a strategic or long-range planning method. Therefore we discuss planning.

Companies commonly have in place a planning process for information technology. It may be informal, meaning the IS director interacts with user management and senior executives and, in the process, develops the agenda for development and investment. The process may be formal with steering committees, long-range hardware and software plans, and data and communications architectures.

From a *results* perspective, an enterprise should work toward a planning and decision process that produces some or all of Figure 16.7.

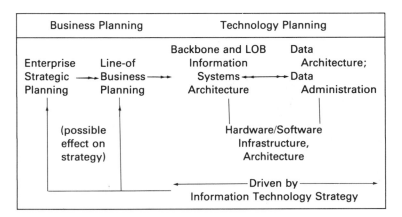

FIGURE 16.7   Planning results.

16-7-1 Conceptual Plan for Putting Together a Process

Figure 16.7 shows a set of planning results and relationships possible in a particular enterprise. Such processes are needed and should be linked. The challenge is to define the appropriate relationships. The results of the planning and decision process are in five categories:

- Enterprise strategy
- Line of business strategies
- Information systems architectures
- Hardware and software infrastructure and architecture
- Data architectures and data administration

Our interest is the planning and decision *process* that produces such results— meaning the activity that creates the projects to define the five products *and* implement them. In particular, we're interested in the application of Information Economics to determine which specific alternatives, in each of the five areas, should be implemented.

16–7–2 Common Planning and Decision Process Characteristics

Although companies are different, a planning process must have common characteristics to adequately drive the decision process.

Project oriented. A planning process should produce a series of application and infrastructure projects rather than a large, monolithic, undifferentiated plan. Appropriate decisions can be made trading off projects against available resources. More pertinently, value can be demonstrated to the line of business and company affected. We acknowledge the critical role of architectures and blueprints to guide technical planning and implementation. These are important tools, but are not the same as planning, and justifying, and communicating to management about each step needed to do them.

Recurrent (perhaps annual) cycle. A planning and decision process must meet two complementary challenges. First, business conditions and requirements change. Second, management awareness of and agreement with current priorities may change and may need reassurance. Further, implementation cycles and time frames have decision points and milestones. Underneath it all is the notion that management needs constant education and development about information technology, and technology management needs constant education and development about business requirements. A recurrent cycle planning process is the appropriate vehicle. Of course, this is usually consistent with other management and planning practices at a particular company.

Limited enterprise resources. We assume that the company or institution does not have unlimited resources. This is, incidentally, one of the flaws of current practices in planning. Approaches that tie project approvals to a hurdle rate or some similar return on investment concept give the impression that the enterprise has infinite resources and the manager merely needs to demonstrate the necessary return to obtain approval. In fact, this is never the case. So a process of priorities is much more appropriate and effective, and emphasizes the crucial linkage to *value* to the business.

Quantifiable decision-making criteria. Management has a bias toward the measurable. Decisions are much more easily sustained when a case can be made on the basis of measurements. We argue that traditional measurements based on ROI cannot adequately deal with information technology investments, but that does not reduce the value of a process that is quantifiable in terms of values and costs and risks.

These are characteristics of the decision process. There are similar appropriate characteristics of the combined planning and decision process.

Consensus. Companies, especially diversified companies with multiple lines of business, consist of a great number of people and organizational units. They all vie for attention and resources. Generally it is better to seek consensus among the largest number of interested people, particularly because of the complexities and multiple interests that can be affected.

Consensus across multiple groups. The value of a consensus-seeking process is particularly valuable where resources are allocated across lines of business. In the constant struggle for resources, forging alliances and creating communities of interest are always better than beating contemporaries over the head with successful appeals to senior management. This sounds naive and trite, but as a condition for success in complex organizations, it is true. Interestingly, this principle is a useful guide to setting values for projects as well. That is, projects that provide *real* value to the enterprise often link multiple units together in common cause. Porter talks about linkages between elements of the value chain as one source of opportunity; he also talks about sharing across lines of business as a potent force for effective corporate strategy (Porter, 1985).

Commonality with other planning processes. We have adopted the sort of planning characterized by the Keep-On Trucking example specifically because it corresponds in many respects to the planning processes used by strategic planning professionals and expected by senior managers. Much of Information Economics, in risk assessment and innovation, is drawn from work done by investment bankers in their assessment of new venture opportunities. The major lesson is that key planning techniques are business based (such as capital planning and new venture assessment) and not technology based. Again, we acknowledge that planning tools such as enterprise-wide data models and data flow diagrams are necessary, and that architectures are an important outcome of planning. Nevertheless, in terms of effectiveness with the real audience—business management—commonality with tools they are familiar with and find useful is paramount.

16–8 DEFINING THE PLANNING PROCESS

We offer seven tests to judge the effectiveness of planning and decision processes.

THE DECISION PROCESS:

1. Project oriented
2. Recurrent (perhaps annual) cycle
3. Assumes limited enterprise resources
4. Uses some form of quantifiable decision-making criteria

THE PLANNING PROCESS:

1. Drive to consensus among differing management functions
2. Drive to consensus across management groups
3. Operates in ways similar to capital budgeting; achieve commonality with corporate management experience, vocabulary, and concepts from capital budgeting and new venture assessment

The key is an emphasis on communication between technology and business domains and persuasion of management about the allocation of scarce corporate resources to the appropriate information systems projects.

16–9 RECOMMENDATIONS FOR PLANNING PROCESSES

Finally, we provide some details that may be helpful in more complex organizations. We offer these recognizing that they may not apply to every organization and that we may be leaning too far into the planning process domain. Nevertheless, we have observed the following criteria for success in establishing a planning and decision process.

1. Backbone (corporate systems) can be planned as a line of business from the information technology perspective.

2. Investment in the backbone is determined by the value of such investment to business performance in the lines of business. This is, we understand, perhaps at variance with traditional views of cost and performance in the overhead function of the business. This isn't to say that backbone activities aren't important *if* they are core areas to the business. Nevertheless, the concept of assessing and evaluating investment based on second-order business value to the individual lines of business remains appropriate.

3. Architectures may exist separately for individual lines of business distinct from the corporate architectures. This is a potential value to lines of business.

4. Corporate cultures are likely different in each LOB. An example is a company that has LOBs chiefly serving government and LOBs with commercial work.

5. There is complexity and difference from company to company based on the dominance of the backbone in the planning processes. This may be the most significant in terms of differences from company to company. This is particularly true when the IS activity is a captive of one element of the corporate backbone (for example, accounting and finance). This will skew the perceptions of value, which further emphasizes the need for the sort of planning and decision processes described here (but may be harder to accomplish).

Understanding what is important is essential to an understanding of the decision-making process. For example, diversified companies tend to make decisions by line of business, and the resulting process needs to follow these lines also. If an executive-level information systems steering committee is to be used to make resource allocation decisions, multiple steering committees and decision processes will most likely need to be established in a company with multiple lines of business. The process or mechanisms used will remain the same, but will be replicated as necessary.

16–10 SUMMARIZING PLANNING AND DECISION PROCESSES

We want ultimately to focus on the decision process itself. We have shown how making decisions is intertwined with the planning process that creates the choices. As such, we want to establish the appropriate process that emphasizes some of these points:

1. A decision process for deciding between alternative investments
2. A decision process that gets line of business management involved; gets the management that makes fiscal investment decisions involved; and makes decisions based on business performance
3. A decision process that seeks out the opportunities
4. A framework for the implementation of the opportunities. This is the role of the IS blueprint and architectures and an implementation that includes:

   bottom-up project planning,
   steering committees,
   consensus,
   IS blueprint,
   and IS architecture

16–10–1 Hurdles in Developing a Planning and Decision Process

It seems easy, perhaps. However, real hurdles of substantial proportion can confront the manager in carrying out the critical role.

- The need to obtain management support for change. Management can be blind to the opportunities, resistant to change, or bound up in politics.
- Resistance to change by all concerned. No one likes change to their job or organization!
- Lack of personal knowledge. The business manager may not be confident of the technology nor the changes needed.
- Getting the IS executive's attention. The IS group can be preoccupied with other problems.
- The inadequate enterprise business plan. There may not be a plan!

These are real problems. The approach to overcoming them is based on defining objectives and establishing strategy.

16–11 ADDING INFORMATION ECONOMICS TO THE DECISION PROCESS

Our view of the planning and decision processes is as follows:

	Bottom-up Projects	Choices: DECISIONS	Plans: execution	
Strategic Planning	Top-down Projects	among projects	of projects	VALUE

The *decision process* part should result in evaluation of individual projects, whatever their source. To support this, we have developed the evaluation process described in

Part Two of the book. Here, we have described considerations in developing a planning process that culminates in decisions. In the next chapter we will discuss the matching of the decision criteria to the specific organization.

QUESTIONS

1. What is the difference between bottom-up and top-down projects?

2. We define characteristics of planning and decision processes:

   The Decision Process:

   1. Project oriented
   2. Recurrent (perhaps annual) cycle
   3. Assumes limited enterprise resources
   4. Uses some form of quantifiable decision making criteria

   The Planning Process:

   1. Drive to consensus among differing management functions
   2. Drive to consensus across management groups
   3. Operates in ways similar to capital budgeting; achieve commonality with corporate management experience, vocabulary, and concepts from capital budgeting and new venture assessment

   Regarding the card catalog project at Old Ivy University, what would be an example of good planning and decision processes for each of the factors, and what would be a bad example of planning and decision processes?

3. How is the decision process complicated when the IS organization serves multiple lines of business?

4. What actions can management take that reduce the complexity of the decision process?

5. What actions might management take that add complexity to decision and planning processes?

6. The success of a particular planning and decision process appears to rest on the simple question, Will the process:

   Derive ideas for the application of IT?

   Seek out the IT opportunities?

   Make the best choices about alternatives?

   Get the right managers involved in decision making?

7. What can management do to create a process that satisfies these requirements?

8. What can management do to create a process that fails in each of the four requirements?

17

Applying Information Economics in a Corporate Setting

We have presented an in-depth examination of a series of concepts whose relationships to each other become readily apparent in a corporate environment. BEAM Parcels will be the vehicle for this study. Although the line of business for BEAM is fictitious, both the cases previously presented and the situation and process in this chapter are based on the experience of an actual company. We first describe the current situation at BEAM and the decision process managers there employ. After an information systems project call, we apply Information Economics to rank the proposed projects. The process of determining the investment priorities is the culmination of Information Economics.

17-1 SITUATION

The current information systems organization at BEAM is a traditional and largely centralized organization. It is also very much a local operation, with little attention paid to out-of-state requirements. Out-of-state processing activities are largely limited to the Sun Belt, and operate independent of the computing activities located in California.

Little attempt was made to integrate the out-of-state systems activities into an overall systems, data, and communications architecture.

The apparent problems inherent in the centralized, largely local information services function located within a regional company were exacerbated when BEAM Parcels established independent divisions as separate profit centers. The managers heading these divisions required systems support tailored to their individual priorities and needs and either received it through the corporate information systems department, or else acquired it on their own.

The technology employed, both inside and outside California, was outdated. To maintain and provide for growth would become an increasing problem. In California, the central mainframe computers were of an older vintage and needed to be replaced by newer equipment. The independent out-of-state data processing activities relied on older minicomputers combined with personal computers of relatively recent vintage. No attempt was being made to determine the proper overall hardware and communications architecture and how it should relate to systems and databases.

Before the selection of the new head of the information systems department, an in-depth study of office automation opportunities at BEAM was commissioned at the instigation of the president. He had read an article in a business magazine on the benefits of office automation and felt that BEAM should evaluate the possibilities. The study was conducted and reached some surprising conclusions. The consultants reported that BEAM was not ready for widespread use of office automation technology and that no broad-ranging program should be started until major problems were resolved. Among the problems identified by the consultants were:

1. The information systems department is incapable of supporting office automation at BEAM. It lacks the needed technical skills, management leadership, and organizational linkages with the company.

2. Data processing applications hold more potential for bottom-line impact than office automation, but there is no comprehensive, approved plan to upgrade the data processing systems and integrate them with office automation.

3. Although office automation opportunities are substantial, the need for better data processing and management information systems is much greater. BEAM should move decisively to upgrade the mainframe data processing systems that support its operation. Although BEAM's business is moving and delivering packages, it is very much driven by, and dependent on, information. If data processing is upgraded with the office automation effort, the impact of better information systems on BEAM will be dramatic and far-reaching.

The consulting company made clear in their report that they considered only California requirements. Noting that the existing information systems environment epitomizes the traditional centralized approach and that BEAM operates in four states, they concluded that this is an outmoded, inappropriate information systems configuration.

The first step toward resolving these problems comes with their recognition and a determination to address them. BEAM recognized that problems existed, and management was determined to address them. The concepts, goals, and priorities outlined in the following scenario were developed at BEAM and received the endorsement and commitment of senior management. Through a collective effort, they were successfully implemented. Through our description of how they ran this process, we will concurrently describe a successful application of the Information Economics process.

17–2 STRATEGIC ISSUES

The president had read "An Unmanaged Computer System Can Stop You Dead" in the *Harvard Business Review* (Allen, 1982). Based on that article, he identified four important strategic issues that required the focus of senior management: organizational design; control of IS, MIS, and IT; architecture of information; and technology architecture.

17–2–1 Organizational Design

The first strategic issue to be raised was organization. How should information systems be organized? BEAM needed to determine how information services should be deployed within the company, and what role the information systems department would play with respect to divisional or regional departments.

Today, the central organizational question for many large companies is how to distribute information resources. This was also the key strategic question in the deployment of information services at BEAM, as it is for many organizations who must now decentralize more of the responsibility for information systems than they have in the past. End-user facilities, decision support systems, information centers, and many of the new nonprocedural systems all require more decisions by users. Yet many of these newer technologies depend on databases and other centrally managed technology.

17–2–2 Aspects of Control of IS, MIS, and IT

The second and a related element of computer strategy at BEAM was control. Top executives must establish who will control which aspects of information resources, how control will be effected, and how and by whom performance will be assessed. Chief issues include:

1. Who plans and approves applications and sets priorities according to what criteria

2. Who selects and approves new technology and on what basis

3. How outside sourcing decisions (and all make-or-buy decisions) are made and by whom

4. Where and how costs are collected and charges rendered

5. Who sets corporate-wide standards and policies and how they will be enforced

Again, this takes us back to the centralization versus decentralization issue, as we must decide which decisions and processing will take place centrally, which will take place locally but be managed centrally, and which will be processed and managed locally. BEAM chose a middle road for their IS organization, decentralizing some responsibilities, but keeping their centralized IS function robust. In this organizational mode, a centralized information systems function shares responsibility with the various users for the primary decisions. A high-level steering committee usually addresses the policy and control questions.

17–2–3 Architecture of Applications and Data

The next strategic issue facing BEAM was to determine the blueprint or master plan for information systems applications. This grand design must decide:

1. What the major data collections will be

2. How they should be related, if at all

3. What types of application systems will feed and draw on these collections

4. How the application systems will be related

The same pressures that lead a company to decentralize functions (e.g., improved response to customers and to changes in market conditions, delegating responsibility to lower levels of the organization) also are reflected in computing, because data flows and information requirements generally mirror a company's organizational structure. Yet the decision is not simple. The data architecture must address what data should be localized, accumulated with data from other divisions, or stored at corporate headquarters. The applications architecture must address which functions to automate, their scope, the use of shared systems, and the mix of traditional data processing, information reporting, and decision support applications.

17–2–4 Technology Architecture

The final strategic issue is to determine the proper architecture of hardware and communications networks—where should it be located and how should it be tied together. Additional issues include:

1. The proper mixture of large host computers, minicomputers, and microcomputers

2. The geographic site of the technology

3. The technological plan for office systems

4. Which software concepts to use for operating systems, communications, databases, and programming

These are the strategic issues facing BEAM, its competitors, and other companies doing business today. The senior management of BEAM decided to address the questions through a policy-making steering group that cut across divisional and departmental lines. The management steering committee at BEAM plays an important role throughout the process. The committee is composed of key members of BEAM's senior management team. The management steering committee is advised of and approves each of the major policy issues along the way and makes the final resource allocation decisions.

17–3 GOALS FOR INFORMATION SYSTEMS

Besides addressing the strategic issues with senior management, the information systems department needed to establish goals and develop plans. With the information systems department now leading the process, senior management at BEAM decided that the primary goals for information systems would be to:

1. Provide high-quality, dependable information systems support. This meant helping the user in identifying opportunities, delivering well-managed projects, and meeting commitments. It also meant moving systems and processing functions closer to the user wherever possible.

2. Organize and protect the corporation's data resources as any other corporate asset and provide tools so that the user can access the data more readily. This is intended to accomplish two purposes: help the user satisfy requirements more readily and release skilled programmers for other tasks.

3. Identify and apply new technology that will give the company a competitive edge in the marketplace. This means that there will be an active search for new ideas and acceptance of the premise that a number of them may not be appropriate.

4. Develop a comprehensive plan for the architecture of the corporation's data, systems, and technology that will guide future development efforts. This will be the key to success, and its development and implementation will require the involvement and commitment of senior management.

The information systems department, with the concurrence of BEAM's senior management, determined that the steps needed to accomplish these goals were:

1. To revise and upgrade the organizational structure of the information systems department, and put in place the key team members who must plan and carry out the actions. This included establishing key functions that were missing, that is, technology planning, database planning and administration, security, control functions, and end-user computing and office automation services.

2. To decentralize or distribute some of these functions where it would improve the overall functioning and productivity of the department or division concerned. This was thought to be no small task, but it became the philosophy behind the subsequent planning efforts. Where doing so made sense, decentralization would occur along divisional lines within an overall integrating information systems structure. Behind this philosophy was an understanding that BEAM would need to determine which aspects or systems should be structured centrally, which located at a distance but designed and managed centrally, and which managed locally. BEAM knew it would also need to decide how and where to link the activities.

3. To provide tools for end-users, along with end-user and office automation standards and educational programs. End-user computing and office automation activities needed to become part of the overall information systems plan. It was decided that the application of technology to the office and other end-user requirements would best be tested through pilot and demonstration projects. Selected sites would be used to demonstrate and evaluate these applications, and seed money would be needed for this purpose. Decisions on future investments would then be made by the individual departments or divisions.

4. To establish how and where different kinds of information systems policy and priority decisions that affect the company are made. This decision-making process required that BEAM establish an effective, policy-level steering group to serve as the ''Board of Directors'' (e.g., a management steering committee) for information systems, to establish company-wide policy, and to guide the overall planning efforts. For this, BEAM needed the personal involvement and commitment of the senior executives of the company.

5. To increase user involvement in information systems activities to improve the quality of information systems services. BEAM decided to establish user-driven processes in the form of user groups to prioritize and monitor systems and end-user activities at a level below the management steering committee, with direct user involvement in steering and managing individual projects.

6. To address the long-range information systems planning needs through a concerted effort that linked the planning for computing to the direction of the business. This included examining various technological architectures (such as database, communications, applications portfolio, and decentralized computing networks) as well as the business strategies for the use of computing for competitive advantage. The product of this planning effort was to be the development of a blueprint for applications and databases that would guide BEAM's future information systems development. This would require an in-depth evaluation of BEAM's automated systems and databases, a framework or structure for the desired environment, and the associated technology to support it.

17-4 TIMING

It was understood at the outset that this was a long-term process. Although benefits will increasingly accrue as progress is made on the overall plan and its implementation, expecting a short-term payoff from this investment would be a mistake. The construction of an information systems plan with a blueprint of the appropriate data, systems, and technological architecture will require upwards of one year. However, it should not begin until the technological planning, database design, and end-user and office systems organization has been established. The time required to redesign the systems and databases will vary with the level of resources employed, but will require several years in any event. Although the corporation will certainly receive near-term benefit from individual applications and office automation projects, this must clearly be viewed as a long-term investment decision. With these understandings outlined in the scenario, BEAM's steering committee adopted a twelve-month action plan as proposed by information systems. They focused on the blueprint development to improve their decision-making process.

17–5 BEAM PARCELS MIS BLUEPRINT: TARGET ARCHITECTURE ORIENTATION

During the year, intense effort was devoted to the development of the blueprint. We present here the fundamental concepts and principles that guided the design of the information systems blueprint (target architectures) for databases and systems. We also present the rationale used to determine the technology infrastructure for these database and system implementations.

17–5–1 Conceptual Foundation of the Information Systems Architecture

An enterprise is fundamentally seen as operating at the operational level to realize its mission, and at the management level to guide the operational activities (Figure 17.1).

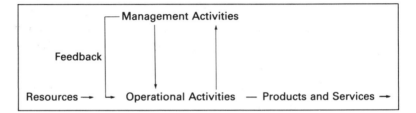

FIGURE 17.1 Two levels of activity within the enterprise.

The information systems of an enterprise automate the processing and storage of data and automate the accessing and manipulation of the accumulated data.

The accumulated data in Figure 17.2 is a representation of the operation of the business. This data is necessary (frequently in an automated form) to perform certain aspects of operational activities, such as scheduling drivers and trucks. Some operational activities would be hindered if automated data were not available.

There are three facets to *management* of an enterprise: operational planning, operational control, and strategic planning. These management facets require access to accumulated operational data and may also require data from external sources (for example,

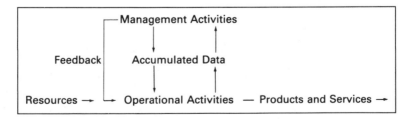

FIGURE 17.2 The operation of the enterprise.

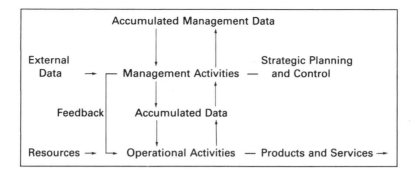

FIGURE 17.3 Facets of management within the enterprise.

data on the competition and the industry). These points lead to the refinement of the model as shown in Figure 17.3.

Ideally, information systems should correspond to the enterprise's activities. So, it is useful to work from a general model of the enterprise's *business activities* to guide the design of the information systems architecture.

17–5–2 BEAM Parcels Business Activity and the Information Systems Architecture

The business activities performed at BEAM Parcels (Figure 17.4) can be grouped into strategic decision-making, planning, operational, and control activities.

BEAM is presented in Figure 17.4 as providing services to the world in which it operates. In providing these services, it utilizes resources, specifically people, money, and material, just as most companies.

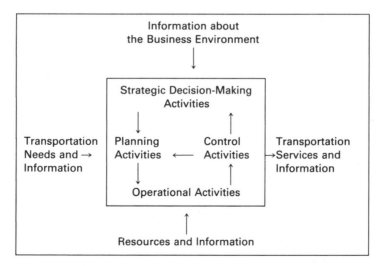

FIGURE 17.4 Business activities within the enterprise.

At the strategic level, BEAM has had to decide:

- What geographic markets it will service with what product types
- With what transportation capacity and what support facilities
- With an estimate of the revenue of the former and cost of the latter, what corporate profit can be expected from a given strategy.

These strategic decisions require information about the business scope of the local and regional package delivery industry, BEAM's performance in the industry relative to competitors, and BEAM's alternatives on how it may deploy its resources and structure its costs.

BEAM's operational activities can be successful only if the resources used in performing them are properly deployed and organized. Thus BEAM management performs *planning activities.*

Planning activities set targets according to criteria defined by the strategic decision-making activities. In addition, knowledge about the specific resources available and the performance of day-to-day operations is required for effective planning.

The planning activities establish how to implement strategic decisions and how to deploy the given resources. In BEAM, these activities provide:

- Volume and revenue targets for specific products in specific markets
- Transportation schedules to satisfy these volumes
- Plans and cost targets in support of the transportation schedule for vehicles, driver teams, fuel, maintenance services, and warehouse operations
- Plans and targets for support resources

BEAM Parcels management also carries out *control activities* to measure its operational performance and provide information to the planning activities. This leads to the redeployment of resources and/or adjustment to targets.

In the current changing business environment, strategic decision-making activities and new and modified planning and control activities are required. If BEAM wishes to broaden its scope of service, experiences significant changes in market needs (as in the recent case with the deregulation of the transportation industry), or experiences changes in the competitive mix (as in the case of BEAM Parcels largest customer now becoming one of its largest competitors), BEAM must review and redefine the set of needs it will attempt to satisfy.

Operational activities deal with the production and delivery of products or services prescribed by the enterprise's mission (Figure 17.5). To understand the relative importance of activities with respect to achieving the mission of the enterprise, the operational activities can be subdivided into core, support, and accounting.

1. *Core* activities are involved in the direct realization of BEAM Parcels mission. They include such things as selling capacity, handling shipments, and scheduling trucks.

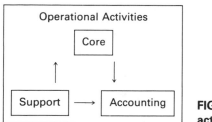

FIGURE 17.5 Operational activities.

2. *Support* activities are concerned with the provision of supporting resources needed by the core activities. They include such things as equipment maintenance, spare parts inventory, and facilities maintenance.

Accounting activities describe the core and support activities in financial terms. These include the operation of the general ledger financial reporting system.

Figure 17.6 includes this dimension into the earlier (Figure 17.5) diagram of BEAM Parcels activities.

This structuring of the activities of BEAM Parcels should be mirrored by its information systems: information systems that automate and/or support the activities in the strategic decision-making, planning and control, and operational activities of the business.

Within the operational activities, systems will automate data flows of either core activities, support activities, or accounting activities.

To be successful, *information systems must be imbedded into the organization* at all levels. Information systems can provide access to data and automated processes for all human "doers of activities" and mechanical "doers" (such as scanners, code readers, and robots).

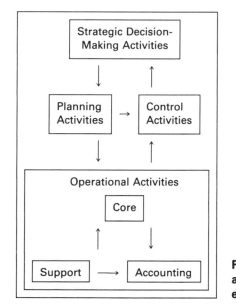

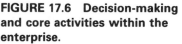

FIGURE 17.6 Decision-making and core activities within the enterprise.

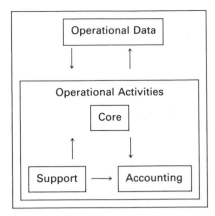

FIGURE 17.7 Operational memory of the enterprise.

Operational activities collect data at the lowest level of detail, for example, customer zip code, subshipment movement, and fuel consumed per delivery route leg. The accumulation of this data represents the operational memory of the business (Figure 17.7).

Automation of operational activities must both accumulate (capture) data and use data accumulated by other operational activities.

Automated planning and control activities also need to use operational data. Planning and control activities need to establish their own accumulated data, for example, summarized operational data, data resulting from what if analysis, and external data about competitors and the industry. These data are captured by the planning and control (and strategic decision support) activities themselves.

Strategic decision support activities also need access to the accumulated management data. A composite of this is represented in the Figure 17.8.

In summary, the desired objective of the blueprint information systems and databases is an integrated database of operational data, serving as the source for all planning, control, and strategic decision-making activities.

It is the responsibility of the operational systems, further classified as *core, support* and *accounting,* to maintain the operational database, which is a snapshot of the enterprise in operation at any moment in time.

The planning, control, and strategic decision support systems may retain the results of operational data aggregations and manipulations for specific reference needs. This would constitute a repository of planning and control data derived from the operational database—the information of the enterprise.

Also, the management activities will collect environment-related data needed for planning and strategic decision-making support.

BEAM's blueprint focused on two levels of activity: operational and managerial. The managerial activities were broken into operational planning, operational control, and strategic planning. They broke the business activities into strategic decision-making, planning, operational, and control activities. With these breakdowns or classifications, the management steering committee, the users, and the information systems department could begin to speak the same language. They began to grapple with issues such as how each system could complement another, and how some systems, although not

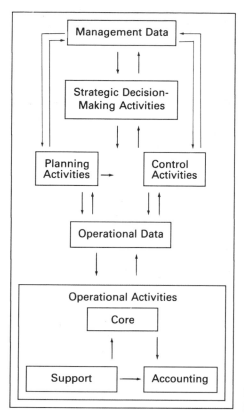

FIGURE 17.8 Strategic management memory of the enterprise.

directly linked, were prerequisite to others. As a result, a sense of common priorities began to emerge. This created an environment in which a new decision-making process could be introduced.

17–6 DECISION-MAKING PROCESS

Next they focused on the decision-making process itself. BEAM decided that their annual resource allocation process must recognize and be guided by a long-range view of systems and data architecture. Within this long-range plan, the near-term or annual resource allocation plan would be open to the needs of the business. It would provide for bottom-up initiatives from the business units that would represent opportunities for systems development. This was, in effect, both a bottom-up approach to identify new projects and a top-down architecture for fitting the proposed projects into a cohesive plan. The timing of the annual plan produced as a result of this process was on a parallel timetable so as to be a part of the annual corporate planning and budgeting process.

Potential projects need to be fitted into the overall architecture. In fact, one of the technology domain factors evaluates the degree to which each project fits. The context for this overall, top-down, architecture plan, was BEAM's architecture blueprint.

17–7 THE PROJECT CALL

With the blueprint in place, BEAM turned its attention to the bottom-up identification of projects for development. They felt that it was important before soliciting the projects to develop and receive concurrence on the criteria to be used in evaluating the candidate projects. The criteria were established by corporate planning and approved by the management steering committee. The criteria may change from project call to project call, depending on areas of emphasis in the corporate business plan. For example, in a constrained economy, short-term ROI may take precedence. On the other hand, long-term management information support may be more important to the more financially secure company.

17–8 TRANSLATING THE CORPORATE STRATEGY INTO THE WEIGHTING SCHEMA

BEAM Parcels is a company whose strategy is based on product differentiation. Although they are in a very cost-competitive industry, they are not planning to compete solely on the basis of cost. Additionally, they are attempting to become a full-service provider serving as many markets as are economically attractive. As a result, ROI will not be the dominant factor in the weighting, to the exclusion of all others. They decided to have the maximum project score equal to 100 as a base. Based on the corporate strategy, the corporate planning department determined the relative value of the categories in which the project candidates were to be evaluated. The results are shown in Figure 17.9.

Each factor is assessed with a score ranging from 0 to 5. Most factors are positive, adding to the desirability of the project. Several are negative, detracting from the desirability of the project; these are indicated with a *minus* maximum score.

Once the weights for the scoring criteria were established to the satisfaction of the management steering committee, a project call was announced. This provided the opportunity for all interested departments to propose candidate projects for development.

In response to the project call, the seven projects that have been previously discussed were submitted. This set of projects is meant to represent a microcosm of the results of a project call of this nature. In reality, a project call would typically result in many times this number of projects. (BEAM actually had over 100 projects to evaluate for its investment prioritization process.)

Once the projects are received, they are reviewed for consistency. They are scored by the previously agreed upon criteria, getting appropriate management signatures (representing concurrence and support) along the way.

The combination of the scoring and the weighting factors provides a project score that reflects not only simple ROI, but also other factors that BEAM management has decided are important to its future.

BUSINESS DOMAIN FACTORS:	Weight	Maximum Score
A. Economic Impact. The project rating depends on calculated simple ROI on the yearly net cash flows for a five-year period.	10	50
B. Strategic Match. The project is rated on the degree to which it is aligned with corporate strategic goals and objectives.	2	10
C. Competitive Advantage. This category reflects the degree to which the project facilities automated interorganizational collaboration or other competitive advantages.	2	10
D. Management Information. The score depends on the degree of management information provided for key corporate activities.	2	10
E. Competitive Response. This category reflects the corporate risk for NOT undertaking the project.	1	5
F. Project or Organizational Risk. This category is rated on the degree to which the system is dependent on new or untested skills, management capabilities, and experience.	−1	−5
TECHNOLOGY DOMAIN FACTORS:		
G. Definitional Uncertainty. This category measures the degree to which the specifications for the project are ill-defined and/or unapproved.	−2	−10
H. Technical Uncertainty. The project is rated on the degree to which the system is dependent on new or untested skills, hardware, software, and systems.	−2	−10
I. Strategic IS Architecture. The project is rated on the degree to which the system is aligned with the MIS and IT strategy, as reflected by the MIS and IT blueprints.	3	15
J. IS Infrastructure Risk. The project is rated on the degree to which technology domain investment in other prerequisite service or environmental facilities is required.	−2	−10
EVALUATION:		
Business Domain: Maximum Positive Score		85
Technology Domain: Maximum Positive Score		15
	TOTAL	100
Business Domain: Maximum Negative Score		−5
Technology Domain: Maximum Negative Score		−30
	TOTAL	−35

FIGURE 17.9 Project evaluation criteria and weighted values.

The weight from Figure 17.10 is then multiplied by the score of each factor. For example, the score of Project 1, automated rating, coding, and billing is found in Chapter Fourteen, Figure 14.8. The resulting product is shown in Figure 17.10. Each of the projects summarized in the previous chapter are weighted by the same process. The seven projects, their weights, and their weighted scores are shown in Figure 17.10. With the project scoring completed, BEAM ranked the projects and summarized their more significant aspects for consideration by the management steering committee. The resulting ranked list of projects shown in Figure 17.11 was presented to the management steering committee.

Evaluator	Business Domain						Technology Domain				Total Score
(weight ——>>)	ROI* +10	SM* +2	CA* +2	MI* +2	CR* +1	OR* −1	SA* +3	DU* −2	TU* −2	IR* −2	
Automated rating, coding, and billing #1	25	8	6	8	5	0	3	−6	−4	−2	(43)
Driver Pay System #2	15	8	0	4	0	0	3	−2	−2	0	(26)
Driver Scheduling (Phase 2) #3	45	10	4	6	4	0	12	−6	−2	0	(73)
Pharmacy Shipment Automation #4	25	4	10	6	5	−3	0	−8	−2	0	(37)
Customer Management Reporting #5	50	10	10	10	5	0	0	−6	−4	0	(75)
Bar Code Project #6	50	10	4	10	4	−2	15	0	−8	−6	(77)
Capacity Project #7	50	10	6	8	4	−1	12	0	−2	−8	(79)

where:
  ROI = Return on investment
  SM = Strategic match
  CA = Competitive advantage
  MI = Management information
  CR = Competitive response
  OR = Organizational or project risk
  SA = Strategic IS architecture
  DU = Definitional uncertainty
  TU = Technical uncertainty
  IR = IS infrastructure risk

FIGURE 17.10 BEAM Project scoring results.

Although these projects represent only a fraction of the number to be expected from a project call, they show a natural grouping. The top four were high in ROI (764–1890 percent). All four were perceived by the business domain as strategic and a competitive risk if not done. Three of the four were ranked by the business domain as high in management information, and by the technology domain as high in supporting the technology strategy.

The second tier projects were not without merit. However, taken as a group, the ROI was significantly lower (211–388 percent). Two of the three were viewed as strategic by business domain management and a competitive risk if not done. Even with many more projects, a tiering, or natural grouping, occurs.

Note in the first tier that the CMRS project would rank higher than the bar code

Rank #	Proj #	Project Name	Sponsoring Department	Cost to Develop	Average Annual Benefit	ROI %	Project Score	Other Risks and Benefits
				\$ 000's				
1	7	Capacity Project	IS	750	14175	1890	79	SM MI CR / SA IR
2	6	Bar Code	Operations	600	5798	966	77	SM MI CR / SA TU
3	5	CMRS	Marketing	55	795	1446	75	SM CA MI CR
4	3	Driver Scheduling	Operations	96	733	764	73	SM CR/SA
5	1	Automated rating, coding, and billing	Finance	247	943	382	43	SM MI CR
6	4	Pharmacy Shipment	Marketing	111	431	388	37	CA CR/DU
7	2	Driver Pay	Finance	37	79	211	26	SM

FIGURE 17.11 Ranked list of proposed development projects.

227

Rank #	Project #	Project Name	Sponsoring Department	$ 000's	
				Cumulative Cost	Cumulative Benefits
1	7	Capacity Project	IS	750	14,175
2	6	Bar Code	Operations	1,350	19,973
3	5	CMRS	Marketing	1,405	20,768
4	3	Driver Scheduling	Operations	1,501	21,501
5	1	Automatic rating, coding, and billing	Finance	1,748	22,444
6	4	Pharmacy Shipment	Marketing	1,859	22,875
7	2	Driver Payroll	Finance	1,896	22,954

FIGURE 17.12   Cumulative cost of proposed projects for BEAM.

project if the projects were judged solely on ROI. Likewise, in the second tier, pharmacy shipment would precede automated rating, coding, and billing based on ROI.

The information systems department reviewed the staff resources available to initiate some or all of these new projects. First, they set aside those resources needed simply to maintain and enhance existing systems, plus the resources required to complete development projects already underway. Some systems were no longer going to be maintained because of this review. Other development efforts would be suspended. They then determined (from Figure 17.12) that there would be sufficient resources to initiate only the first three projects on the ranking list. They decided to ask the management steering committee to authorize the first four ranked projects. Projects ranked fifth, sixth, and seventh would not be recommended, but could be reconsidered later.

Were finance and marketing satisfied with the decision? Yes, because they understood the process, had participated in the scoring, and could see that the projects being recommended for funding had greater benefit to BEAM Parcels than those they had nominated. They did, however, believe that perhaps a more appropriate ranking approach could be developed that would give more emphasis to the size of the investment required, rather than the return on investment. They all agreed to work on this problem over the next year, and have a solution in place prior to the next project call.

17–9 SOME FINAL THOUGHTS ON APPLYING INFORMATION ECONOMICS

The scoring process is designed to achieve a quantified measure of utility—the projects' value to the company. The resulting ranking must be developed not only on relative value (i.e., benefit) of each project, but also on the cost to achieve each measure of benefit. The examples shown in this book are simplified for the purposes of presentation. A more sophisticated application of these concepts needs to go beyond the examples and consider the following points.

Time Value of Money. The time value of money needs recognition, and this can be done in several ways. For example, a computation of return on investment (ROI) normally uses the internal rate of return (IRR) method, and not the simple ROI calculations used here. IRR is defined as the rate of return at which the discounted future cash flows equal the initial cash outlay. IRR is the discounted rate at which net present value (NPV) is zero. The value of IRR relative to the present value discount rate also indicates the desirability of the investment, e.g., if IRR is equal to the desired rate of return the investor is indifferent to the investment (HP-12c Owners' Handbook, 1986).

The time value of money is represented by using a present value (PV) calculation for the average annual benefits of a project, in lieu of simple average annual benefit used in the examples. The PV will use an assumed discount rate to more heavily discount those benefits that are relatively more distant in the future.

Cost-Value Ranking. An alternative and technically more correct method of calculating the economic score and the resulting overall project score and cost-value ratio of the proposed projects would be to first calculate the present value of the anticipated value stream of each project. The highest value is then set to equal the highest score given to the economic impact, and the other projects' present value benefits are scored relative to this benchmark project. For example, if we only had the following projects:

Reference Figure #	Project Number	Project Name	($000's) Benefit	($000's) NPV @ 10%	Revised Economic Score
10.8	1	Automated rating, coding and billing	4,715	3,604	5.0
11.7	2	Driver payroll	394	299	0.4
12.6	4	Pharmacy	2,156	1,634	2.3

Billing becomes the benchmark project, as its benefit (value) stream produces the highest NPV (i.e., $3,604,000). This thus receives a 5 as the score, as the economic scores of the other projects are set relative to the benchmark score.

When the economic score is computed on this alternative basis and is combined with the scores for the other evaluation categories, it results in an overall value total for each project that is independent of the cost of producing it. This score is then divided by the project cost to produce a ratio, which is the basis for producing the project ranking.

Order of Precedence. Sometimes one IS project is dependent on another, and the projects must be done in that sequence despite the fact that the value-sequenced rankings suggests that the first project ranks significantly lower than the second project.

This order of preference issue may be addressed in the value ranking process in one of two ways. First, the two (or more) interdependent projects may be combined and treated for ranking purposes as one project. Second, the projects may remain separate, with the linkages made explicit. When the ensuing project plans are developed, the lower-ranked project is included over higher-ranked projects, but the order of preference issue is acknowledged. Practitioners seem to prefer the latter way of handling the issue, as it preserves the integrity of individual projects.

Additional Risk Factors. There may be additional risks to be acknowledged in the analysis, beyond those discussed in previous chapters. For example, a projects' revenue stream may fluctuate with seasonal weather, e.g., sales of mittens in the winter, and a particularly mild winter might have a disastrous effect on sales. This "out of control" risk may be handled by attaching a probability to the risk factor(s). For example, one year in ten the winters will be particularly mild. This probability factor could be used to more conservatively estimate the projects' value.

Changing Weights. The weights attached to the project evaluation criteria can (and probably should) change from year to year. New areas of emphasis, or changing values will need to be reflected and the weights attached to each factor are the means for so doing.

Not-For-Profit Companies. The Information Economics principles are equally as applicable in the not-for-profit environment as they are for profit-making companies. A different set of values may be required in the not-for-profit company, as any difference in emphasis may be reflected by further changes to the weights attached to the project evaluation factors. Even the factors themselves could be amended to fit a particular situation, although this generally will not prove necessary.

QUESTIONS

1. Refer to Chapter Ten. There, BEAM Parcels automated rating, coding, and billing scored 504 percent simple ROI. Should the project have been submitted without the productivity package included? Why?

2. What approach would you advise to justify the investment in the productivity package?

3. If $150K additional funds were made available, what would be your strategy for projects currently ranked fifth, sixth, and seventh?

18

Summing Up Information Economics

Information Economics goes beyond traditional methods of evaluating information systems (MIS) projects that are usually based loosely on the return on investment capital budgeting model. We have examined other dimensions that we argue may have considerable long-term value to the firm and that are usually ignored by the traditional processes.

In this book, we introduced the ideas of Information Economics in three parts. Part One discusses the relationships that need developing to effectively link business performance and information technology. Part Two expands the concepts of cost-benefit analysis by adding four new methods of evaluating benefits and costs. It expands the concept of benefit to six classes of *value* of information technology, and introduces four classes of *risk*. Part Three applies these new concepts in a corporate setting. The result of this process is the ability to assign a value to each project's perceived contribution to corporate goals (Parker and Benson, 1986).

18–1 COST-BENEFIT ANALYSIS

Traditional cost-benefit analysis is no longer adequate for most applications that are innovative or that produce or enhance revenue. Nor is it completely adequate for justifying the long-term investments necessary for developing information architectures and infrastructures. Previous cost-benefit methods for evaluating investments dealt with discrete projects. These methods depend on a linkage directly to cost avoidance or cost displacement. Management now expects information technology to contribute to the success of a product or product line or to create a product that will be offered as a service by the line of business. These systems are most closely associated with LOB (and enterprise) success. They link to the bottom-line performance of the LOB, and they contain new elements of risk that are not addressed by the typical information systems proposal.

To address this wide range of investment opportunities in an even-handed manner, the justification process must expand to embrace new techniques to quantify the new risks, and the quantification techniques must be easy to use. Information Economics meets both demands. Its structure encompasses three categories of factors: economic impact quantifications, business domain assessments, and technology domain assessments. These factors combine to portray a true economic value for the project. The innovative, revenue producing or revenue enhancing applications designed to gain competitive advantage can then be prioritized along with investments in architectures, infrastructure support, and maintenance of current systems. The results of that prioritization must be intuitively obvious to the business domain manager during the decision-making process. Information Economics provides a taxonomy and action plan for this purpose by assuring that the information technology plans support the tactical, long-range, and strategic goals of the LOB and enterprise.

Managers using current methods rely heavily on some form of return on investment (ROI) to evaluate information systems projects. ROI has been popular because it matches the capital investment evaluation framework with which managers in industrial companies are familiar. We believe that capital budgeting techniques in addition to ROI should be applied to information systems projects, but that the traditional techniques by themselves are inadequate. Furthermore, the additional techniques we introduced, although under the heading of Information Economics, should also apply to the capital budgeting process and will further question the adequacy of that process as it is commonly practiced.

Even the commonly used return on investment calculation may require special consideration when applied to information systems (MIS) projects. The usual difficulties in carrying out this analysis—for example, choosing an appropriate discount rate and evaluating correctly all relevant investment alternatives—apply with special force to the consideration of such projects as an investment in computer-integrated manufacturing. MIS projects of this nature typically have a longer useful life than non-MIS projects and provide many additional benefits—such as better quality, greater flexibility, and technological expertise that can be leveraged into other strategic investments for competitive advantage—that the typical capital justification process does not begin to quantify.

Furthermore, MIS projects can extend the concepts of improved operational efficiency and functional effectiveness beyond the boundaries of a single firm. These interorganizational systems (IOS) are a new phenomenon (Cash and Konsynski, 1985). Using electronic data interchange (EDI) between companies, firms integrate their information-related activities (vertical information integration) and use these systems as part of their strategic plan. Methodologies of Information Economics can identify opportunities for interorganizational systems by viewing the unit of analysis as two (or more) organizations instead of one.

18–2 EMERGENCE OF INFORMATION ECONOMICS REQUIREMENTS

Two new concepts have emerged to be used as descriptors by the information systems professional: *competitive advantage* and *backbone architectures*. Competitive advantage (Porter, 1985) focuses on the competitive value of computing and information technology to the line of business and enterprise. Current marketplace pressures have led senior business managers to pressure their information systems managers to accomplish computer implementations that will gain competitive advantage. At the same time, greater attention has been focused on the backbone systems of the organization.

These two emphases pose difficult choices, particularly when resources available to managers are limited. How does one balance the maintenance of current systems with the support of new LOB or enterprise infrastructures, or investment in information architectures with the creation of competitive advantage applications for the line of business? How does one plan for computing that supports the business planning of the enterprise? How can one address the many associated problems in information technology and business in a cost-justifiable manner? The key is new techniques for financial justification that expand the concept of tangible costs and benefits and address truly intangible costs and benefits by building consensus.

18–3 COST AND EVALUATION TOOLS HAVE LACKED CONTEXT

CEOs and financial officers show little interest in state-of-the-art information technologies unless they demonstrate improved financial performance for the LOB or enterprise. Justification of an information technology application links to one of two conditions: either it improves performance of the current organization or it improves the outlook for new business opportunities and strategies (Benson and Parker, 1985).

Traditional cost-benefit analysis (Chapter Eight), based on easily measurable and tangible benefits, presents a limited view of the costs and benefits of information availability within the enterprise. The new Information Economics context must assess benefits previously not thought to be quantifiable. The quantification must be demonstrable to be accepted by executives in the business domain and the CEO. Information Economics works to achieve cost and benefit quantification through *communication* and *consensus* between and among the business and technology domains of the enterprise.

For example, Appleton (1986), who has written extensively on information resource management, proposes an asset-based life cycle model for information systems. He believes that basic changes should occur in the way that information systems are justified and managed. First, information systems should be managed as the assets they are. Second, information systems should be as financially justified as assets in procurement and development. This concept of *asset* helps define the problem Information Economics seeks to solve, for ROI works to define costs and benefits as a current period impact on net current cash flows. To achieve an *asset* perspective on information systems requires basic changes in the way information systems are currently justified.

New techniques supplement the traditional cost-benefit approach. By focusing on cost and performance, they demonstrate new value that can be added to the LOB. The combination of techniques ranges from traditional cost displacement to evaluating risk and uncertainty associated with gaining and sustaining competitive edge. It embraces both alignment- and impact-oriented applications. All ROI calculations must link to and support the spectrum of strategic information technology applications. The boundaries are traditional cost-benefit analysis techniques and innovation valuation. We also use value acceleration, value linking, and value restructuring.

18–3–1 The Techniques

Information Economics uses several financial justification techniques to assess potential information technology applications as input to simple ROI calculations. They are traditional cost-benefit analysis, value linking, value acceleration, value restructuring, and innovation valuation.

Traditional cost-benefit analysis and architecture-based cost-benefit analysis fit most easily with the views of financial planners. They support the traditional views of the business domain for capital investment and consumption. It is useful for supporting tactical plans. The technology manager can apply his or her enterprise's method of justifying long-term capital investment to architecture- and infrastructure-based projects. (This is successful if technical management knows business strategy and has information systems strategy, master plan, and blueprint in place to support the firm.)

Value linking and value acceleration analysis (Chapter Ten) are techniques to assess costs that enable benefits received by other departments. This can occur via a ripple effect (value linking), or by causing benefits to be received more quickly (value acceleration), accelerating a measurable effect on the bottom-line performance of the line of business or enterprise. Both approaches are rooted in economics rather than in business finance.

Value restructuring analysis (Chapter Eleven) assumes that because a function exists within an organization, it has some recognized value. Like value linking and value acceleration analysis, the basis for value restructuring is economic theory. The model assists in estimating the effects of modifying an existing job function. By restructuring employee or department efforts from lower- to higher-value activities, the value of the employee or department contribution increases. This technique is useful when direct linkage to bottom-line performance is obscure or not established. Research and development, legal, and personnel departments are examples because they are support functions of the LOB or enterprise.

Several financial justification techniques for developing a simple ROI for alignment applications have been introduced. For displacing costs, traditional and architecture- and infrastructure-based investment techniques are best. If costs are not displaced, value linking, value acceleration, and value restructuring techniques are more appropriate.

Innovation valuation (Chapter Twelve) is applied when the financial issues change from measuring to evaluating and choosing among new, untried, and unproven alternatives. It is useful for new, unprecedented applications of information technology, because it considers the value and benefit of gaining and sustaining competitive advantage, the risk or cost of being first, and the risk or cost of failure. It is applied to functions of the LOB or enterprise Value Chain involving innovation.

Value acceleration, value linking, and value restructuring are additive approaches

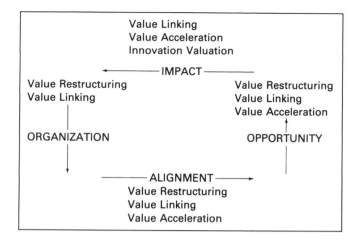

FIGURE 18.1   The Enterprise-wide information management planning and financial justification process.

to gain better insights into both costs and benefits of information technology applications. We have used innovation valuation in an attempt to size the impact of new ventures for information technology, we have associated these ROI supplementary techniques with the appropriate planning processes (Figure 18.1).

The goal is to be better able to develop rational investment priorities for decision-making among *all* of the investment alternatives. Thus an enterprise is successfully able to make the business perform better, make the business compete more effectively, differentiate the business, or add market share, that effectively supports the business strategy with information technology.

Simple ROI calculations encompass both alignment and impact applications. Alignment-oriented applications of information technology focus on off-the-shelf software (through functional packages and linked databases) and have limited technical risk. The risk that does apply is the ability of the management and technical team to apply proven information technology practices. Impact-oriented applications of information technology aimed at gaining competitive advantage focus on prototypes and custom software. They have high risks both technically and organizationally, because success requires innovation and invention.

All of these techniques are additive to traditional cost-benefit analysis (see Figure 18.2). Risk and uncertainty and competitive edge are added to the ROI calculation. The simple ROI calculation and assessments of other factors beyond cost-benefit factors in the business and technology domain are assessed. The sum of these evaluations

Traditional Cost- Benefit	+	Value Link- ing	+	Value Accel- eration	+	Value Restruc- turing	+	Innovation	=	Input to Simple ROI Calculations

FIGURE 18.2   Information economics techniques for developing simple ROI calculations.

| Simple ROI (BENEFITS | + | Business Domain (Assessment) | + | Technology Domain (Assessment) | = | VALUE |

FIGURE 18.3 Factors for computing the project value.

becomes the means of ranking alternative information technology projects (see Figure 18.3).

18–4 SHIFTING FROM BENEFITS TO VALUES

The fundamental impact of information technology is the change it causes in the competitive strength and capability of the business. For example, a company that invests in its back office (its infrastructure) does so to reduce unit operating costs, enable future growth, and add to its capacity to manage the business. The investment strengthens the company and may be a source of competitive advantage. The investment adds value to the enterprise.

The source of **value** lies in the character of the business itself and is commonly not definable in strict fiscal terms. For example, we have read about the "information economy." This idea is based on the increasingly complex and powerful capabilities of information technology that provide substantial value to the enterprises that use it. Commentators forecast a new competitive order based on information and information-based services: information becomes the foundation of competition. Consequently the basis for planning and justifying information technology projects must reflect the new value of information to the business (Chapters One and Three).

As a result, Information Economics works to measure and justify the value of information technology based on the business and not the technology, and based on effect on business performance and not just previous concepts of benefit. True economic impact can be determined, and projects and investments considered and approved with confidence, by considering justification separately from technical viability. The challenge to managers is to assure that Information Economics in fact links business performance—the basis for value and thus justification—to the proposed information technology applications (Chapters Two and Seven).

We define *value* as the true economic impact of information technology, and *process* as the means a company uses to make its decisions about information technology investments. Underneath it all is an undercurrent of change. First, we propose that the real benefit of information technology results from change in the business. Information technology changes products, markets, management styles, and organizational structures. Without change there is no benefit (Chapter Four). Second, we propose that the ways a company plans and manages IT and MIS also change, particularly in its decision-making about priorities and investments in its infrastructure (Chapter Five). Finally, we propose that the **use** of IT and MIS should be directly linked to its impact on business performance (Chapters Six, Seven, and Seventeen). To us, this is the key to Information Economics. Without a link, information technology is irrelevant. With it, information technology becomes a powerful tool with which management can improve economic performance and hence the overall strength and vitality of the organizations for which they are responsible.

18–4–1 Challenges for Information Economics

The problem we address with Information Economics is the traditionally limited view of economic benefits. Rather, the appropriate focus is on value.

A company gains value from information technology in diverse ways. The idea of **value**—the 'benefits' in cost-benefit analysis—originated with cost reduction. We have expanded the idea of value to include **six classes of value:** enhanced ROI, strategic match, competitive advantage, management information, competitive response, and strategic IS architecture.

Enhanced ROI. (Chapters Eight through Twelve). The measurement of this factor is through the simple ROI calculation result, employing value acceleration, value linking, value restructuring, and innovation valuation.

Strategic Match. (Chapter Thirteen). The strategic alignment dimension assesses the degree to which the proposed project corresponds to established corporate strategic goals. This dimension emphasizes the close relationship between MIS planning and corporate planning and measures the degree to which a potential project contributes to the strategy. Projects that are an integral and essential part of the corporate strategy will be assigned a higher strategic alignment score than those projects which are not, regardless of the return on investment (ROI) calculations. Obviously, there are many ways to obtain a favorable ROI; however, there is a cumulative effect of obtaining the ROI *and* moving toward a broader corporate purpose. This dimension assesses the value of moving toward that long-term direction (and implicitly requires its existence).

Competitive Advantage. (Chapter Thirteen). The competitive advantage dimension assesses the degree to which the proposed project provides an advantage in the marketplace—such as, interorganizational collaboration through electronic data interchange. Michael Porter identifies three basic objectives that a company must achieve if it is to gain a competitive advantage, and this dimension measures the extent to which a project contributes toward these goals (Porter, 1985).

1. Alter the industry structure. The project must change the degree to which buyers, suppliers, new entrants, and substitutes or rivals influence competition.

2. Improve the organization's position in its existing businesses. In general, this measures the extent to which a project can differentiate a company's products or services, or change the competitive scope of its business.

3. Create new business opportunities. Under this heading, a project can contribute to competitive advantage in several ways, including the sale or use of information as a by-product of the current business and the use of internal information processing capability to start a new line of business.

The competitive advantage dimension requires that we place a value on a project's contribution to achieving one or more of these objectives.

Management Information. (Chapter Thirteen). This assesses a project's contribution to management's need for information on **core activities:** efforts involved in the direct realization of the firm's mission, as distinguished from support and accounting activities. Support functions supply resources such as spare parts inventory and truck maintenance to the core activities. Accounting activities translate the core and support functions into financial terms.

The ability of management to make informed decisions is important to all companies. Measuring a project's contribution to the *core* activities of the business implies that the company has identified its critical success factors. Measurement of this dimension is obviously somewhat subjective because improved management information is an intangible, but the benefit measurement can be improved if the company first defines those core activities that are critical to its success, then selects a general strategy to address these issues.

Competitive Response. (Chapter Thirteen). This dimension assesses the degree of corporate risk associated with *not* undertaking the project. Although similar to the concepts of both opportunity cost and competitive advantage, this dimension also measures the risk of losing the market share that, once lost, may be difficult or impossible to recover later. This dimension looks at timely implementation of an information systems project as a possible preemptive move to prevent the competition from gaining a foothold.

Strategic IS Architecture. (Chapter Fourteen). This dimension measures the degree to which the proposed project fits into the overall information systems direction. It assumes the existence of a long-term information systems plan—an architecture or blueprint that provides the top-down structure into which future data and systems must fit.

Each of the value classes has an underlying basis for its value to the company, and Information Economics recognizes this with an appropriate measurement. For example, a truck leasing company obtains new competitive impact from a system that improves the route and service station information provided to its customers. This system neither reduces costs nor creates revenues, yet has a profound impact and hence adds value to the company's competitive position. Information Economics provides methods to measure the worth of such a system to the company.

18–5 VALUE AS AN ALTERNATIVE TO INTANGIBLE BENEFITS

The classes of value provide the appropriate methods to assess the importance of benefits previously classed as intangible. In the traditional methods, simple ROI calculations represent an attempt to quantify as much as possible. Nevertheless, simple ROI alone cannot represent all of the factors that management must consider in the investment decision-making process. Quasi-tangible benefits are most often cited in support of alignment projects (Parker, 1982). Value restructuring and value acceleration techniques are a way of quantifying some, but not all, of these benefits. Value, with its six categories, links all forms of benefits to business performance. This measures the true economic impact of information systems, a true basis for value.

18–6 ADDRESSING THE PROBLEM OF RISK AND UNCERTAINTY

Fully defining value isn't enough to make the best choices among information systems projects. We also need to consider the full dimensions of cost. Just as Information Economics looks beyond benefits to value, it looks beyond simple costs to risk and uncertainty.

Information Economics recognizes four classes of risk and uncertainty, organizational risk, IS infrastructure risk, definitional uncertainty, and technology uncertainty.

Organizational Risk (Chapter Thirteen). This category measures the degree to which an information systems project depends on new or untested corporate skills, management capabilities, and/or experience. Although a project may look attractive on other dimensions and the technical skills may be available, there may be an unacceptable risk associated with the project if other required skills are missing. It also focuses on the extent to which the organization is capable of carrying out the changes required by the project, that is, the user and business requirements. This does not include the technical organization, which will be measured on another dimension.

IS Infrastructure Risk (Chapter Fourteen). This measure evaluates the degree of nonproject technical support investment necessary to accomplish the project. It is essentially an environmental assessment, involving such factors as data administration, communications, and distributed systems. It measures the degree to which the entire IS organization is both required to support the project and prepared to do so. A project that requires the support of many functional areas is inherently more complex and difficult to supervise; it depends on factors that may not be under the direct control of the project manager.

Definitional Uncertainty (Chapter Fourteen). Generally, this criterion assesses the degree of specificity of the user's objectives that are communicated to the information systems project personnel. Essentially another measure of risk, this dimension associates the potential to obtain objectives with the specificity in which they can be expressed. Projects lacking proper definition or firm specifications will be assessed a penalty associated with their uncertainty.

Technical Uncertainty (Chapter Fourteen). This evaluates a project's dependence on new or untried technologies. It may involve one or a combination of new technical skill sets, hardware, or software tools. A project may be inherently risky if it requires introduction of an untried technology.

18–7 A DECISION-MAKING PROCESS

How do managers successfully choose between alternative investments?

The problem is complicated. Some investment decisions improve the infrastructure: the mainframe computer, a collection of personal or departmental computers, a communications network, the database and systems development software. These investments create the *capability* for many individual application projects, much as a manufacturing building and its utility and heating systems provide the infrastructure for the production of a company's product lines. Other investment decisions are between individual projects. Should we install an order-entry system or a marketing intelligence system? Both infrastructure and application project decisions are ultimately priority decisions: Which of the many possibilities are the best and deserve support?

Information Economics has been developed to give management the tools to answer the question. The tools include new definitions for cost and benefit, explicit consideration of the potential of failure through risk, and a comprehensive yet simple decision process to rank projects and make investment decisions.

At one level, Information Economics is simply a collection of computational tools to rank benefits and costs for information technology projects. This is the traditional role of cost-benefit analysis (CBA). However, Information Economics looks beyond CBA to deal with projects that have previously been difficult or impossible to handle, such as those that have strategic impact on the company. Information Economics also looks at supply side investment in the infrastructure.

At a second level, Information Economics is a new conceptualization of the decision-making process (Chapters Fifteen and Sixteen). Every proposed investment—programmer, application, hardware—should be justified, but every potential investment has unique characteristics. Resource allocation means choosing among alternative investments. For example, should we install a relational database management system, buy the Financial Reporting System, or hire a personal computer support professional? The bases for *discriminating* among alternatives is extremely difficult to determine. Yet managers must regularly make these decisions. Our purpose is to expand the set of economic tools beyond CBA to embrace competitive advantage and infrastructure and at the same time provide guidance to the decision-making process itself.

Information Economics applies a decision framework that separates the *business justification* for information technology from the *technology viability* for the proposed application. Conceptually, this is a crucial distinction. Both are necessary, but the measurements and considerations are different and should be determined separately. From the business perspective, justification is based on project value compared to cost. There are two key questions. The first is, What is the project worth to the business? From the technology viewpoint, viability is based on the project resources available compared to the resources needed to provide the services. Therefore, the second is, Does the business have the resources to complete the project? Does it have the resources to overcome all of the identified risks and uncertainties associated with the proposed project?

Separation into two perspectives allows evaluation of information technology value and priorities for the business as distinct from the infrastructure, staff, and facilities required.

New Information Economics tools help to define value (Chapters Eight through Fourteen), and we also, more importantly, create an Information Economics *decision process* (Chapters Fifteen through Seventeen). The process develops a measure of value and an understanding of costs and potential sources of failure or risk. In addition, the process creates consensus among management groups. The evaluation covers both business feasibility—value and effect on business performance—and technical viability, including risk analysis. By grading feasibility as perceived by each of the affected management groups, Information Economics helps to develop consensus and enhance each group's awareness of the others' concerns and evaluations.

Information Economics provides a persuasive tool for analyzing and allocating resources to support business strategy and performance. Information technology has the potential of being a fundamental force in reshaping the business world. It is crucial that every manager be able to determine the value of information technology in his or her organization.

APPENDIX A

Glossary of Accounting Terms

Breakeven month The month in the analysis that the positive cumulative cash flow equals the negative cumulative cash flow. Also known as the pay back month.

Discounted cash flow The after-tax cash flow discounted from the payment date back to the present value date, using the discount rate defined by the user. For BEAM Parcels, the consultant defined the rates.

Expensed A cost that is accounted for at the time it is incurred.

Fiscal year The twelve month period for record keeping, accounting, and tax purposes. The fiscal year does not have to coincide with the calendar year.

Future value (FV) The future value of money today plus accrued interest.

Internal rate of return (IRR) The rate of return on an asset investment. IRR is calculated by finding the discount rate that equates the present value of future cash flow to the cost of the investment.

Payment timing Payments can be made in advance or arrears. Payments made in advance are due on the first day of a month. Payments made in arrears are due on the last day of the month.

Present value The value today of a future payment, or stream of payments, discounted at the specified discount rate.

APPENDIX B

Generation of Monthly Cash Flows

Internal Rate of Return.   The internal rate of return (IRR) is the rate, between zero and 100, at which the addition of the discounted after-tax monthly cash flow equals zero.

Present Value.   Present value (PV) is the worth of money today for the cost of future expenditures. For example, $100,000 two years from today has a PV of $82,645 based on annual compounding and a discount rate of 10%.

$$
\begin{array}{ll}
\text{Year 1} & \$82645.00 \times 10\% = 8264.50 \\
 & \underline{+\ \ 8264.50} \\
\text{Year 2} & \$90909.50 \times 10\% = 9090.95 \\
 & \underline{+\ \ 9090.95} \\
 & \$100000.45
\end{array}
$$

Future Value.   The inverse of PV is Future Value (FV). $100,000 is the two year FV of $81,940 today for monthly compounding with a discount rate of 10%. The discount rate is .10 divided by 12 (.008333) and the frequency of compounding is 24 (12 months times 2 years).

$$FV = 81940 \times (1 + .008333)^{24}$$
$$= 81940 \times 1.008333^{24}$$
$$= 81940 \times 1.2204$$
$$= 99{,}999.58$$

Calculations. To calculate the monthly PV, we:

1. Require the following user specified information:

Discount start date: Typically, the discount date is the same as the analysis start date. However, the discount date can be any date within the analysis period.

Discount rate: We can either use the industry discount rate or use an approximation (about one half the cost of borrowing money).

Monthly expenditures: Each expenditure occurs in a specific month. For example, the down payment for a Purchase acquisition occurs in the month of purchase. A lease charge would occur in the month of acquisition and each month for the term of the lease.

Payment timing: For the following calculations, we discount payments made in advance in the month of expenditure. Payments made in arrears are offset by one month, as if they were made one month later.

2. Find the monthly discount rate, discount factors, and multiply the factors by the FV.

Finding the monthly discount rate: We find the monthly discount rate by solving for I in the standard FV formula:

1. $FV = PV (1 + I)^N$

2. $\dfrac{FV}{PV} = (1 + I)^N$

3. $\sqrt[N]{\dfrac{FV}{PV}} = 1 + I$

4. $\sqrt[N]{\dfrac{FV}{PV}} - 1 = I$

For example, if we have a 12% after-tax discount rate, the monthly discount rate would be:

$$I_{Monthly} = \sqrt[12]{\dfrac{1.12}{1.00}} - 1 = .94887929\%$$

With a discount factor of 12%, $1.00 today would be worth $1.12 in exactly 12 months. The monthly discount rate which, after compounding, yields $1.12 in 12 months is .94887929%.

Note that we calculate monthly factors using the 12th root. This reflects an accurate 12% discount rate. An annual percentage of 12% does not yield a monthly percentage of 1%. A 1% monthly discount rate compounded 12 times yields an annual rate of 12.682%, not 12%.

Finding the discount factors: With the monthly discount rate determined, the basic formula is rewritten as follows to find the monthly discount factors:

$$PV = \left[\frac{1}{(1 + I)^N} \right] \times FV$$

The discount factor is the quantity 1 divided by $(1+I)^N$.

With a discount rate of 12%, I = .94887929% or .009887929% and $1 + 0.009887929 = 1.009887929$.

The monthly discount factors are:

Month		Factor
0	$\dfrac{1}{1.009887929^0}$	1.0000
1	$\dfrac{1}{1.009887929^1}$	.9906
2	$\dfrac{1}{1.009887929^2}$	.9813
3	$\dfrac{1}{1.009887929^3}$	.9712
4	$\dfrac{1}{1.009887929^4}$	.9629

Multiplying factors by FV: We now calculate the PV. The discount factors are multiplied by the monthly FV expenditures (down payments, lease charges, etc.). The FVs used are the after-tax monthly cash flow. The monthly amounts generated are summed for each fiscal year. These numbers are called the *discounted cash flow.*

Reports. The discounted cash flow and the cumulative discounted cash flow appear in the cash flow report that follows. The Monthly Cash Flow report displays detailed discounted cash flow information. For each month in the analysis, the following information is displayed separately for expenditures paid in advance and those paid in arrears:

Nondiscounted cash flow times Factor equals discounted cash flow (non-discounted cash flow times factor)

Also, the combined advance and arrear nondiscounted and discounted cash flows are displayed.

The assumptions for BEAM Parcels Automated Rating, Coding, and Billing are:

- The analysis and the report period are from 1/YR1 through 12/YR6.
- Discount rates are 4.50 in YR1, 5.00 in YR2, 6.00 in YR3, 6.50 in YR4, and 7.00 in YR5 and YR6.
- No taxes of any kind are included in the calculations.
- Costs and benefits are:

Cost/Benefit	Growth Rate	Mo	Yr	Amount	Mo	Yr
Cost:						
Development	Compounded monthly	1	YR1	14,200	1	YR2
Testing	Compounded monthly	7	YR1	1,743	1	YR2
Operations	Compounded monthly	1	YR2	1,743	1	YR2
Benefit:						
Labor savings	Compounded monthly	1	YR2	10,417		

- All payments are made in arrears (at end of month).

MONTHLY CASH FLOWS

BEAM Parcels (A') Automated Rating, Coding, and Billing

ANALYSIS PERIOD 1/YR1 THROUGH 12/YR6
REPORT PERIOD 1/YR1 THROUGH 12/YR6

FISCAL YEAR-END:	DEC	YR1	YR2	YR3	YR4	YR5	YR6
MOS IN REPORT		12	12	12	12	12	12
DISCOUNT RATES		4.50	5.00	6.00	6.50	7.00	7.00

	ADVANCE			ARREARS			ADVANCE AND ARREARS	
	NON-DISC. CASHFLOW	FACTOR	DISC. CASHFLOW	NON-DISC. CASHFLOW	FACTOR	DISCOUNTED CASHFLOW	NON-DISC. CASHFLOW	DISC. CASHFLOW
YEAR 1								
JAN	0	.0000	0	14,200	.9963	14,148	14,200	14,148
FEB	0	.0000	0	14,200	.9927	14,096	14,200	14,096
MAR	0	.0000	0	14,200	.9891	14,045	14,200	14,045
APR	0	.0000	0	14,200	.9854	13,993	14,200	13,993
MAY	0	.0000	0	14,200	.9818	13,942	14,200	13,942
JUN	0	.0000	0	14,200	.9782	13,891	14,200	13,891
JUL	0	.0000	0	15,943	.9747	15,539	15,943	15,539
AUG	0	.0000	0	15,943	.9711	15,482	15,943	15,482
SEP	0	.0000	0	15,943	.9675	15,425	15,943	15,425
OCT	0	.0000	0	15,943	.9640	15,368	15,943	15,368
NOV	0	.0000	0	15,943	.9605	15,312	15,943	15,312
DEC	0	.0000	0	15,943	.9569	15,256	15,943	15,256
TOTALS	0		0	180,856		176,497	180,856	176,497

	ADVANCE			ARREARS			ADVANCE AND ARREARS	
	NON-DISC. CASHFLOW	FACTOR	DISC. CASHFLOW	NON-DISC. CASHFLOW	FACTOR	DISCOUNTED CASHFLOW	NON-DISC. CASHFLOW	DISC. CASHFLOW
YEAR 2								
JAN	0	.0000	0	−8,674	.9485	−8,227	−8,674	−8,227
FEB	0	.0000	0	−8,674	.9447	−8,194	−8,674	−8,194
MAR	0	.0000	0	−8,674	.9408	−8,161	−8,674	−8,161
APR	0	.0000	0	−8,674	.9370	−8,128	−8,674	−8,128
MAY	0	.0000	0	−8,674	.9332	−8,095	−8,674	−8,095
JUN	0	.0000	0	−8,674	.9294	−8,062	−8,674	−8,062
JUL	0	.0000	0	−8,674	.9257	−8,029	−8,674	−8,029
AUG	0	.0000	0	−8,674	.9219	−7,997	−8,674	−7,997
SEP	0	.0000	0	−9,674	.9182	−7,964	−8,674	−7,964
OCT	0	.0000	0	−9,674	.9144	−7,932	−8,674	−7,932
NOV	0	.0000	0	−8,674	.9107	−7,900	−8,674	−7,900
DEC	0	.0000	0	−8,674	.9070	−7,868	−8,674	−7,868
TOTALS	0		0	−104,088		−96,555	−104,088	−96,555
YEAR 3								
JAN	0	.0000	0	−8,674	.8857	−7,682	−8,674	−7,682
FEB	0	.0000	0	−8,674	.8814	−7,645	−8,674	−7,645
MAR	0	.0000	0	−8,674	.8771	−7,608	−8,674	−7,608
APR	0	.0000	0	−8,674	.8729	−7,571	−8,674	−7,571
MAY	0	.0000	0	−8,674	.8686	−7,535	−8,674	−7,535
JUN	0	.0000	0	−8,674	.8644	−7,498	−8,674	−7,498
JUL	0	.0000	0	−8,674	.8603	−7,462	−8,674	−7,462
AUG	0	.0000	0	−8,674	.8561	−7,426	−8,674	−7,426
SEP	0	.0000	0	−8,674	.8519	−7,390	−8,674	−7,390
OCT	0	.0000	0	−8,674	.8478	−7,354	−8,674	−7,354
NOV	0	.0000	0	−8,674	.8437	−7,319	−8,674	−7,318
DEC	0	.0000	0	−8,674	.8396	−7,283	−8,674	−7,283
TOTALS	0		0	−104,088		−89,772	−104,088	−89,772
YEAR 4								
JAN	0	.0000	0	−8,674	.8235	−7,143	−8,674	−7,143
FEB	0	.0000	0	−8,674	.8192	−7,106	−8,674	−7,106
MAR	0	.0000	0	−8,674	.8149	−7,069	−8,674	−7,069
APR	0	.0000	0	−8,674	.8107	−7,032	−8,674	−7,032
MAY	0	.0000	0	−8,674	.8064	−6,995	−8,674	−6,995
JUN	0	.0000	0	−8,674	.8022	−6,958	−8,674	−6,958
JUL	0	.0000	0	−8,674	.7980	−6,922	−8,674	−6,922
AUG	0	.0000	0	−8,674	.7938	−6,886	−8,674	−6,886
SEP	0	.0000	0	−8,674	.7897	−6,849	−8,674	−6,849
OCT	0	.0000	0	−8,674	.7855	−6,814	−8,674	−6,814
NOV	0	.0000	0	−8,674	.7814	−6,778	−8,674	−6,778
DEC	0	.0000	0	−8,674	.7773	−6,743	−8,674	−6,743
TOTALS	0		0	−104,088		−83,293	−104,088	−83,293
YEAR 5								
JAN	0	.0000	0	−8,674	.7586	−6,580	−8,674	−6,580
FEB	0	.0000	0	−8,674	.7543	−6,543	−8,674	−6,543
MAR	0	.0000	0	−8,674	.7501	−6,506	−8,674	−6,506
APR	0	.0000	0	−8,674	.7459	−6,470	−8,674	−6,470
MAY	0	.0000	0	−8,674	.7417	−6,433	−8,674	−6,433
JUN	0	.0000	0	−8,674	.7375	−6,397	−8,674	−6,397
JUL	0	.0000	0	−8,674	.7334	−6,361	−8,674	−6,361

ADVANCE			ARREARS			ADVANCE AND ARREARS	
NON-DISC. CASHFLOW	FACTOR	DISC. CASHFLOW	NON-DISC. CASHFLOW	FACTOR	DISCOUNTED CASHFLOW	NON-DISC. CASHFLOW	DISC. CASHFLOW
AUG 0	.0000	0	−8,674	.7292	−6,326	−8,674	−6,326
SEP 0	.0000	0	−8,674	.7251	−6,290	−8,674	−6,290
OCT 0	.0000	0	−8,674	.7211	−6,255	−8,674	−6,255
NOV 0	.0000	0	−8,674	.7170	−6,219	−8,674	−6,219
DEC 0	.0000	0	−8,674	.7130	−6,184	−8,674	−6,184
TOTALS 0		0	−104,088		−76,565	−104,088	−76,565
YEAR 6							
JAN 0	.0000	0	−8,674	.7090	−6,150	−8,674	−6,150
FEB 0	.0000	0	−8,674	.7050	−6,115	−8,674	−6,115
MAR 0	.0000	0	−8,674	.7010	−6,081	−8,674	−6,081
APR 0	.0000	0	−8,674	.6971	−6,047	−8,674	−6,047
MAY 0	.0000	0	−8,674	.6932	−6,013	−8,674	−6,013
JUN 0	.0000	0	−8,674	.6893	−5,979	−8,674	−5,979
JUL 0	.0000	0	−8,674	.6854	−5,945	−8,674	−5,945
AUG 0	.0000	0	−8,674	.6815	−5,912	−8,674	−5,912
SEP 0	.0000	0	−8,674	.6777	−5,878	−8,674	−5,878
OCT 0	.0000	0	−8,674	.6739	−5,845	−8,674	−5,845
NOV 0	.0000	0	−8,674	.6701	−5,813	−8,674	−5,813
DEC 0	.0000	0	−8,674	.6663	−5,780	−8,674	−5,780
TOTALS 0		0	−104,088		−71,556	−104,088	−71,556

Appendix B: Generation of Monthly Cash Flows

APPENDIX C

Benefits, Costs, and Risks

The original taxonomy was developed by P. Mertens, R. Anselstetter and Th. Eckardt at the University of Erlangen-Nuremberg. The taxonomies listed in Appendix B.1 through B.12 were compiled from the following publications:

Anselstetter, R. Betriebswirtschaftliche Nutzeffekte der Datenverarbeitung, Anhaltpunkte fuer Nutzen-Kosten-Schaetzungen, 2ed., Springer, Berlin 1986.

Mertens, P. Anselstetter, R. Eckhardt, Th. Nickel, R. Betriebswirtschaftliche Nutzeffekte und Schaeden der EDV—Ergebnisse des NSI-Projektes, Zeitschrift fuer Betriebswirtschaft, Vol. 52, 1982, 135–153.

Mertens, P. Zeitler, P. Schumann, M. Koch, H. Untersuchungen zum Nutzen-Kosten-Verhaeltnis der Bueroautomation, H. Krallmann (editor), Planung, Einsatz und Wirtschaftlichkeitsnachweis, Erich Schmidt Verlag GmbH, 1986, 103–134.

Dr. M. Schumann and U. Roesch, University of Erlangen-Nuremberg, added and improved some parts. Editing was done by M. M. Parker. The table below identifies the appendix in which a particular taxonomy can be found.

APPENDIX C.1

Individual as Employee

Change in Work Contents, Organization and Conditions

Humanizing the work (lighter physical labor, reduction of monotony and repetitive activities, less stress, fewer unpleasant responsibilities, less routine work)

Job enrichment (expansion of the operational realm, enrichment of work contents, suspension of task-sharing processes)

Greater supply of information for the individual

Fewer administrative functions (debureaucratizing)

Possibility to spend more concentrated time on the work

Greater contentment with the work place, better environment

Possibility for self-supervision (example: among autonomous groups)

Better work coordination

Less fear of making mistakes

Better work and worker relations (better labor exchange, better employment market transparency, better vocational guidance, more objective judgement of employees)

Safer work places

Increased number of new work places (eventually with more responsibility for minorities; example: handicapped)

Better possibility of substitution, easier training, flexible work hours

Possibility for reduced work hours (reduction of overtime)

New possibilities for outwork

Better health protection and health provisions at the work place

APPENDIX C.2

Change in Qualifications

Revaluation of the work place (higher self-confidence, improved status)

Releasing of creative productivity

APPENDIX C.3

Change of the Operational Social Structure

Better communication (breaking down of psychological barriers, more social communication)

Fewer differences between laborers and salaried personnel

Improved equal opportunity (example: fairer representative areas, fairer income opportunities)

APPENDIX C.4

Business Area—Overlaps Include Public Agencies

Better risk politics (early detection and warning system)

Better accounting (cost transparency, more exact calculations)

Better and more exact coefficients (better budget supervision)

More exact planning of the solvency

Fewer deficits in receivables (better supervision of debtors)

Lower planning costs

More efficient employment of managerial factors (employment of operational resources)

Higher productivity

Lower costs (example: wages and material costs)

Personnel economizing

Energy saving

Better capacity employment (less time loss)

Less tie-up of capital

Interest reduction

Increase in sales or return

Security of competitive position and marketability

Image improvement

Better advertisement, better planning of publicity means, more exact market analysis

Longer contractual relationships for employees (less fluctuation)

Shorter periods of vocational adjustment

Less overtime

Greater building security, better property (or project) supervision

Greater flexibility

Time savings (example: production and execution time)

Higher performance and production quality

Fewer errors

Possibility for decentralization of tasks and decisions (individual responsibility for divisional departments)

Faster tabulation of votes

APPENDIX C.5

Administrative Area

Better information handling (fewer telephone calls, fewer memoranda, greater transparency, increased information service, acceleration of information, more convenient analyses)

Improved documents, faster document creation

Better and faster decision-making

Greater planning and prognosis accuracy

Better execution of planning and clarity of executions (avoidance of work repetition)

Restraint of paper build-up

Less documentation expenditure, better quality of documentation

Less use of capital, faster return of capital (faster task completion)

Satisfied customers

Shorter run-through time (job time)

APPENDIX C.6

Industry

Sales

Better control of field service

Better response to customer wishes

Faster supply and provision of bids

Better preparation for delivery, shorter delivery time, faster contract transactions

Better observance of deadlines

Better service

Better adjustment to peak production

Less reclamation

APPENDIX C.7

Material Management and Purchasing

Better selection of suppliers and distributors

Surer control over reception of goods

Less inventory, higher turnover of inventory and supplies

Better inventory control

Better flow of material in storage

Better management of stock

Less loss in the stock

Less risk of obsolescence, decay, and scrapping

Better storage use, less spatial need

APPENDIX C.8

Production

Greater multiplicity of variants

More exact capacity planning

Better flow of material in production

Less intermediate storage, maintenance resources

Shorter job time

Better care of facilities (maintenance upkeep)

Higher security against breakdown in production

Less blending, scrap material

Better production control

Higher quality of output

APPENDIX C.9

Assembly

Increase in work productivity regarding product components

Better flow of materials in the factory

Lower material, manufacturing costs, installation and assembly costs (standardization and restriction or reduction of planning alternatives)

Decrease of production space

Better planning of resources

Better use of machinery, longer use of equipment

Higher quality of output

APPENDIX C.10

Research and Development

Higher quality of planning, in time and mistake-free procurement of manufacturing records

Elimination of bottlenecks in the construction

Improvement of the basis of decision-making

Better termination, reduced shutdown time and delivery time, shortening of development times

Automatic supply of numerical control programs, parts lists, and work organization; automatic sending of information (example: numeric control equipment)

Lower ordering costs, savings in measuring devices, tools, equipment, (avoidance of replanning)

Reduced routine tasks

Less manual and administrative costs

Good documentation immediately following the product design

Easy system to store the information

Simplified control of assembly times and phases (detailed additional data)

Faster completion of changes

Decreased supervision of norms

Standardization of parts (possibly for production of substitutive or variant parts)

Shorter development times

Better optimization through simulation (playing through of different variants or scenarios)

APPENDIX C.11

Banking and Insurance

Better, faster, more accommodating service for bank customers, higher operative preparedness

Faster business transactions, customer service

Relieving pressure on tellers (example: routine tasks)

Exemption for qualified consultation

Faster funds transfer, greater transaction security

Less backlog (example: the processing of vouchers)

Fewer payment bearers (paper-saving)

Possibility for absorbing shorter work hours

Fewer peak loads (disassembly or leveling)

Better planning and control of field work

Less risk of theft (example: because of lower cash balance at automatic tellers)

Image and competition advantages

APPENDIX C.12

Trade

A more current and detailed analysis of assortments

Better delivery service, readiness to deliver, less inventory, shorter delivery time

Easier inventory

Less overstock

Better control and determination of outcome for special actions

Easier personnel placement

Better and more optimal tour planning

Longer visiting periods for the representatives (example: due to better announcement of offers)

Unified settling of accounts, evaluation and bookkeeping by branch offices

APPENDIX C.13

Agriculture

Higher foodstuffs production, crop surplus

Better food quality

APPENDIX C.14

Hospital

Higher capacity for medical treatment, shorter treatment time

Faster reaction possibility, improved emergency assistance, faster emergency agencies assistance

Better possibilities for analysis and diagnosis

Less examination and notation time, fewer instruments for examinations

Better therapy possibilities

Fewer measurement and diagnosis errors

Less danger of administering incorrect doses, nondangerous doses

Better knowledge of side effects and integrated effects

Better protection against infection; infection prevention through early detection

Less use of medications

Less loss of medications and blood plasma due to expiration (dates)

Better training possibilities for hospital personnel

Fewer administrative costs

Faster administrative procedures, including billing and insurance claims

Fewer accounting mistakes

Less in-patient treatment (due to better therapy possibilities)

APPENDIX C.15

Individual as Employee

Elimination or Displacement of Human Labor

Loss of work place security

Dismissal, release of manpower

Internal job rotation

APPENDIX C.16

Change of Work Contents, Organization and Conditions

Consolidation of hierarchical authority structures

Establishing a hierarchy through data processing access

Accumulation of power, stronger establishment of hierarchy, centralization, dependency

Stronger supervision of dispositive activities

Change in the balance of information between the workers' council and the employer (disparity)

Dependency upon electronic data processing or data processing specialists

Influence of the work organization by data processing or data processing producers

Greater division of work, separation of work

Higher work monotony, pacification

Formalization, systematization, and reduction of operational phases and work objects

Outside determination of the work rhythm, less individual margin for decision-making procedures

One-sided workload (example: only mental work)

Higher physical stress or burdens

Higher psychological stress (example: permanent education stress)

Fear of the consequences of rationalization

Greater performance pressure, increasing work intensity or work tempo

Introduction of shift work to use the capacity of data processing systems

Income loss, regrouping

Breaking down of social communications, relations, and interaction possibilities

Depersonalizing of the work, no relations to work or to the product, alienation, estrangement, discontent

Less transparency of the work process

Higher sickness quota

Higher fluctuation quota

APPENDIX C.17

Change in Qualifications

Disqualifying (depreciation of educational or training contents and job prospects or descriptions)

Restricting specialization, less chance for mobility and flexibility

Destruction of learning capability, creativity, and initiative

Polarizing of qualification requirements

Fewer promotion opportunities; value depreciation of skills (forfeiture of status and authority)

No monetary increase or gain despite higher qualification requirements

APPENDIX C.18

Changes of the Operational Social Structure

A worse social environment (example: because of polarizing)

Stronger individual competition and promotion struggles

Growing strike potential

Danger of individual power concentration because of information advantages

APPENDIX C.19

Micro-level (Enterprise Level)

Implementation and conversion difficulties

Communication problems between data processing and divisional departments

Higher costs

Less flexibility

More errors, less work discipline

Image defamation or damage because of delays and errors

Data-processing as an alibi for other errors

Higher susceptibility or vulnerability of the enterprise

Greater dependency on suppliers

Data-processing causes hampering of innovation

Less turnover

Bankruptcy of smaller and middle-level enterprises and operations

APPENDIX C.20

Administration and Office Automation

Poorer security, safety, and confidentiality

Recipient must be provided with compatible equipment

Injury to work flow with technological failure or breakdown

Greater dependency on the clerical staff and secretary

Impairing of the work completion in the case of personnel absences

APPENDIX C.21

Research, Development, and Manufacturing

Relations to manually conducted tasks is lost (overlapping department applications)

Problems of interdisciplinary collaboration and co-operation

High acquisition costs force a high system capacity (worktime scheduling)

Longer response times with complex operational production lines and burdening of the computer because of more users

APPENDIX D

Cost Curves for Data-Managed Systems

Information systems exist to provide cost-justified quality and coherent information in support of the management objectives of the enterprise. Quality information is needed by management to make quality decisions. Coherent and cohesive information is necessary as interactions between functions within an enterprise are emphasized. What is quality information? How do we know when information is important enough to be required to pass the test of coherency and cohesiveness? These are attributes of value that have not been addressed in the techniques to date, yet these are the benefits on which the perceived success or failure of an information technology application often rests.

DATA-DRIVEN AND DATA-MANAGED SYSTEMS

As the recognition of the requirement for quality and cohesiveness of information grows, many companies evolved their information systems from the traditional stand-alone systems to those more closely aligned with data-driven or data-managed systems. A *data-driven system* is defined here as one in which an attempt is made to isolate data from the software. A *data-managed system*, going a step further, is one in which an attempt is made to shield knowledge of the data from the software. In this ideal environment, information volatility is hidden from the applications and the applications development people. This evolution has brought about a realignment of data processing into functional areas of data management and information and application development centers. Also, more precise methods of projecting and measuring programmer productivity by function points are being applied. (Function point analysis is based on the identification of functional areas of a project and provides a more accurate evaluation of work product output than the traditional and more easily measurable lines of code.)

Typically, the information center focuses on end-user productivity and quick and easy applications. Data administration provides and maintains information distribution and data integrity. The development center focuses on (improved) application programmer productivity and the development of the more complex applications.

These are technical solutions to the technical problems of managing the data and providing better estimates for development times and costs. They may only incidentally provide identifiable tangible benefits for the business domain.

Today, the major application systems to be managed have increased tenfold. Small desktop systems abound. Terminals providing end-user support exist by the thousands in a large LOB or enterprise. To assess the change in the cost structure caused by these types of investments, we present a cost model of more traditional systems (Figure A.1) and a model more closely representing the new structure (Figure A.2). The comparison provides a clear illustration of the differences in the cost elements of both systems.

AN ABSTRACT SET OF COST MODELS

Typically, cost curves (or models) of a product considered in their most abstract sense are depicted as sets of two. Each represents an extreme case. In the one extreme, the

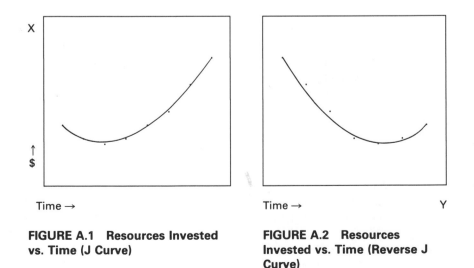

FIGURE A.1   Resources Invested vs. Time (J Curve)

FIGURE A.2   Resources Invested vs. Time (Reverse J Curve)

Appendix D: Cost Curves for Data-Managed Systems

product is built in the most inexpensive manner possible. This provides the opportunity to minimize the initial investment, but brings with it the exposure for a significant investment in maintenance during the life of the product. The first case cost model, a J curve, is illustrated in Figure A.1. In the figure, the x-axis depicts the amount of resources invested, and the y-axis depicts a progression over time. (In this and subsequent figures, resource costs include personnel costs, equipment costs, and organizational costs. Also, no attempt has been made to calibrate the x or y coordinates.)

In the other extreme, the product is built in anticipation of maintenance avoidance. This requires a high initial cost, but brings with it the anticipation of lower maintenance costs over the life of the product. This is illustrated in the reverse J curve in Figure A.2. Again, we use the x-axis to depict resources invested, and the y axis to depict a progression over time. Both the theory and application of these cost models are compatible with the economic concept of replacement theory.

APPLICATION OF THE ABSTRACT SET OF COST MODELS TO INFORMATION SYSTEMS

If only the abstract view is desired, these cost models are adequate to show the trade-off between two approaches used for systems design and implementation. By applying these cost models to the costs of information systems, the cost model representing small, incremental, up-front cost with exposure for large investments in product maintenance (Figure A.1) describes the traditional stand-alone systems involving application design, implementation, and maintenance. The large up-front investment coupled with the anticipation of maintenance cost avoidance (Figure A.2) describes the data-managed system.

However, more precise cost models maintaining the same relative abstraction level can be developed. This increasing precision illustrates some of the specific considerations affecting the life-cycle costs of information systems and can be used as a vehicle for communication between the management teams of the enterprise. Consider the second set of cost curves shown in Figures A.3 and A.4. These figures show the difference in cost curves in a technology-driven environment and a data-managed environment.

Here, the x-axis remains the same as in Figures A.1 and A.2 and represents the magnitude of the investment of resources. However, the y-axis in Figures A.3 and A.4 has been modified to reflect the number of applications added to an information system over time. In comparing Figure A.3 to Figure A.1, the change of the y-axis does not change the general J curve cost model. Yet in comparing Figure A.4 to Figure A.2, the difference is marked. This change is due to one of the attributes of the data-managed system. Although the very large up-front investment is absorbed by the first product (application), only small incremental costs are required for the addition of subsequent functions (applications).

Whereas in a data-managed system, data is separated from software, no such division is formally made in the technology-driven system. Indeed, no attempt is made to assess the impact of data on software. With this in mind while comparing Figures A.1 and A.3, it might be noted that although the general J curve cost model does not change, a limit on the number of additional applications that can be implemented in

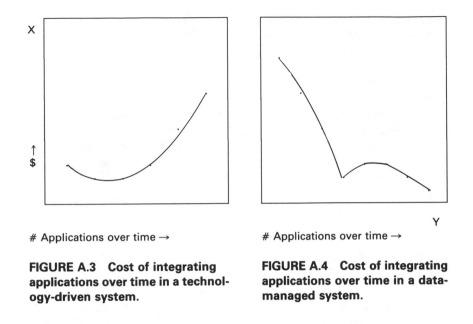

Applications over time →

FIGURE A.3 Cost of integrating applications over time in a technology-driven system.

Applications over time →

FIGURE A.4 Cost of integrating applications over time in a data-managed system.

the technology- hardware- driven system exists. This limit will be due to the increasingly higher cost to integrate each additional application, or the impossibility of physically integrating one more application, or both. This is the syndrome of the ''straw that broke the camel's back.'' The traditional reaction of adding more hardware may or may not provide an interim solution and certainly does not provide the long-term solution. Only good planning accomplishes this.

DATA ADMINISTRATION AND INFORMAL SYSTEMS

To provide a more appropriate abstraction of the information systems an additional attribute of the cost models must be considered. This additional attribute is the cost of data administration and its reflection in the costs of an informal information system. An informal information system, as opposed to a formal one, is the system that evolves at the end-user level to accommodate the needs of the enterprise as they arise. It may be implemented with a hand-held calculator, or a desktop personal computer. It may be a reorganization of data from computer output into a significant context by the end-user. The scope of its components is narrow, at its worst being limited to one product, one application, or one department. It is usually not documented. This Band-Aid approach to tying up the information needs can be riddled with duplication and redundancy.

On imposing the cost of the functions of data administration, the issue of costs of the informal support system will surface. Traditionally, the costs of formal systems have been included in cost projections, but the cost of supporting the informal systems, which are often necessary to make the formal system function, have been ignored. The informal system, by its very nature, exacerbates attempts at cost measurement (Parker,

1982). Because of this, unfortunately very little cost data is available from the business domain about the informal system. Such a cost curve is, at best, an estimate. When informal costs are overlaid on the set of curves depicted in Figures A.3 and A.4, we develop the set of Figures A.5 and A.6. To show the ambiguities in the area of costs of informal support systems, three possible cost curves are shown. They differ primarily in proportional costs of informal systems.

For example, in evaluating the costs of the formal system at point n in time (Figure A.5), curve A reveals that the system is only starting to become saturated. However, when the informal system costs are imposed on (added to) the formal system, comparing point 3 on the informal system curve B with point 2 on the formal system curve A, a much higher level of system saturation exists for the informal system.

In Figure A.6 the addition of the data administration function, which in effect formalizes the informal systems, does not significantly affect the cost model illustrated in Figure A.4. Data administration is usually the prime contributor to that large, up-front investment. For illustration, the variation and complexity of the individual application's impact on the cost of development and maintenance is depicted by the somewhat inconsistent and wavy line over time. The flat line representations of Figures A.4 and A.6 can be supported. Experience has demonstrated that structured reuseable code, an integral element in data administration concepts, is more impervious to technological (hardware and software) changes than traditional coding techniques are to changes in technology-driven systems.

We view attributes of systems about the relationship of data to the overall system. Notice that the data-managed system is least vulnerable to the technological changes that usually affect the operating environment (Figure A.7).

The obvious next question is, What does the current (and projected) cost curve or model look like? If the progressions of Figures A.1 through A.6 have been reasonably

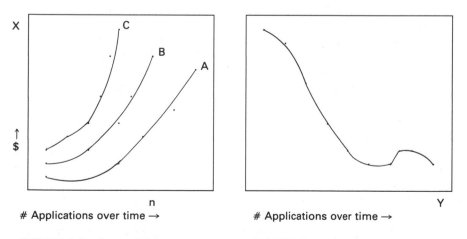

FIGURE A.5 Cost of data management in a technology-driven system.

FIGURE A.6 Cost of data management in a data-managed system.

SYSTEM ATTRIBUTE	COST ATTRIBUTE	DATA	EFFECT OF TECHNOLOGY CHANGE
Technology Driven	• Inexpensive to build • Expensive to maintain	• Multiple acquisition and control points	• Maximum vulnerability
Data Driven	• Expensive to build • Moderately inexpensive to maintain	• Few acquisition and control points	• Moderate protection
Data Managed	• Expensive to build • Optimally expensive to maintain	• Single acquisition and control points	• Optimum protection

FIGURE A.7 Comparison of systems characteristics

accurate about form (without benefit of calibration) the bell-shaped curve to represent the resource consumption life cycle is no longer adequate. As data integration becomes necessary due to the basic change in information systems architecture, the costs associated with the maintenance of the old systems and the development of the new systems are not adequately reflected.

Further, most systems that are currently being planned for future implementation are not purely data-managed, but a hybrid of the two alternatives and are called data-driven. This has come about through a gradual evolution from traditional stand-alone systems and because of some very practical reasons. The scope of requirement specification for information systems design currently is limited to the application, where the data structure is dictated by that application. Company-wide requirements are best fulfilled when the data structure is general enough to serve many applications. However, this approach is not without its problems.

New, as yet nonexistent systems can be designed, developed, and implemented under the umbrella of a newly created data-managed structure. Yet such luxuries seldom exist in the real world. Many data processing users are faced with the formidable task of updating large existing systems. To cite an example, one such user in trying to modernize one of its information systems created four models (old physical, old logical, new logical, new physical) describing the system as it currently exists, inserting new requirements, and describing the system as it will be. It soon became obvious that implementation of the final step (new logical to new physical) could not be accomplished without seriously disrupting the business at hand. Thus, the system was implemented in stages revising the format of the system's data structure along the way to minimize the impact of a change and to ensure the existence of backup facilities.

SUMMARY

Over the past several years, there has been a gradual movement from systems design and implementation of stand-alone, application-oriented systems, supporting primarily the operational and functional levels of management, to data-base oriented, data-managed systems, designed to support the information needs of the enterprise as a whole. This gradual change has recently become more accelerated due to a variety of factors, the prime one being the reversal of the traditional constraint as applied to the resource mix. Previously, hardware costs were focused upon for conservation, and personnel costs were secondary. Today, the hardware is becoming progressively less expensive, and personnel costs for maintenance and development are becoming critical cost issues.

It was suggested that, because of the costs of the *underground* informal systems, the industry may be past the knee of the cost curve of the traditional stand-alone system, with little chance of recovery. One cannot simply move straight across from one curve to another without incurring the costs, during one increment of time, of both maintaining the old system and developing the new system—a very substantial investment of time and money. An enterprise must understand and evaluate the risk of remaining status quo.

The success of any business enterprise is measured by its profitability and part of the profitability potential of any enterprise is the control and management of its data. Data needs to be perceived as a resource and managed as such. It should be incorporated into an enterprise plan of management by objectives, and be an integral part of the business strategy. When applied to data as a resource, as compared to any other kind of resource that is an integral part of a business enterprise, risk management has been exceptionally onerous to a non-data processing oriented user/manager. The models presented were developed in an effort to assist in risk management of Information Systems.

APPENDIX E

Conversion of Scores to Project Weighted Values

Institution One

Application	ROI 10	SA 2	CA 0	MI 6	CR 0	OR −0	SA 2	DU −0	TU −4	IR −4	Score
Library Card Catalog	0	4	2	0	3	2	3	1	3	2	
	0	8	0	0	0	0	6	0	−12	−8	− 7
Information Center	0	1	0	4	0	4	4	0	2	0	
	0	2	0	24	0	0	8	0	− 8	0	26
New Payroll System	4	2	0	3	0	3	4	2	1	3	
	40	4	0	18	0	0	8	0	− 4	−12	54
Accounts Payable Upgrade	3	2	1	3	0	2	4	2	1	3	
	30	4	0	18	0	0	8	0	− 4	−12	44
Student Records P/F	3	3	2	1	3	3	0	3	1	2	
	30	6	0	6	0	0	0	0	− 4	− 8	30
Admissions Network	0	5	3	3	4	4	5	0	3	4	
	0	10	0	18	0	0	10	0	−12	−16	10
Instructional Support	0	5	4	0	5	3	2	4	4	4	
	0	10	0	0	0	0	4	0	−16	−16	−18

Institution Two

Application	ROI 4	SA 2	CA 4	MI 8	CR 0	OR −2	SA 2	DU −4	TU −4	IR −4	Score
Library Card Catalog	0	4	2	0	3	2	3	1	3	2	
	0	8	8	0	0	−4	6	− 4	−12	− 8	− 6
Information Center	0	1	0	4	0	4	4	0	2	0	
	0	2	0	32	0	−8	8	0	− 8	0	26
New Payroll System	4	2	0	3	0	3	4	2	1	3	
	16	4	0	24	0	−6	8	− 8	− 4	−12	22
Accounts Payable Upgrade	3	2	1	3	0	2	4	2	1	3	
	12	4	4	24	0	−4	8	− 8	− 4	−12	24
Student Records P/F	3	3	2	1	3	3	0	3	1	2	
	12	6	8	8	0	−6	0	−12	− 4	− 8	2
Admissions Network	0	5	3	3	4	4	5	0	3	4	
	0	10	12	24	0	−8	10	0	−12	−16	20
Instructional Support	0	5	4	0	5	3	2	4	4	4	
	0	10	16	0	0	−6	4	−16	−16	−16	−24

Appendix E: Conversion of Scores to Project Weighted Values   **269**

Institution Three

Application	ROI 3	SA 4	CA 6	MI 0	CR 4	OR −8	SA 3	DU −2	TU −2	IR −4	Score
Library Card Catalog	0	4	2	0	3	2	3	1	3	2	
	0	16	12	0	12	−16	9	−2	−6	− 8	17
Information Center	0	1	0	4	0	4	4	0	2	0	
	0	4	0	0	0	−32	12	0	−4	0	−20
New Payroll System	4	2	0	3	0	3	4	2	1	3	
	12	8	0	0	0	−24	12	−4	−2	−12	−10
Accounts Payable Upgrade	3	2	1	3	0	2	4	2	1	3	
	9	8	6	0	0	−16	12	−4	−2	−12	1
Student Records P/F	3	3	2	1	3	3	0	3	1	2	
	9	12	12	0	12	−24	0	−6	−2	− 8	5
Admissions Network	0	5	3	3	4	4	5	0	3	4	
	0	20	18	0	16	−32	15	0	−6	−16	15
Instructional Support	0	5	4	0	5	3	2	4	4	4	
	0	20	24	0	20	−24	6	−8	−8	−16	14

Appendix E: Conversion of Scores to Project Weighted Values

Institution One

Application	ROI 7	MI 7	SA 6	TU −6	Score
Library Card Catalog	0	0	3	3	
	0	0	18	−18	0
Information Center	0	4	4	2	
	0	28	24	−12	40
New Payroll System	4	3	4	1	
	28	21	24	− 6	67
Accounts Payable Upgrade	3	3	4	1	
	21	21	24	− 6	60
Student Records P/F	3	1	0	1	
	21	7	0	− 6	22
Admissions Network	0	3	5	3	
	0	21	30	−18	33
Instructional Support	0	0	2	4	
	0	0	12	−24	−12

Appendix E: Conversion of Scores to Project Weight Values

Institution Two

Application	SA 7	CA 7	CR 6	OR −6	Score
Library Card Catalog	4	2	3	2	
	28	14	18	−12	48
Information Center	1	0	0	4	
	7	0	0	−24	−17
New Payroll System	2	0	0	3	
	14	0	0	−18	− 4
Accounts Payable Upgrade	2	1	0	2	
	14	7	0	−12	9
Student Records P/F	3	2	3	3	
	21	14	18	−18	35
Admissions Network	5	3	4	4	
	35	21	24	−24	56
Instructional Support	5	4	5	3	
	35	28	15	−18	60

Appendix E: Conversion of Scores to Project Weighted Values

Institution Three

Application	ROI 10	SA 10	OR −4	DU −4	IR −4	Score
Library Card Catalog	0	4	2	1	2	
	0	40	− 8	− 4	− 8	20
Information Center	0	1	4	0	0	
	0	10	−16	0	0	− 6
New Payroll System	4	2	3	2	3	
	40	20	−12	− 8	−12	28
Accounts Payable Upgrade	3	2	2	2	3	
	30	20	− 8	− 8	−12	22
Student Records P/F	3	3	3	3	2	
	30	30	−12	−12	− 8	22
Admissions Network	0	5	4	0	4	
	0	50	−16	0	−16	18
Instructional Support	0	5	3	4	4	
	0	50	−12	−16	−16	6

References

CHAPTER ONE

BENSON, ROBERT J., and MARILYN M. PARKER, "Enterprise-wide Information Management: An Introduction to the Concepts," G320–2768, IBM Corp., Los Angeles Scientific Center, 11601 Wilshire Blvd., Los Angeles, CA 90025–1738, May, 1985.

CHAPTER TWO

ALLEN, BRANDT, "Making Information Services Pay Its Way," *Harvard Business Review*, 65, no. 1 (January/February 1987), pp. 57–65.

ANTHONY, ROBERT N., *Planning and Control Systems: A Framework for Analysis*, Cambridge, MA: Harvard University Press, 1965.

GILLENSON, MARK L., and ROBERT GOLDBERG, *Strategic Planning, Systems Analysis, and Data Base Design: The Continous Flow Approach*, New York: Wiley, 1984.

NOLAN, RICHARD L., and THOMAS R. MANTZ, "The Missing Ingredient: Executive Awareness," *Stage by Stage*, 6, no. 6 (November–December 1986), pp. 1–8.

SHANKLIN, WILLIAM L., and JOHN K. RYANS, JR., *Thinking Strategically: Planning for Your Company's Future*, New York: Random House, 1985.

STRASSMAN, PAUL A., *Information Payoff: The Transformation of Work in the Electronic Age*, New York: Free Press, 1985.

WISEMAN, CHARLES, *Strategy and Computers: Information Systems as Competitive Weapons*, Homewood, IL: Dow Jones-Irwin, 1985.

CHAPTER THREE

BENSON, ROBERT J., and MARILYN M. PARKER, "Enterprise-wide Information Management: An Introduction to the Concepts," G320–2768, IBM Corp., Los Angeles Scientific Center, 11601 Wilshire Blvd., Los Angeles, Ca. 90025–1738, May, 1985.

"Employment Policies: Looking to the Year 2000," National Alliance of Business, 1015 15th Street NW., Washington, D.C. 20005, 1986.

HAMERMESH, RICHARD G., *Making Strategy Work,* New York: Wiley, 1986.

"High Tech to the Rescue," *Business Week,* June 26, 1986, pp. 100–108.

IVES, BLAKE, GENE SAKAMOTO, and PATRICIA GONGLA, "A Facilitative System for Identifying Competitive Applications of Information Technology," G320–2789, IBM Corp., Los Angeles Scientific Center, 11601 Wilshire Blvd., Los Angeles, CA 90025–1738, May 1986.

MILES, RAYMOND E., and CHARLES C. SNOW, "Organizations: New Concepts for New Forms," *California Management Review,* 27, no. 3, (Spring 1986), pp. 62–73.

PORTER, MICHAEL, *Competitive Advantage,* New York: Free Press, 1985.

ROCKART, JOHN, "Chief Executives Define Their Own Data Needs," *Harvard Business Review,* 57, no. 2, (March/April 1979), pp. 81–93.

STRASSMAN, PAUL A., *Information Payoff: The Transformation of Work in the Electronic Age,* New York: Free Press, 1985.

CHAPTER FOUR

ALLEN, BRANDT, "Making Information Services Pay Its Way," *Harvard Business Review,* 65, no. 1 (January/February 1987), pp. 57–65.

DIEBOLD, JOHN, *Business in the Age of Information,* New York: ANACOM, a division of the American Management Association, 1985.

HERBERT, MARTIN, and CURT HARTOG, "MIS Rates the Issues," *Datamation,* November 15, 1986, pp. 79–86.

KANTER, ROSABETH MOSS, *The Change Masters,* New York: Simon and Schuster, 1983.

NOLAN, RICHARD N., "Business Needs a New Breed of EDP Manager," *Harvard Business Review,* 54, no. 2 (March/April 1976), pp. 46–59.

———, "Managing the Computer Element from the Top," *Stage by Stage,* 6, no.1, (January–February 1986), p. 4.

———, and W. E. KELVIE, "Installing Venture Portfolio Management," *Stage by Stage,* 6, no.4, (July–August 1986), pp. 1–11.

ZACHMAN, JOHN, "A Framework for Information Systems Architecture," G320–2785, IBM Corp., Los Angeles Scientific Center, 11601 Wilshire Blvd., Los Angeles, CA 90025–1738, March 1986.

CHAPTER FIVE

MCFARLAN, WARREN, ed., *Current Research Challenges in Information Systems,* Boston, MA: Harvard Business School Press, 1984, p. 273.

ORR, KEN, "Breaking Big Ones into Little Ones," *Proceedings, Third International Conference in Enterprise-wide Information Management,* June 4–6, 1986, St. Louis, MO: Washington University Center for the Study of Data Processing, pp. 99–110.

McLean, Ephraim R., and John Z. Soden, *Strategic Planning for MIS.* New York: Wiley, 1977.

CHAPTER SIX

Anthony, Robert N., *Planning and Control Systems: A Framework for Analysis,* Cambridge, MA: Harvard University Press, 1965.

Barrett, Stephanie S., "Strategic Alternatives and Inter-organizational System Implementations: An Overview," *Journal of Management Information Systems* 3, no. 3, (Winter 1986–87), pp. 6–16.

Bhide, Amar, "Hustle as Strategy," *Harvard Business Review,* 65, no. 5, (September/October 1986), pp. 59–66.

Cash, James I., and B. R. Konsynski, "IS Redraws Competitive Boundaries," *Harvard Business Review,* 63, no. 2, (March–April 1985), pp. 134–142.

Doherty, Walt J., and W. G. Pope, "Computing as a Tool for Human Augmentation," *IBM Systems Journal,* 25, no. 3/4, (1986), pp. 306–320.

Ghemawat, Pankaj, "Sustainable Advantage," *Harvard Business Review,* 64, no. 5 (September/October 1986), pp. 53–58.

Jenster, Per V., "Firm Performance and Monitoring of Critical Success Factors in Different Strategic Contexts." *Journal of Management Information Systems/* 3, no. 3, (Winter 1986–87), pp. 17–33.

Mills, Peter K., *Managing Service Industries,* New York: Ballinger, 1986.

Norton, David P., "The Economics of Computing in the Advanced Stages," *Stage by Stage,* 4, no. 2 (Summer 1984), pp. 1–5.

_____, "A Case Study: Hercules Incorporated," *Stage by Stage,* 6, no. 5, (September–October 1986), pp. 11–17.

_____, "The Economics of Computing in the Advance Stages, Part V: Describing the I/S Investment," *Stage By Stage,* 4, no. 4 (Winter 1985).

_____, "The Economics of Computing in the Advance Stages: Part III Managing the Benefits," *Stage by Stage,* 5, no. 2 (Summer 1985) pp. 1–12.

_____, "The Economics of Computing in the Advanced Stages," *Stage by Stage Supplement,* January 1987, pp. 1–26.

Porter, Michael E., *Competitive Advantage,* New York: Free Press, 1985.

_____, *Competitive Strategy: Techniques for Analyzing Industries and Competitors,* New York: Free Press, 1980.

Rowe, Alan J., Richard O. Mason, and Karl Dickel, *Strategic Management and Business Policy: A Methodological Approach,* Reading, MA, Addison Wesley, 1982.

Robinson, David G., "Synchronizing Systems with Business Values," *Datamation* June 15, 1984, pp. 152–158.

CHAPTER EIGHT

Cheek, L. M., *Zero-based Budgeting Comes of Age, AMACOM,* A Division American Management Association, New York, 1977.

SASSONE, PETER G., "Cost Benefit Analysis of Information Systems: A Survey of Methodologies," Georgia Institute of Technology, Atlanta, GA 30332, Working Paper, March, 1986.

WOLFE, J. N., *Cost Benefit and Cost Effectiveness: Studies and Analysis,* George Allen & Unwin Ltd., Ruskin House-Museum Street, London (1973).

CHAPTER NINE

BENSON, ROBERT J., and MARILYN M. PARKER, "Enterprise-wide Information Management: An Introduction to the Concepts," G320–2775, IBM Corp., Los Angeles Scientific Center, 11601 Wilshire Blvd., Los Angeles, CA, May 1985.

CASH, JAMES I., and B. R. KONSYNSKI, "IS Redraws Competitive Boundaries," *Harvard Business Review,* 63, no.2, (March–April 1985), pages 134–142.

MCFARLAN, F. WARREN, J. L. MCKENNEY and P. PYBURN, "The Information Archipelago— Plotting a Course," *Harvard Business Review,* 61, no. 1, (January–February 1983), pp. 145–156.

NOLAN, RICHARD, "The Computer Edges," *Stage by Stage, UPDATE,* December 1985.

PARKER, MARILYN M., "Enterprise Information Analysis: Cost-Benefit Analysis and the Data-Managed System," *IBM Systems Journal,* 21, no. 1, pp. 108–123.

PORTER, MICHAEL E. *Competitive Advantage: Creating and Sustaining Superior Performance,* The Free Press, New York, 1985.

CHAPTER TEN

DONOHUE, J. F., Integration Strategies: It's up to Systems Integrators to Implement Just-In-Time," *Micro-Mini Systems,* no. 2, February 1987, page 46.

SCHWARTZ, A. PERRY, and PETER G. SASSONE, "Management Technology: From Promise to Payoff," Georgia Institute of Technology, Atlanta, Ga. 30332, Working Paper.

CHAPTER ELEVEN

BAIN, D., *The Productivity Prescription: The Manager's Guide to Improving Productivity and Profits,* McGraw-Hill Book Company, New York, 1982, Chapter 5: Developing Appropriate Measures, pages 51–75, and Chapter 6: Design Aids, pages 76–83.

DRUCKER, PETER F., *The Frontiers of Management: Where Tomorrow's Decisions Are Being Shaped Today,* Truman Talley Books, E. P. Dutton, New York, 1986, Chapter 14: Measuring White-Collar Productivity, pages 129–133.

HAMPTON, W. J., and J. R. NORMAN, "General Motors: What Went Wrong?" *Business Week,* March 16, 1987, number 2989, pages 102–110.

SASSONE, PETER G., and A. P. SCHWARTZ, "Cost-Justifying OA: A Straightforward Method for Quantifying the Benefits of Automated Office Systems," *DATAMATION,* 32, no. 4, February 15, 1986, pages 83–88. In the article, the authors describe their application of the Hedonic Wage Model as it applies to the justification of Office Automation.

STRASSMANN, P. A., *Information Payoff: The Transformation of Work in the Electronic Age,* The Free Press, New York, 1985, Chapter 5: The Economics of Office Work, pages 79–99; Chapter 7: The Effectiveness Approach to Productivity, pages 116–135; and Chapter 8: Value-Added Productivity Measurement, pages 136–149.

CHAPTER TWELVE

ARNOLD, J. H., "Assessing capital risk: you can't be too conservative," *Harvard Business Review,* 64 no. 6, (September–October 1986), pages 113–121.

BENSON, ROBERT J. and MARILYN M. PARKER, "Enterprise-wide Information Management: An Introduction to the Concepts," G320–2775, IBM Corp., Los Angeles Scientific Center, 11601 Wilshire Blvd., Los Angeles, Ca., May 1985.

COSTELLO, D. R., *New Venture Analysis: Research, Planning and Finance,* Dow Jones-Irwin Homewood, IL, 1985.

McFARLAN, F. WARREN, J. L. McKENNEY and P. PYBURN, "The Information Archipelago— Plotting a Course," *Harvard Business Review,* 61, no. 1, (January–February 1983), pages 145–156.

NOLAN, RICHARD L., and W. E. KELVIE, "Installing Venture Portfolio Management," *Stage by Stage,* 6, no. 4, (July–August 1986), pages 1–11.

PARKER, MARILYN M. and ROBERT J. BENSON, "Enterprise-wide Information Economics; Investment Evaluation Techniques for Information Technology," G320–2782, and "Enterprise-wide Information Economics (EwIE): Latest Concepts," G320–2798, IBM Corp., Los Angeles Scientific Center, 11601 Wilshire Blvd., Los Angeles, Ca. 90025–1738, November 1986.

RICH, S. R., and D. GUMPERT, *Business Plans that Win $$$: Lessons From the MIT Enterprise Forum,* Harper and Row, New York, 1985.

CHAPTER THIRTEEN

NOLAN, RICHARD L., "The Computer Edges," *Stage by Stage, UPDATE,* December 1985.

PORTER, MICHAEL E., *Competitive Advantage: Creating and Sustaining Superior Performance,* The Free Press, New York, 1985.

CHAPTER FIFTEEN

CHURCHMAN, C. WEST, *The Design of Inquiring Systems: Basic Concepts of Systems and Organization,* New York: Basic Books, 1971.

DONALDSON, GORDON, and JAY W. LORSCH, *Decision Making at the Top,* New York: Basic Books, 1983.

VAN NIEVELT, M. C. AUGUSTUS, "Management Productivity and Information Technology," *Information Strategy: The Executive's Journal,* 1, no.1, (Summer 1984) pp. 39–46.

SHANKLIN, WILLIAM L., and JOHN K. RYANS, JR., *Thinking Strategically: Planning for Your Company's Future,* New York: Random House, 1985.

CHAPTER SIXTEEN

ANSOFF, H. IGOR, "Corporate Capability for Managing Change," Advances in Strategic Management, Vol. 2, Greenwich, Ct: JAI Press, 1983, pp. 1–30.

BENSON, ROBERT J., and MARILYN M. PARKER, "Enterprise-wide Information Management—The State of the Art," Working Paper 87–2, St. Louis, MO: Washington University Center for the Study of Data Processing, 1987.

BENSON, ROBERT J., and MARILYN M. PARKER, "Enterprise-wide Information Management: An Introduction to the Concepts," G320–2768, IBM Corp., Los Angeles Scientific Center, 11601 Wilshire Blvd., Los Angeles, Ca. 90025–1738, May, 1985.

HAMERMESH, RICHARD G., Making Strategy Work, New York: Wiley, 1986.

PORTER, MICHAEL E., "From Competitive Advantage to Corporate Strategy," Harvard Business Review, 65, no. 3, (May/June 1987), pp. 43–59.

———, Competitive Advantage, New York: Free Press, 1985.

CHAPTER SEVENTEEN

ALLEN, BRANDT, "An Unmanaged Computer System Can Stop You Dead," Harvard Business Review, 60, no. 6, (November–December 1982), pages 77–87.

HP-12c Owner's Handbook, Hewlett Packard Corp., Corvallis, OR., 1986, page 66.

CHAPTER EIGHTEEN

APPLETON, D. S., "Very Large Projects," DATAMATION, 32, no. 2, January 15, 1986, pages 63–70.

BENSON, ROBERT J. and MARILYN M. PARKER, "Enterprise-wide Information Management: An Introduction to the Concepts," G320–2775, IBM Corp., Los Angeles Scientific Center, 11601 Wilshire Blvd., Los Angeles, Ca. 90025–1738, May 1985.

CASH, J. I., and B. R. KONSYNSKI, "IS Redraws Competitive Boundaries," Harvard Business Review, 63, no.2, (March–April 1985), pages 134–142.

PARKER, MARILYN M., and ROBERT J. BENSON, "Enterprise-wide Information Economics; Investment Evaluation Techniques for Information Technology," G320–2782, and "Enterprise-wide Information Economics EwIE): Latest Concepts," G320–2798, IBM Corp., Los Angeles Scientific Center, 11601 Wilshire Blvd., Los Angeles, Ca. 90025–1738, November 1986.

PARKER, MARILYN M., "Enterprise Information Analysis: Cost-Benefit Analysis and the Data-Managed System," IBM Systems Journal, 21, no. 1, 1982.

PORTER, MICHAEL E., Competitive Advantage: Creating and Sustaining Superior Performance, The Free Press, New York, 1985.

Index